AIRCRAFT OF THE COLD WAR
1945–1991

THE ESSENTIAL
AIRCRAFT IDENTIFICATION GUIDE

AIRCRAFT OF
THE COLD WAR

1945–1991

THOMAS NEWDICK

amber
BOOKS

This edition published in 2010 by
Amber Books Ltd
Bradley's Close
74–77 White Lion Street
London N1 9PF
United Kingdom
www.amberbooks.co.uk

A catalogue record for this book is available from the British Library.

ISBN: 978-1-906626-63-1

Distributed in the UK by
Casemate Ltd
17 Cheap Street
Newbury
RG14 5DD
www.casematepublishing.co.uk

Project Editor: James Bennett
Design: Hawes Design
Picture Research: Terry Forshaw

Printed in Thailand

PICTURE CREDITS
All artworks courtesy of Art-Tech/Aerospace
Photographs:
Art-Tech/Aerospace: 16, 18, 60, 71, 107, 115, 157
Art-Tech/MARS: 56, 110
Cody Images: 6, 49, 81, 82, 128, 132, 145, 172, 185 (both)
U.S. Department of Defense: 40, 76, 138

Contents

Chapter 1

Europe

'From Stettin in the Baltic to Trieste in the Adriatic
an iron curtain has descended across the Continent. Behind
that line lie all the capitals of the ancient states of Central
and Eastern Europe. Warsaw, Berlin, Prague, Vienna,
Budapest, Belgrade, Bucharest and Sofia; all these famous
cities and the populations around them lie in what I must
call the Soviet sphere, and all are subject, in one form or
another, not only to Soviet influence but to a very high and,
in some cases, increasing measure of control from Moscow.'
Winston Churchill, Fulton, Missouri,
March 1946

◀ Soviet Su-9 Interceptors

In a shot redolent of the Cold War, Soviet airmen discuss their next mission while maintainers ready a trio
of Su-9 interceptors. The dawn of the nuclear age and increasing East–West tensions meant that fighters
such as these played a vital role in national defence in the post-war period.

The Iron Curtain Descends
1945–1955

Having fought together to bring about the defeat of Nazi Germany, the uneasy alliance between the communist Soviet Union and the Western powers broke down irrevocably after World War II.

SPEAKING AT FULTON in March 1946, British war leader Winston Churchill coined a phrase that has since come to be seen by some historians as signalling the starting point of the Cold War. Many of the realities of the postwar world had been defined previously – notably in successive conferences between the Allied powers at Yalta and Potsdam – but the terminology in Churchill's 'iron curtain' speech would define the tense years of East-West standoff that would follow.

After its surrender in May 1945, Germany lay in ruins. The liberation of nations from Nazi occupation in 1944-45 had established the battle lines of the Cold War in Europe, an ideological confrontation that would endure until the fall of the Berlin Wall in 1989 – an event that would in turn be followed by the collapse of the communist bloc and the USSR.

With Nazi resistance finally extinguished in 1945, much of Europe was now divided along lines drawn up at Yalta by the three major Allied powers: the Soviet Union, the U.S. and the UK. While the two victorious Western Allies (together with France) set about reinstating national governments, and ensuring a return to democracy in their respective occupation zones, the Soviets took a very different approach. Under Soviet leader Josef Stalin's guidance, the USSR established control zones and then created 'satellite' states within its zones of occupation. For Stalin, the territory in Eastern Europe that had been liberated by the Red Army represented legally agreed 'possessions', while the West viewed its occupation zones as more flexible 'spheres of influence'.

Soviet expansion

When Stalin prohibited Eastern European satellites from benefiting from Marshall Plan reconstruction aid in 1947, U.S. President Harry S. Truman announced that the U.S. would help defend Western Europe against communist aggression. In response, Soviet military strength was retained at 'wartime' levels, with a force of 5 million troops.

Differing attitudes came to a head when the three German zones occupied by the Western Allies were combined in September 1949. This development,

▲ **Republic P-47 Thunderbolt**

512th Fighter Squadron, 406th Fighter Group, USAAF / Nordholz, 1945

Typical of the USAAF fighters operating over Western Europe in the months immediately after VE-Day, this P-47D-30-RA was part of the occupation forces in Germany in summer 1945. Having helped the Allied air forces roll back the Germans, the brightly marked Thunderbolt flew with the 512th Fighter Squadron from Nordholz in northwest Germany.

Specifications

Crew: 1	Dimensions: span 12.42m (40ft 9in); length
Powerplant: 1 x 1891kW (2535hp) Pratt &	11.02m (36ft 2in); height 4.47m (14ft 8in)
Whitney R-2800-59W Double Wasp	Weight: 7938kg (17,500lb) loaded
Maximum speed: 697km/h (433mph)	Armament: 8 x 12.7mm (.5in) MGs in wings,
Range: 3060km (1900 miles)	plus provision for 1134kg (2500lb) external
Service ceiling: 12,495m (41,000ft)	bombs or rockets

together with Western plans to rebuild Germany's industry and economy, was a source of great concern to Stalin. The situation deteriorated further with the establishment of NATO in April 1949, and the acceptance of the now independent West Germany into the Alliance in May 1955.

As a direct result of West Germany's entry into NATO, the Soviets established the Warsaw Pact military alliance in May 1955. This created a buffer zone across Eastern Europe that would serve to protect the USSR from another invasion from the west. Based on earlier military agreements, the Warsaw Pact was inevitably viewed in the West as a

Moscow-led, expansionist initiative. For the Soviets, the Warsaw Pact was necessary to counter perceived Western imperialist aims.

In the event, the battles of the Cold War were fought almost exclusively outside Europe, between client states. Germany, however, was the front line. Here, NATO and Warsaw Pact aircraft were ranged on many of the same airfields that had been captured from the Nazis in 1944-45. Although the political landscape would change, and military strategies would be revised, these aircraft would remain at a high level of readiness until the final reunification of Germany in October 1990.

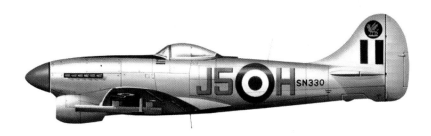

▲ Hawker Tempest Mk V

3 Sqn, RAF / Gütersloh, late 1940s

Represented by the commander's aircraft, 3 Sqn moved to Germany after the war, and retained its Tempests for another three years before transitioning to the Vampire in mid-1948, as the first RAF jet fighter unit in Germany. This particular aircraft wore a silver scheme combined with the squadron's green markings.

Specifications

Crew: 1

Powerplant: 1 x 1626kW (2180hp) Napier Sabre IIA H-type piston engine

Maximum speed: 686km/h (426mph)

Range: 2092km (1300 miles)

Service ceiling: 10,975m (36,000ft)

Dimensions: span 12.5m (41ft); length 10.26m (33ft 8in); height 4.9m (16ft 1in)

Weight: 6142kg (13,540lb) loaded

Armament: 4 x 20mm (.78in) Hispano cannon in wings, plus up to 907kg (2000lb) of stores consisting of either 2 bombs or 8 rockets

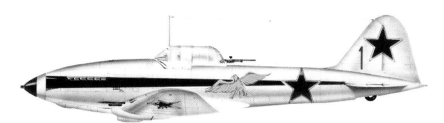

Specifications

Crew: 2

Powerplant: 1 x 1320kW (1770hp) Mikulin AM-42 liquid-cooled V-12 engine

Maximum speed: 550km/h (342mph)

Range: 800km (550 miles)

Service ceiling: 4000m (13,123ft)

Dimensions: span 13.40m (44ft); length 11.12m

(36ft 6in); height 4.10m (13ft 5in)

Weight: 6345kg (14,000lb) loaded

Armament: 2 x 23mm (0.9in) Nudelman-Suranov NS-23 cannons; 1 x 12.7mm (0.5in) UBST cannon in the BU-9 rear gunner station; up to 600kg (1320lb) bomb load

▲ Ilyushin Il-10

Group of Soviet Forces in Germany / mid-1940s–early 1950s

With the end of the war, Soviet aviation units remained stationed in the eastern part of Germany, frequently occupying the airfields that had previously served the wartime German Luftwaffe. This specially marked Il-10 was typical of those aircraft that formed the initial equipment of the GSFG in the early 1950s.

Berlin Airlift
1948–1949

The first major confrontation of the Cold War occurred in Berlin, where Stalin hoped to force the Western Allies out of Germany's former capital, eventually subjecting the city to a blockade.

WHILE BRITAIN AND the U.S. intended that Germany would eventually be rehabilitated, Stalin feared a revival of German power and sought to strip its assets through reparations. British and U.S. occupation zones in the west saw the establishment of trade unions, a free press and a fledgling political framework. British and U.S. zones were then merged, later to be joined by the French zone, and a federal government was eventually established, together with currency reform – another bugbear for the Soviets.

The blockade begins

The major problem, however, was Berlin, isolated 160km (100 miles) within the Soviet zone and divided in turn between the four Allied powers. Stalin wanted the other three powers out and had begun to restrict access to the Western sectors. From 31 March 1948, road traffic to Berlin was subject to Soviet inspection. When the Western powers refused to comply, Stalin severed all links with the West, with the exception of food and freight trains.

Finally, at midnight on 18 June, all passenger traffic between Berlin and the Western zones was banned; 24 hours later, all food trains were stopped. The only option open to the Western powers was to maintain their garrisons and the local population by air. This mammoth task required an estimated 2000

USAF AND U.S. NAVY, BERLIN AIRLIFT		
Aircraft	Unit	Base
C-47, C-54, C-82	60th TCG	Rhein-Main, Wiesbaden
C-47, C-54	61st TCG	Rhein-Main
C-54	313rd TCG	Fassberg
C-54	513rd TCG	Rhein-Main
R5D	VR-6, VR-8	Rhein-Main
B-29A	2nd BG	Lakenheath
B-29A	28th BG	Scampton
B-29A	301st BG	Fürstenfeldbruck, Scampton
B-29A	307th BG	Marham, Waddington
F-80A/B	36th FG, 56th FG	Fürstenfeldbruck
WB-29A	18th WS	Rhein-Main

▲ Lockheed F-80A Shooting Star

62nd Fighter Squadron, 56th Fighter Group, USAF, Fürstenfeldbruck, 1948

Harassment by Soviet Yak-3s and La-9s in the Berlin air corridors during the airlift saw 42 dive-strafe incidents reported by U.S. aircrew, plus 14 more of gunfire close to transports, and 96 near-misses. The U.S. response was to deploy two groups of B-29 bombers to the UK, and a wing of F-80s to Fürstenfeldbruck airbase in Bavaria. This F-80A was one of those deployed to Fürstenfeldbruck.

Specifications

Crew: 1

Powerplant: 1 x 17.1kN (3,850lb) J33-GE-11 or J33-A-9 turbojet engine

Maximum speed: 792km/h (492mph)

Range: 2317km (1440 miles)

Service ceiling: 13,716m (45,000ft)

Dimensions: span 11.81m (38ft 9in); length 10.49m (34ft 5in); height 3.43m (11ft 3in)

Weight: 6350kg (14,000lb) loaded

Armament: 6 x 12.7mm (0.5in) MGs, 10 x 127mm (5in) rockets or 907kg (2000lb) bombs tons of food and supplies per day, simply to prevent the city's 2.5 million Western inhabitants starving.

At the time, the RAF transport fleet was in poor shape, with just 153 aircraft available, primarily obsolescent Dakotas and Yorks. A full-scale airlift was nevertheless put into action, and by 29 June RAF Transport Command's entire Dakota fleet was in Germany, supported by Australian, New Zealand and South African personnel. From 1 July, Yorks and Sunderland flying boats became involved, together with the recently introduced Hastings, and the entire front-line RAF transport force was now dedicated to the operation, codenamed Plainfare by the British.

The RAF was supplemented by large numbers of civilian transports, including converted Haltons, Lancastrians and Liberators. Civil aircraft were active from August, but the major contribution was made by the USAF, which initially provided 102 C-47s and soon began to mobilize its more capable C-54 fleet. Eight C-54 squadrons were involved in the operation from 23 July, and at the same time Maj Gen William H. Tunner took command, with his reorganization maximizing the effect of the airlift. By mid-August, U.S. aircraft had begun operating from airfields in the British zone, Celle and Fassberg, which reduced the flying time to the beleaguered city.

RAF, BERLIN AIRLIFT		
Aircraft	**Unit**	**Base**
Dakota IV	30 Sqn, 46 Sqn, 18 Sqn, 240 OCU	Wunstorf, Fassberg, Lübeck
Dakota IV, Hastings C.Mk 1	53 Sqn	Wunstorf, Fassberg, Lübeck, Schleswigland
Dakota IV	77 Sqn	Fassberg, Lübeck
Dakota IV	238 Sqn, 10 Sqn	Wunstorf, Fassberg
Dakota IV	27 Sqn	Schleswigland, Wunstorf, Fassberg, Lübeck
Dakota IV	62 Sqn	Fassberg, Lübeck
Dakota IV, York C.Mk 1	24 Sqn	Lübeck, Bückeburg
York C.Mk 1	40 Sqn, 51 Sqn, 59 Sqn, 99 Sqn, 242 Sqn, 511 Sqn, 241 OCU, 206 Sqn	Wunstorf
Sunderland Mk V	201 Sqn, 230 Sqn	Finkenwerder
Hastings C.Mk 1	47 Sqn, 297 Sqn	Schleswigland
Tempest Mk II	135 Wing	Gütersloh

▲ **Tempest Mk II**

33 Sqn, RAF / Gütersloh, 1948

At the time of the Berlin Airlift, half of the 10 RAF fighter squadrons that equipped the British Air Force of the Occupation (BAFO) were equipped with Tempest day fighters. This Tempest Mk II served with 33 Sqn at Gütersloh, part of the Western effort to counter Soviet aggression during the months of the blockade.

Specifications

Crew: 1

Powerplant: 1 x 1931kW (2590hp) Bristol Centaurus V 17-cylinder radial engine

Maximum speed: 708km/h (440mph)

Range: 2736km (1700 miles)

Service ceiling: 11,430m (37,500ft)

Dimensions: span 12.49m (41ft); length 10.49m (34ft 5in); height 4.42m (14ft 6in)

Weight: 5352kg (11,800lb) loaded

Armament: 4 x 20mm (.0.78in) cannon, external bomb and rocket load of 907kg (2000lb)

Original estimates concerning required tonnage turned out to be far too low: at least 4000 tons was required each day, especially with winter approaching. In July over 2000 tons of supplies were flown in daily, before averages of 3839 and 4600 tons were achieved in September and October.

Tunner established the Combined Air Lift Task Force (Provisional) in mid-October, improving coordination, and 300 C-54s replaced the remaining USAF C-47s. The RAF contribution became less important, with Dakotas and Yorks departing Celle and Fassberg to make way for C-54s. The British effort thereafter focused on transport of awkward cargo, passengers and export of Berlin-made goods.

At the peak of operations, aircraft were taking off or landing at Berlin's Tempelhof and Gatow airports every 90 seconds, with a break in operations only for a brief period in November. Eventually, almost one ton of supplies was flown into the city for every Berliner, including 1,586,530 tons of coal, 92,282 tons of wet fuel and 538,016 tons of food, part of an overall total of over 2.3 million tons.

Soviet intimidation was countered by Western resolve, and Stalin lifted the blockade one minute after midnight on 12 May 1949, although the airlift continued until September. No longer in any doubt about the threat posed by the Soviets, the Western powers established NATO in August 1949.

Specifications

Crew: varied	Dimensions: span 31.60m (103ft 8in);
Powerplant: 4 x 1205kW (1615hp) Bristol	length 22.43m (73ft 7in); height 6.32m
Hercules XVI radial engines	(20ft 9in)
Maximum speed: 515km/h (320mph)	Weight: 30,844kg (68,000lb) loaded
Range: n/a	Armament: none
Service ceiling: 7620m (25,000ft)	

▲ Handley Page Halton

BOAC (later Bond Air Services) / late 1940s

One of 12 Halifax C.Mk 8 transports converted by Shorts for civilian use by BOAC, G-AHDN was later used in the Berlin Airlift, operated by Bond Air Services. The aircraft completed 139 sorties during the operation, carrying over 750 tons of cargo. The aircraft carried additional freight in its ventral pannier.

▲ Avro Lancaster Mk 3

Flight Refuelling Ltd / Wunstorf/Schleswigland, 1948

One of the more specialist aircraft employed by civilian operators during the Berlin Airlift was this Lancaster Mk 3. The aircraft was one of two that had been converted as an aerial tanker by Flight Refuelling, and undertook 40 sorties during the operation, transporting liquid fuels into Berlin.

Specifications

Crew: 7	Dimensions: span 31.09m (102ft);
Powerplant: 4 x 1088kW (1460hp) Rolls-Royce	length 21.18m (69ft 5in); height 5.97m
Merlin 28 or 38 piston engines	(19ft 7in)
Maximum speed: 452km/h (281mph)	Weight: 32,658kg (72,000lb) loaded
Range: 5567km (3459 miles)	Armament: none
Service ceiling: 7467m (24,500ft)	

Berlin Crisis
1961

With the superpowers still at loggerheads over Berlin, Soviet Premier Nikita Khrushchev saw an opportunity to push for a demilitarization plan in Germany, ending Western rights to Berlin.

WITH U.S. PRESIDENT John F. Kennedy only in office for a matter of months, Khrushchev hoped to force the Berlin issue. But West Germany was now a cornerstone of NATO, and the U.S. refused to give it up. Khrushchev issued an ultimatum: if the Berlin issue were not resolved by December 1961, the USSR would be forced to take action over the city.

The Vienna Summit to discuss the issue failed. In July 1961, the Soviet military budget was increased, so Kennedy built up conventional military forces and mobilized Reserve and National Guard units.

Kennedy saw a Soviet threat to take control of the city, and intimated nuclear war if West Berlin were lost. With the border between East and West Germany already secure, the USSR now set about building the Berlin Wall. Construction began in mid-August, and would conclusively separate the city and prevent further emigration from East to West.

As tensions increased, aircraft reserves were sent to Europe from the U.S. In October, 18,500 ANG personnel reported for duty, and 216 home-based USAF and ANG aircraft took up their war stations in Europe, together with an F-104A wing transported by air. Further reinforcements were provided by the RAF, which sent Lightning and Javelin fighter detachments from the UK. Eventually the Berlin Crisis subsided, but the city was now divided.

USAF AND ANG DEPLOYMENTS, BERLIN CRISIS		
Aircraft	**Unit**	**Base**
F-100D	55th TFS	Chaumont, France
F-104A	151st FIS	Ramstein AB, Germany
F-104A	157th FIS	Moron AFB, Spain
F-86H	102nd FW	Phalsbourg, France
F-84F	110th TFS	Toul-Rosières, France
F-84F	141st TFS	Chaumont, France
F-84F	163rd TFS	Chambley, France
F-84F	166th TFS	Etain, France
RF-84F	106th TRS	Dreux/Chaumont, France

Specifications

Crew: 1

Powerplant: 1 x 45kN (10,200lb) Pratt & Whitney J57-P-21/21A turbojet

Maximum speed: 1380km/h (864mph)

Range: 3210km (1995 miles)

Service ceiling: 15,000m (50,000ft)

Dimensions: span 11.8m (38ft 9in); length 15.2m (50ft); height 4.95m (16ft 3in)

Weight: 13,085kg (28.847lb) loaded

Armament: 4 x 20mm (0.79in) M39 cannon, 4 x AIM-9 Sidewinder missiles, provision for 3190kg (7040lb) nuclear bombs

▲ **North American F-100D Super Sabre**

20th TFW, USAFE / Wethersfield, 1961

This F-100D strike fighter was based at Wethersfield, England, during the Berlin Crisis. At the time, USAFE operated two tactical F-100D wings in the UK, plus a further two wings in West Germany. Additional fighter-bombers based in Europe comprised one wing each of F-105D Thunderchiefs and F-101C Voodoos.

NATO's Central Front
1949–1989

Had the Cold War ever turned hot, there is little doubt that Europe's Central Front theatre would have been the crucible in which NATO and Warsaw Pact forces went to war.

IN STARK CONTRAST to the postwar situation in the Soviet occupation zones, in Germany's Western zones demobilization was the order of the day. After the war, USAAF combat groups were reduced from 218 to just two, and troop numbers of the Western Allies were slashed from five million to one million in 12 months. What remained in occupied Germany's Western zones was essentially a 'policing' force. By way of example, at the end of 1947, the British Air Force of Occupation (BAFO) had just 10 front-line squadrons in Germany, reduced from 34.

The situation changed in the wake of the Berlin Airlift, as superpower relations in Europe increasingly began to be defined by paranoia and mistrust, and opposing military alliances began a tense standoff. Air arms re-equipped and expanded, with jet aircraft coming on line in large numbers. After the Berlin Airlift, units were moved forward, towards the east, in

Specifications
Crew: 1
Powerplant: 1 x 32.3kN (7275lb) Avro
Orenda Mark 14 engine
Maximum speed: 975km/h (606mph)
Range: n/a
Service ceiling: 15,450m (50,700ft)
Dimensions: span 11.58m (38ft);
length 11.58m (38ft); height 4.57m (15ft)
Weight: 6628kg (14,613lb) loaded
Armament: 6 x 12.7mm (0.50in) M2
Browning machine guns; 2 x AIM-9
missiles; 2400kg (5300lb) of payload

▲ **Canadair Sabre Mk 6**
Jagdgeschwader 71 'Richthofen', Luftwaffe / Wittmund, 1963
After Canada, West Germany was the major operator of the Sabre Mk 6, this example being flown by the Wittmund-based JG 71, an air defence wing, in 1963. Luftwaffe Sabre day fighters served with a total of three fighter wings (*Jagdgeschwader*), two of which were re-formed as fighter-bomber wings (*Jagdbombergeschwader*) in 1964.

Specifications
Crew: 1
Powerplant: 1 x 32.3kN (7275lb) Avro
Orenda Mark 14 engine
Maximum speed: 975km/h (606mph)
Range: n/a
Service ceiling: 15,450m (50,700ft)
Dimensions: span 11.58m (38ft);
length 11.58m (38ft); height 4.57m (15ft)
Weight: 6628kg (14,613lb) loaded
Armament: 6 x 12.7mm (0.50in) M2
Browning machine guns; 2 x AIM-9
missiles; 2400kg (5300lb) of payload

▲ **Canadair Sabre Mk 6**
439 Sqn, Royal Canadian AF / Marville, late 1950s
Prior to the arrival of the CF-104, the RCAF maintained a wing of Canadian-built Sabre Mk 6s at bases in France (Gros Tenquin, Marville) and West Germany (Baden-Söllingen, Zweibrücken). 439 'Sabre-Toothed Tiger' Sqn flew this Sabre from Marville in the latter half of the 1950s. In the mid-1950s, each wing replaced a squadron of Sabres with CF-100s.

order to defend the air corridors to Berlin and to protect a 48-km (30-mile) deep air defence zone along the border with Soviet-controlled territory.

NATO establishment

NATO's predecessor was the Western Union, a military alliance created in March 1948 and comprising the UK, France, Belgium, Luxembourg and the Netherlands. The North Atlantic Treaty was signed in April 1949, with Denmark, Iceland, Italy, Norway and Portugal joining the U.S. and Canada plus the Western Union nations. Greece and Turkey would join the Alliance in 1952, followed by West Germany in 1955. With the creation of NATO, any aggression against its members was to be met by a coordinated military response.

With the Korean War, NATO's European forces were further bolstered, with the Western powers fearing Soviet expansionism. One expression of this was the 13 RAF Vampire FB.Mk 5 units stood up in Germany between 1950 and 1951, to counter the MiG-15 that had debuted over Korea. In April 1951,

Specifications

Crew: 1
Powerplant: 2 x 72.7kN (16,360lb) Rolls-Royce
 Avon 301 engines
Maximum speed: 2112km/h (1312mph)
Range: 1290km (802 miles)
Service ceiling: 16,770m (55,020ft)

Dimensions: span 10.62m (34ft 11in);
 length 16.84m (55ft 3in); height 5.97m
 (19ft 7in)
Weight: 12,717kg (28,036lb) loaded
Armament: 2 x 30mm ADEN cannon; up to
 2721kg (6000lb) of external ordnance

▲ English Electric Lightning F.Mk 2A

92 Sqn, RAF / Gütersloh, 1975

From the mid-1960s, RAF Germany provided two squadrons of Lightnings for air defence duties. This F.Mk 2A, armed with Firestreak air-to-air missiles, was based at Gütersloh in 1975. The other operator was 19 Sqn, also at Gütersloh. Both units re-equipped with the Phantom FGR.Mk 2 at Wildenrath in the mid-1970s.

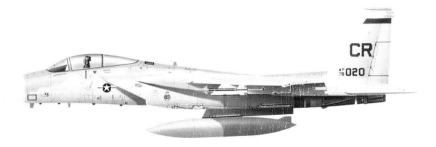

Specifications

Crew: 1
Powerplant: 2 x 105kN (23,810lb) Pratt &
 Whitney F100-PW-100 turbofans
Maximum speed: 2655km/h (1650mph)
Range: 1930km (1200 miles)
Service ceiling: 30,500m (100,000ft)

Dimensions: span 13.05m (42ft 9in); length
 19.43m (63ft 9in); height 5.63m (18ft 5in)
Weight: 25,424kg (56,000lb) loaded
Armament: 1 x 20mm M61A1 cannon, provision
 for up to 7620kg (16,800lb) of stores

▲ McDonnell Douglas F-15C Eagle

32nd TFS, USAFE / Soesterberg, early 1980s

During the 1980s, USAFE maintained a single F-15 air superiority squadron operating from Soesterberg in the Netherlands. The Eagle introduced a powerful new beyond-visual-range engagement capability and also equipped three squadrons of the 36th TFW at Bitburg in West Germany.

▲ **Fairchild A-10A Thunderbolt II**

Northern Germany was 'tank country', and here USAFE's A-10s would have tackled Warsaw Pact armour, which included some 16,400 tanks by the mid-1980s.

Allied Command Europe became operational under Gen Dwight D. Eisenhower, while Allied Air Forces Central Europe stood up under Lt Gen Lauris Norstad. In September 1951 the former BAFO was subordinated to NATO's Supreme Allied Commander Europe (SACEUR) as the 2nd Tactical Air Force.

After the Mutual Defense Assistance Program (MDAP) had supplied many of the Alliance's European air arms with their initial equipment, NATO's posture on the Central Front was further strengthened starting in the late 1950s through the introduction of supersonic aircraft. By now, West Germany had been brought within the fold, with the Luftwaffe being re-established in September 1956. There followed an immense build-up programme, as

Specifications

Crew: 2	17.55m (57ft 7in); height 4.96m (16ft 3in)
Powerplant: 2 x 91.2kN (20,515lb) Rolls-Royce	Weight: 26,308kg (58,000lb) loaded
Spey 202 turbofans	Armament: 4 x AIM-7 Sparrow missiles; two
Maximum speed: 2230km/h (1386mph)	wing pylons for 2 x AIM-7, or 4 x AIM-9
Range: 2817km (1750 miles)	Sidewinders, provision for 20mm cannon;
Service ceiling: 18,300m (60,000ft)	pylons for stores to a maximum weight of
Dimensions: span 11.7m (38ft 5in); length	7257kg (16,000lb)

▲ **McDonnell Douglas Phantom FGR.Mk 2**

17 Sqn, RAF / Brüggen, 1970–75

Formerly a Canberra reconnaissance unit at Wahn, 17 Sqn reformed in September 1970 to operate the Phantom from Brüggen, home of a three-squadron strike wing. Phantoms were retained until December 1975, by which time the squadron had begun conversion to the Jaguar. In January 1985 the squadron began to convert to the Tornado GR.Mk 1.

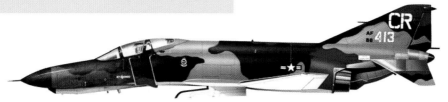

▲ **McDonnell Douglas F-4E Phantom II**

32nd TFW, USAFE / Soesterberg, 1970s

For many years the backbone of USAFE, this F-4E was operated by the 32nd TFW based at Soesterberg (also known as Camp New Amsterdam). The 32nd TFW was part of the 17th Air Force, which was concentrated in West Germany, but this particular unit was unique in being stationed in the Netherlands.

Specifications

Crew: 2	length 17.76m (58ft 3in); height 4.96m
Powerplant: 2 x 79.6kN (17,900lb) General	(16ft 3in)
Electric J79-GE-17 turbojets	Weight: 26,308kg (58,000lb) loaded
Maximum speed: 2390km/h (1485mph)	Armament: 1 x 20mm M61A1 Vulcan cannon;
Range: 817km (1750 miles)	4 x AIM-7 Sparrow or other weapons up to
Service ceiling: 19,685m (60,000ft)	1370kg (3020lb); 2 x AIM-7, or 4 x AIM-9 air-
Dimensions: span 11.7m (38ft 5in);	to-air missiles

the Luftwaffe was reinstated, with 62,000 personnel enrolled within four years, including 1300 pilots.

Division of power

NATO's Central Front air power was ultimately divided more or less evenly between the 2nd Allied Tactical Air Force (2nd ATAF) in the north and the 4th Allied Tactical Air Force (4th ATAF) in the south. Ground forces were divided into Northern and Central Army Groups (NORTHAG and CENTAG), which were analogous to the 2nd and 4th ATAFs.

Both air forces were commanded by Allied Air Forces Central Europe (AAFCE) at Ramstein, West Germany. By the mid-1980s, around 45 squadrons of NATO combat aircraft were based on the Central Front.

Command positions were shared between nations. Supreme Allied Powers Europe (SHAPE) at Mons, Belgium, (formerly Paris) was under the command of SACEUR – always a U.S. officer. The chain of command included AAFCE, directing all air arms in theatre, while HQ Allied Forces Central Europe (AFCENT) at Brunssum in the Netherlands was coordinated land and air operations. In wartime, flying units would revert from national control to NATO, with the exception of the interceptor units, which were always under NATO control.

NATO's 2nd ATAF included Belgium, the UK, the U.S. and West Germany. The area of responsibility stretched from the East German border north to the Danish border and North Sea, from the

Specifications

Crew: 2	9.8m (32ft 2in) (swept); length 22.4m
Powerplant: 2 x 112kN (25,100lb) Pratt &	(73ft 6in); height 5.22m (17ft 1.6in)
Whitney TF30-P-100 afterburning turbofans	Weight: 37,577kg (82,843lb) loaded
Maximum speed: 2655km/h (1650mph)	Armament: 1 x 20mm (0.78in) M61 Vulcan
Range: 2140km (1330 miles)	Gatling cannon (optional) and 14,300kg
Service ceiling: 17,270m (56,650ft)	(31,500lb) bomb load
Dimensions: span 19.2m (63ft) (spread),	

▲ **General Dynamics F-111D**

20th TFW, USAFE / Upper Heyford, early 1980s

Arguably the most potent strike assets available to SACEUR, USAFE F-111s were based in England. The 2nd ATAF included F-111Es from three squadrons of the 20th TFW at Upper Heyford, while the more advanced F-111Fs of the 48th TFW at Lakenheath were assigned to the 4th ATAF. Both were supported by EF-111As.

Specifications

Crew: 1	Dimensions: span 9.45m (31ft); length 15.09m
Powerplant: 1 x 105.7kN (23,770lb) Pratt &	(49ft 6in); height 5.09m (16ft 8in)
Whitney F100-PW-200 turbofan	Weight: 16,057kg (35,400lb) loaded
Maximum speed: 2142km/h (1320mph)	Armament: 1 x General Electric M61A1 20mm
Range: operational radius 925km (525 miles)	multi-barrelled cannon; provision for up to
Service ceiling: above 15,240m (50,000ft)	9276kg (20,450lb) of stores

▲ **Lockheed Martin F-16A Fighting Falcon**

311 Sqn, Royal Netherlands AF / Volkel, mid-1980s

By 1984, the Netherlands had replaced its F-104s with the F-16. Lack of standardization was long an irritant for NATO's Central Front air arms, and the arrival of the F-16 helped address this issue. Armed with AGM-65 Maverick air-to-surface missiles, this F-16A served with a strike/fighter-bomber unit at Volkel.

Franco-German border to the northern end of Luxembourg, and across West Germany along an axis between Kassel and Göttingen. The wartime commander of the 2nd ATAF would have been the commander of RAF Germany (formerly the RAF's 2nd Tactical Air Force), with headquarters at Rheindahlen.

2nd ATAF numbers would have been boosted by deployments from the mainland U.S., while USAFE A-10As would leave the UK for West German soil in wartime, joining RAF Harriers at forward operating locations and dispersed sites, respectively.

▲ **Harrier GR.Mk 3**

Representing nothing less than a revolution in air warfare, the vertical take-off and landing Harrier provided RAF Germany with a uniquely survivable warplane.

Specifications

Crew: 1

Powerplant: 2 x 32.5kN (7305lb) Rolls-
  Royce/Turbomeca Adour Mk 102 turbofans

Maximum speed: 1593km/h (990mph)

Range: 557km (357 miles)

Service ceiling: 14,020m (45,997ft)

Dimensions: span 8.69m (28ft 6in); length
  16.83m (55ft 2.5in); height 4.89m (16ft 0.5in)

Weight: 15,500kg (34,172lb) loaded

Armament: 2 x 30mm DEFA cannon; provision
  for 4536kg (10,000lb) of stores, including a
  nuclear weapon or conventional loads

▲ **SEPECAT Jaguar GR.Mk 1**

14 Sqn, RAF / Brüggen, 1975–85

The RAF's 14 Sqn flew Mosquitos from Wahn until these were replaced by Vampires in 1951, supplemented two years later by Venoms. In 1955, the unit received Hunters, before re-forming at Wildenrath with Canberras in the strike role. Phantoms arrived in 1970, and Jaguars replaced these in 1975.

▲ **Fiat G.91R/3**

Waffenschule der Luftwaffe 50, Luftwaffe / Erding, mid-1960s

Developed to meet a NATO requirement for a light tactical fighter, the G.91R served with two 'light' reconnaissance wings and four light combat wings (*Leichtes Kampfgeschwader*) from 1960 until 1980, when replaced by Alpha Jets. This aircraft served with a Luftwaffe training establishment based at Erding.

Specifications

Crew: 1

Powerplant: 1 x 22.2kN (5000lb) Bristol-
  Siddeley Orpheus 803 turbojet

Maximum speed: 1075km/h (668mph)

Range: 1150km (715 miles)

Service ceiling: 13,100m (43,000ft)

Dimensions: span 8.56m (28ft 1in);
  length 10.3m (33ft 9in); height 4m (13ft 1in)

Weight: 5440kg (11,990lb) loaded

Armament: 4 x 12.7mm (0.5in) M2 Browning
  MGs, provision to carry up to 1814kg (4000lb)
  bomb payload

The southern edge of the Central Front was covered by NATO's 4th ATAF, with an area of responsibility that comprised the lower half of West Germany, below a line running from Luxemburg northeast to Kassel. The 4th ATAF included air arms from Canada, Belgium, the Netherlands, the UK, the U.S. and West Germany, and was commanded by a U.S. officer, with his headquarters based in Heidelberg. The U.S. contribution included the 17th Air Force in the Netherlands and West Germany, and part of the UK-based U.S. 3rd Air Force.

Pending the arrival of British-built swept-wing fighters, the RAF acquired 430 Sabres from Canada, all but two squadrons of the type serving in Germany. The Sabre provided a three-year stopgap pending the delivery of Hunters to 13 squadrons. Meanwhile, night-fighters appeared in the form of Meteor NF.Mk 11s, replaced in turn by Javelins in 1957. By 1961, two squadrons of Javelin FAW.Mk 9s provided the RAF's forward defence in Germany. Later, RAF interceptors comprised Lightnings, and then Phantoms, the latter being switched from their previous strike role to undertake air defence

Specifications
Crew: 1

Powerplant: 2 x 15.56kW (3500lb) Rolls Royce Derwent 8 turbojets

Maximum speed: 925km/h (575mph)

Range: 2253km (1400 miles)

Service ceiling: n/a

Dimensions: span 13.11m (43ft 0in); length 13.49m (44ft 3in); height n/a

Weight: 6954kg (15,330lb) loaded

Armament: none

▲ Gloster Meteor PR.Mk 10
541 Sqn, RAF / Bückeburg, 1954
By the end of 1947, BAFO had just one Spitfire fighter-reconnaissance unit. In 1950-51, three squadrons of Meteors arrived for reconnaissance, with longer-range reconnaissance requirements met by Canberras from 1956. This photo-reconnaissance Meteor served with 541 Sqn at Bückeburg, Germany, in 1954.

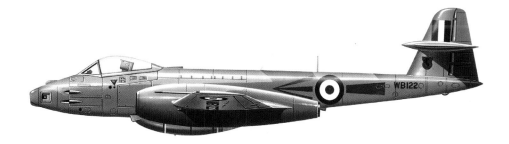

▲ Gloster Meteor FR.Mk 9
79 Sqn, RAF / Bückeburg, 1951-56
79 Sqn reformed with Meteor FR.Mk 9s at Bückeburg in late 1951, and supported unarmed Meteor PR.Mk 10s and Canberras. The fighter-reconnaissance Meteor was replaced by the Swift FR.Mk 5 and the Hunter. Later, RAF Germany included one tactical reconnaissance Phantom unit, which subsequently received Jaguars.

Specifications
Crew: 1

Powerplant: 2 x 15.56kN (3500lb) Rolls Royce Derwent 8 turbojets

Maximum speed: 956km/h (595mph)

Range: 1110km (690 miles)

Service ceiling: n/a

Dimensions: span 11.33m (37ft 2in); length 13.26m (43ft 6in); height n/a

Weight: 7103kg (15,660lb) loaded

Armament: 4 x 20mm cannon

Specifications

Crew: 2

Powerplant: 2 x 79.4kN (17,845lbf) General

Electric J79-GE-17A turbojets

Maximum speed: 2370km/h (1472mph)

Range: 2600km (1615 miles)

Service ceiling: 18,300m (60,000ft)

Dimensions: span 11.7m (38ft 4.5in);

length 19.2m (63ft); height 5m (16ft 6in)

Weight: 18,825kg (41,500lb) loaded

Armament: Up to 8480kg (18,650lb) of

weapons on nine external hardpoints

▲ **McDonnell Douglas RF-4E Phantom II**

Aufklärungsgeschwader 52, Luftwaffe / Leck, late 1970s

Throughout most of the Cold War, the Luftwaffe provided NATO commanders with two reconnaissance wings, initially equipped with 108 RF-84Fs. These were replaced by RF-104Gs, before the arrival of the RF-4E. This RF-4E served with AG 52 at Leck, northern Germany, the wing being assigned to NATO's 2nd ATAF.

duties, and serving the 2nd ATAF with two units at Wildenrath.

Royal Canadian AF units in Europe were initially equipped with Sabres and CF-100s and were based in France and Germany, until the former withdrew from NATO. France itself had provided tactical fighters for the 4the ATAF, as well as fulfilling obligations under Berlin's four-power air traffic agreement. By 1962, the French AF included Mirage III interceptors and fighter-bombers, but France announced its intention to leave NATO in March 1966.

The reborn Luftwaffe was mainly devoted to offensive duties, but also included 225 Canadair Sabres for air defence. The all-weather F-86K was also supplied to the Luftwaffe, as well as the Netherlands. Ultimately, the Luftwaffe air defence capability was provided by two wings, one each assigned to the 2nd and 4th ATAFs, and equipped with F-104G interceptors, and later F-4Fs.

Belgium and the Netherlands both received Hunter day fighters in the 1950s. A beneficiary of the U.S. Offshore Procurement Act, which supported European aircraft for European air arms, the Hunter was built in Belgium and the Netherlands, and provided a replacement for Dutch-built Meteor F.Mk 8s. The Act also funded RAF Javelins and Canberras.

By 1961, the USAFE air defence contribution was spearheaded by a wing of F-102As in West Germany and a squadron of the same type in the Netherlands. Significant change came in the first half of the 1980s, with modernization through the introduction of the F-15 and F-16. Eventually, USAFE declared one

F-15C unit at Soesterberg, the Netherlands, to the 2nd ATAF, while F-15Cs of the 36th TFW at Bitburg were assigned to the 4th ATAF.

In 1978 the Alliance announced plans to establish the NATO Airborne Early Warning Force, with the acquisition of 18 E-3A Airborne Warning And Control System (AWACS) aircraft starting in 1983. Registered in Luxembourg, these were based in Geilenkirchen, West Germany, and were operated by multinational NATO crews.

Strike and close support

The development and subsequent fielding of tactical nuclear weapons was the most critical factor in the development of NATO strike formations on the Central Front. Initially, the capability of the Western powers to launch offensive air operations over Germany was strictly limited. At the end of 1947, for instance, the BAFO had just four squadrons of Mosquito light bombers on strength.

Tactical nuclear weapons began to appear in the mid-1950s, with the U.S.-produced Mk 5, Mk 7 and Mk 12 lightweight bombs. By now, MDAP had ensured that F-84Es (and by 1952) F-84Gs were supplied in their hundreds to NATO air arms, including Belgium and the Netherlands on the Central Front. Swept-wing F-84Fs and RF-84Fs arrived later, and these also served with West Germany. France received F-100s, Thunderjets and Thunderstreaks under MDAP, before withdrawing from NATO, by which time indigenous jets had been introduced to replace U.S.-supplied equipment. The

▲ **Rockwell OV-10A Bronco**

601st Tactical Control Wing, USAFE / Sembach, 1970s

Based at Sembach, West Germany, in the 1970s, this OV-10A forward air control aircraft was on strength with the 601st TCW, which also maintained a squadron of CH-53C helicopters. In the 1980s, the base was also a forward operating location for A-10A close support aircraft and was home to electronic warfare C-130s.

Specifications
Crew: 2

Powerplant: 2 x 533kW (715hp) Garrett T76-G-410/412 turboprop engines

Maximum speed: 452km/h (281mph)

Range: 358km (576 miles)

Service ceiling: 7315m (24,000ft)

Dimensions: span 12.19m (40ft); length 12.67m (41ft 7in); height 4.62m (15ft 2in)

Weight: 6552kg (14,444lb) loaded

Armament: 4 x 7.62mm M60C MGs; pods for 70mm (2.75in) or 125mm (5in) rockets; up to 226kg (500lb) of bombs

Specifications
Crew: 2

Powerplant: 2 x 634kW (850hp) Pratt & Whitney Canada PT6A-41 turboprop engines

Maximum speed: 491km/h (306mph)

Endurance: 5 hours

Service ceiling: 9449m (31,000ft)

Dimensions: span 16.92m (55ft 6in); length 13.34m (43ft 9in); height 4.57m (15ft)

Weight: 6412kg (14,136lb) loaded

Armament: none

▲ **Beechcraft RC-12D**

1st Military Intelligence Brigade, US Army, Wiesbaden, 1980s

An electronic intelligence (ELINT) platform, this RC-12D served with the U.S. Army at Wiesbaden in the 1980s. Charged with battlefield surveillance duties, the RC-12D served with the U.S. Army in both West Germany and Korea, and was equipped with an extensive antenna array for its Improved Guardrail ELINT suite.

'new' Luftwaffe emerged with a backbone provided initially by 375 F-84Fs in five wings, with a primary strike tasking.

Supersonic strike/attack equipment appeared in the form of the F-100, first deployed by the USAFE to Bitburg, West Germany, in March 1956. In 1960, France requested that nuclear-capable USAF aircraft be removed from its territory, so by 1961 there were two wings of USAFE F-100Ds in West Germany, together with a single wing of F-105Ds. At the same time, the UK hosted two wings of USAFE F-100Ds, one F-101 wing, and a bomb wing with the B-66. Offensive assets were supported by a smaller number of tactical reconnaissance units, with USAF RF-101s first deployed in France, and then in the UK. At the time of the Berlin Crisis, the 66th TRW was in France, with the RF-101, while the UK hosted a reconnaissance wing with RB-66s.

With an urgent need to procure more advanced equipment, West Germany ordered the 'multi-role'

Specifications

Crew: 2

Powerplant: 1 x 662kW (888shp) Rolls-Royce
BS 360-07-26 engine

Maximum speed: 296km/h (184mph)

Range: 1850km (999 miles)

Service ceiling: n/a

Dimensions: rotor diameter 12.8m (42ft);
length 12.34m (40ft 6in); height 3.4m
(11.25ft)

Weight: 3878kg (8551lb) loaded

Armament: 8 x BGM-71 TOW anti-tank missiles

▲ **Westland Lynx AH.Mk 1**

1 Wing (BAOR), British Army Air Corps / early 1980s

Helicopters were initially deployed on the Central Front in an observation, casualty evacuation or army cooperation capacity, before undertaking battlefield transport and ultimately anti-armour roles. The British Army Lynx AH.Mk 1 served in the latter, armed with eight TOW anti-tank guided missiles.

F-104G for the nuclear strike, fighter-bomber, air defence and reconnaissance roles, and 916 examples were eventually delivered. Benefiting from European assembly, the F-104G was also selected by Belgium, Canada and the Dutch for Central Front service.

No. 1 Canadian Air Group replaced its Sabres and CF-100s with CF-104s to equip a strike wing starting in 1962, before these began to give way to the CF-188 in the mid-1980s. Canada's eight squadrons were cut back to three in the first half of the 1980s, with the nuclear role now removed. The last three squadrons were assigned a conventional ground-attack role, operating from Baden-Söllingen, West Germany, under Commander, Canadian Forces Europe.

Before France withdrew from NATO, the French AF Mirage III fighter-bomber had been fielded, armed with indigenous tactical nuclear bombs.

British nuclear assets

After Korea, re-equipment of the British 2nd TAF was prioritized, and it grew to 25 squadrons, including Venom FB.Mk 1s for conventional ground attack. Four squadrons of Canberra B(I).Mk 6s and B(I).Mk 8s provided a tactical nuclear capability by 1958, each unit maintaining one aircraft on 15-minute readiness. Britain's 2nd TAF was reduced by half after the 1957 Defence White Paper, and the surviving 18 front-line squadrons were relocated to bases close to the Dutch border, offering improved protection against an initial Warsaw Pact thrust.

Valiants and Vulcans based in the UK supplemented RAF Germany Canberras in the low-level free-fall tactical role. Fatigue saw the Valiants withdrawn in 1964, while the Canberra interdictors continued into the early 1970s, armed with single Mk 28 tactical nuclear bombs. Replacing the Canberra in the offensive role was the Phantom, with three strike/attack squadrons equipped starting in 1970. When the Jaguar arrived as a replacement from 1975–76, the Phantoms were reassigned to air defence.

Towards the end of the Cold War, the USAFE strike force comprised two wings of F-111s at Lakenheath and Upper Heyford in England, divided between 2nd and 4th ATAFs and supported by EF-111As for defence suppression. Nuclear-capable F-4Es and F-16s were based in West Germany and, in addition, 100 or so more F-111s were available in the U.S. for deployment to Europe. At the time, the U.S. maintained around 1,850 free-fall nuclear bombs in Europe, including those provided to other NATO air arms under the 'dual-key' arrangement.

By the mid-1980s, the 2nd ATAF's strike/attack force included eight RAF Tornado squadrons at Brüggen and Laarbruch in West Germany (one for reconnaissance), and single Luftwaffe wings equipped with the Tornado and the F-4F fighter-bomber. Two squadrons of RAF Harriers would operate from dispersed sites near the front line, together with A-10As. Normally based with the 81st TFW at Bentwaters and Woodbridge in England, the A-10s were divided between 2nd and 4th ATAFs and

Specifications

Crew: 3

Powerplant: 2 x 1070kW (1435shp) Turbomeca
Turmo IIIC4 turbo-shafts

Maximum speed: 263km/h (163mph)

Range: 570km (360 miles)

Service ceiling: 4800m (15,750ft)

Dimensions: rotor diameter 15m (49ft 3in);
length 18.15m (59ft 6in); height 5.14m
(16ft 10in)

Weight: 7400kg (16,300lb) loaded

Armament: 20mm (0.8in) cannon and 7.62mm
(0.30in) MGs

▲ Aérospatiale Puma HC.Mk 1

230 Sqn, RAF / Gütersloh, early 1980s

RAF Germany support helicopter forces were technically assigned to 2nd ATAF but normally operated in support of the British Army of the Rhine (BAOR). This RAF Puma was based at Gütersloh, West Germany, and wears Tiger stripes associated with a NATO Tiger Meet. In the 1980s, Gütersloh also hosted two RAF Harrier squadrons and one Chinook squadron.

Specifications

Crew: 3

Powerplant: 2 x 2927kW (3925shp) General
Electric T64-GE-413 turboshaft

Maximum speed: 395km/h (196mph)

Range: 1000km (620 miles)

Service ceiling: 5106m (16,750ft)

Dimensions: rotor diameter 22.01m (72ft 3in);
length 26.97m (88ft 6in); height 7.6m
(24ft 11in)

Weight: 15,227kg (33,500lb) loaded

Armament: 2 x 7.62mm MG3 MGs

▲ Sikorsky CH-53G

Mittleres Transporthubscrauberregiment 35, Heeresflieger / Mendig, early 1980s

The German Army and Luftwaffe provided a significant transport force for NATO's battlefield commanders, eventually centered on a fleet of around 90 Transalls and 110 CH-53 transport helicopters. Heavy-lift CH-53Gs served with front-line *Heeresflieger* regiments at Rheine Bentlage, Lauphiem and Niedermendig.

Specifications

Crew: 1 or 2 (+ 4 passengers)

Powerplant: 2 x 313kW (420shp) Allison
250-C20B turboshaft engines

Maximum speed: 270km/h (168mph)

Range: 550km (342 miles)

Service ceiling: 5182m (17,000ft)

Dimensions: rotor diameter 9.84m
(32ft 3in); length 11.86m (38ft 10in);
height 3m (9ft 11.77in)

Weight: 2400kg (5291lb) loaded

Armament: none

▲ Messerschmitt Bo 105

300 Sqn, Royal Netherlands AF / Deelen, late 1970s

By the mid-1980s, the Netherlands provided army cooperation and liaison on the Central Front through a force of Alouette III helicopters (two units, at Soesterberg and Deelen) and Bo 105s (one unit, 300 Sqn based at Deelen from 1976). The Netherlands also maintained a single fixed-wing transport squadron, 334 Sqn, equipped with F.27 Troopships.

operated rotating detachments at four forward operating locations in West Germany. Conventional ground-attack assets included a wing of Luftwaffe Alpha Jets, three Belgian Mirage 5BA units and four squadrons of Dutch NF-5As. Tactical recce needs were addressed by one Dutch F-16 unit, one Belgian Mirage 5BR unit, USAFE RF-4Es of the 1st TRS at Alconbury, a wing of Luftwaffe RF-4Es, a squadron of RAF Jaguars and half a squadron of RAF Harriers.

The 4th ATAF offensive capability ultimately rested with three Luftwaffe Tornado wings, three Canadian CF-188 squadrons, F-16s of the USAFE's 50th TFW at Hahn and the 86th TFW at Ramstein, plus single wings of Luftwaffe Alpha Jets and F-4Fs. Electronic warfare and special operations support were provided by Spangdahlem-based Wild Weasel F-4Gs and F-4Es, EF-111As at Upper Heyford and MC-130Es at Ramstein. 4th ATAF recce missions were tasked to the 38th TRS RF-4Es at Zweibrücken, and a single Luftwaffe RF-4E wing.

The withdrawal of 35,000 U.S. personnel from Europe from 1967 increased the importance and

Specifications
Crew: 1/2
Powerplant: 1 x 236kW (317shp) Allison
  T63-A-700 turboshaft
Maximum speed: 222km/h (138mph)
Range: 481km (299 miles)
Service ceiling: 5800m (19,000ft)
Dimensions: span 10.77m (35ft 4in);
  length 9.8m (32ft 2in); height 2.92m
  (9ft 7in)
Weight: 1360kg (3000lb) loaded
Armament: 1 x 7.62mm (0.3in) M134
  minigun or 1 x 40mm (1.57in) M129
  grenade launcher

▲ **Douglas OH-58A Kiowa**
25th Aviation Company, U.S. Army / 1980s
In addition to the AH-1G and the TOW-equipped AH-1Q/S close support helicopters, U.S. Army formations in Europe were equipped with the OH-58A for observation and liaison. Additional U.S. Army helicopter types were dedicated to air mobility, and included the CH-47 Chinook and the UH-60A Black Hawk, 150 examples of which were in Germany by the mid-1980s.

Specifications
Crew: 6
Powerplant: 4 x 1834kW (3800hp) Pratt &
  Whitney R-4360 engines
Maximum speed: 520km/h (320mph)
Range: 3500km (2175 miles)
Service ceiling: 10,000m (34,000ft)
Dimensions: span 53.06m (174ft 1in);
  length 40m (130ft); height 14.7m (48ft 4in)
Weight: 98,000kg (216,000lb) loaded
Armament: none

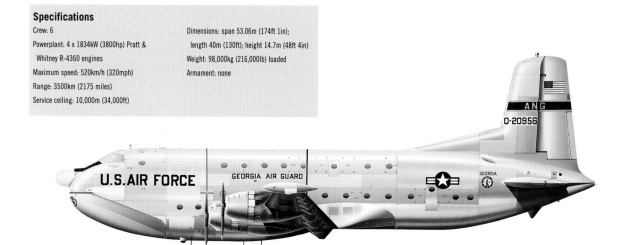

▲ **Douglas C-124C Globemaster II**
63rd TCW, USAF / early 1960s
In times of tension, the sea lines of communication between the U.S. and Europe were reinforced by airlift. This C-124 was one of those involved in the deployment of troops, equipment and fighters to Europe during the 1961 Berlin Crisis. Also active were C-97s, both types flying into ex-13th Air Force bases in France.

urgency of upgrading the 'dual basing' concept and improving rapid reinforcement by home-based air and ground units. Deployments were regularly practised, with one of the first major exercises being Crested Cap I in 1969, when 96 F-4Ds and 3500 USAF personnel deployed to West Germany.

NATO standardization

After MDAP had paved the way in establishing postwar Western European air arms, NATO began issuing its own requirements, most notably resulting in the G.91 light attack aircraft, which served on the Central Front with West Germany.

Standardization of NATO air arms was never successfully addressed. For example, Belgium and the Netherlands selected different aircraft to replace the RF/F-84F in the late 1960s, opting for the Mirage 5 and NF-5 respectively. Things improved when both procured the licence-produced F-16 to replace the F-104. By 1982, Belgium and the Netherlands had placed orders for 116 and 124 respectively. Belgium's F-16s equipped four Cold War squadrons, though two wings of Mirage 5 fighter-bombers also survived into the 1980s. Assigned to NATO's 2nd ATAF, the Dutch Tactical Air Command eventually fielded five F-16 units, plus four squadrons of NF-5s.

▲ Lockheed C-5A Galaxy

436th Military Airlift Wing, USAF / Dover AFB, 1970s

Europe's NATO contingent would have been unable to sustain a robust defence in wartime without significant reinforcement from the U.S. Movement of U.S. troops and materiel to Europe was reliant on the USAF's Military Airlift Command, the backbone of which was eventually provided by C-5s and C-141s.

Specifications

Crew: 6

Powerplant: 4 x 191kN (43,000lb) General Electric TF39-GE-1C turbofan engines

Maximum speed: 908km/h (564mph)

Range: 9560km (5940 miles)

Service ceiling: 10,895m (35,745ft)

Dimensions: span 67.88m (222ft 9in); length 75.54m (247ft 10in); height 19.85m (65ft 1in)

Weight: 379,657kg (837,000lb) loaded

Armament: None

Specifications

Crew: 5–6

Powerplant: 4 x 93.4kN (21,000lb) Pratt & Whitney TF33-7 turbofans

Maximum speed: 912km/h (567mph)

Range: 4723km (2935 miles)

Service ceiling: 12,500m (41,000ft)

Dimensions: span 48.74m (159ft 11in); length 51.29m (168ft 3.5in); height 11.96m (39ft 3in)

Weight: 155,582kg (343,000lb) loaded

Armament: none

▲ Lockheed C-141B StarLifter

438th Military Airlift Wing, USAF / McGuire AFB, early 1980s

Deployments of U.S.-based units to the Central Front were practised through regular Reforger (Reinforcement of Forces in Germany) exercises. During one such exercise in 1976, the U.S. 101st Airborne Division deployed to West Germany, with 11,000 troops being ferried in the course of 125 C-141 sorties.

Greece and Turkey
1946–1974

While both Greece and Turkey became NATO members, the long-standing tensions between them more than once led to the outbreak of fighting, becoming a thorn in the side of the Alliance.

COMPARED TO NATO's Central and Northern Fronts, the Southern Front was assigned much lower strategic importance. However, apathy between Greece and Turkey resulted in problematic relations with the U.S., numerous disputes and open conflict.

One of the earliest flashpoints of the Cold War, Greece saw a communist-inspired revolution gain a foothold immediately after the war. British air power was deployed, and Greece remained within the British sphere of influence. Aided by U.S. military deliveries, the Greek Monarchists eventually put down the communist rebellion.

War in Cyprus

After Cyprus was granted independence by the UK in 1960, Greek and Turkish troops remained on the island, watched by UN peacekeepers. Seeking amalgamation with Greece, Greek-Cypriot factions attacked villages near the Cypriot capital, Nicosia, in August 1963, triggering a response by Turkey, which sent F-84G and F-100C/D fighter-bombers to attack Greek-Cypriot positions.

TURKISH AF AND ARMY, 1974		
Aircraft	Unit	Base
F-100D/F	111 Filo, 132 Filo, 181 Filo	Adana
F-104G	141 Filo	Adana
C.160D	221 Filo	Erkilet
C-47	223 Filo	Etimesgut
UH-1, AB.204	Army	Antalya

In the wake of a Greek-Cypriot coup attempt in July 1974, Turkey invaded the island, with troops being delivered by AB.204 helicopters and C.160D and C-47 transports. An amphibious landing was accompanied by air strikes by F-100s and F-104s.

A Turkish destroyer was sunk in a 'friendly fire' incident by Turkish warplanes, while RAF transports and Royal Navy and U.S. Marine Corps helicopters mounted an evacuation for foreign nationals. After a renewed Turkish offensive in August – during which F-100s again attacked Greek-Cypriot targets – a ceasefire was declared, leaving the island divided.

Specifications

Crew: 1

Powerplant: 1 x 45kN (10,200lb) Pratt & Whitney J57-P-21/21A turbojet

Maximum speed: 1380km/h (864mph)

Range: 3210km (1995 miles)

Service ceiling: 15,000m (50,000ft)

Dimensions: span 11.8m (38ft 9in); length 15.2m (50ft); height 4.95m (16ft 3in)

Weight: 13,085kg (28,847lb) loaded

Armament: 4 x 20mm (0.79in) M39 cannon, 4 x AIM-9 Sidewinder missiles, provision for 3190kg (7040lb) nuclear bombs

▲ **North American F-100C Super Sabre**

111 Filo, Turkish AF / Eskisehir, mid-1960s

A former USAF aircraft, this F-100C normally served in the ground-attack role from Eskisehir. In 1964, the unit was based at Adana, and was among those involved in attacks against Greek targets in Cyprus. By the time of the 1974 fighting, the F-100C had been withdrawn, although F-100D/Fs remained in use.

Warsaw Pact on the Central Front
1955–1989

Forward-deployed U.S. and British air power rapidly contracted after VE-Day, but in the east, aircraft numbers were reduced only marginally and would form the backbone of the Warsaw Pact.

NINE DAYS AFTER West Germany joined NATO in May 1955, the Soviets organized the signing of the Treaty of Friendship, Mutual Assistance and Cooperation – better known as the Warsaw Pact. Under the terms of this treaty, the USSR was aligned militarily with Albania (which later withdrew from the Alliance), Bulgaria, Czechoslovakia, East Germany, Hungary, Poland and Romania. Together, these nations were committed to the defence of the socialist states in Central and Eastern Europe, and their air arms formed a counter to those of NATO, arranged on the opposite side of the iron curtain. More importantly for Moscow, the new Alliance ensured that the Soviet satellite states in Eastern

▲ Ilyushin Il-10
Soviet Frontal Aviation / late 1940s–early 1950s

Soviet ground-attack regiments began to replace the Il-2 Shturmovik with the improved Il-10 from October 1944. The type remained an important asset for the Soviet air arms in the immediate postwar period, and examples were forward-deployed with the Group of Soviet Forces in Germany.

Specifications

Crew: 2

Powerplant: 1 x 1320kW (1770hp) Mikulin
AM-42 liquid-cooled V-12 engine

Maximum speed: 550km/h (342mph)

Range: 800km (550 miles)

Service ceiling: 4000m (13,123ft)

Dimensions: span 13.40m (44ft);

length 11.12m (36ft 6in); height 4.10m (13ft 5in)

Weight: 6,345kg (14,000lb) loaded

Armament: 2 x 23mm (0.9in) Nudelman-
Suranov NS-23 cannons; 1 x 12.7mm (0.5in)
UBST cannon in the BU-9 rear gunner station;
up to 600kg (1320lb) bomb load

▲ Mikoyan-Gurevich MiG-21PF
Soviet Frontal Aviation / mid-1960s

In the days of 'massive retaliation', the focus of Soviet frontal air power was placed on air defence, with limited close support and ground-attack capabilities. In the 1970s, the MiG-21 was dominant among Soviet fighter units on the Central Front, this example being a MiG-21PF, which introduced a new R-11 engine.

Specifications

Crew: 1

Powerplant: 1 x 60.8kN (13,668lb) thrust
Tumanskii afterburning turbojet

Maximum speed: 2050km/h (1300mph)

Range: 1800km (1118 miles)

Service ceiling: 17,000m (57,750ft)

Dimensions: span 7.15m (23ft 5.5in); length

(including probe) 15.76m (51ft 8.5in);
height 4.1m (13ft 5.5in)

Weight: 9400kg (20,723lb) loaded

Armament: 1 x 23mm cannon, provision for
about 1500kg (3307lb) of stores, including air-
to-air missiles, rocket pods, napalm tanks or
drop tanks

Specifications

Crew: 1

Powerplant: 1 x 88.2kN (19,842lb) Lyulka AL-7F
turbojet

Maximum speed: 1700km/h (1056mph)

Range: 320km (199 miles)

Service ceiling: 15,150m (49,700ft)

Dimensions: span 8.93m (29ft 3.5in); length

17.37m (57ft); height 4.7m (15ft 5in)

Weight: 13,500kg (29,750lb) loaded

Armament: 2 x 30mm NR-30 cannon; four
external pylons for 2 x 750kg (1653lb) and
2 x 500kg (1102lb) bombs, but with two tanks
on fuselage pylons, total external weapon load
is reduced to 1000kg (2205lb)

▲ Sukhoi Su-7BMK

Soviet Frontal Aviation / early 1970s

The Su-7 was the first dedicated ground-attack jet to be deployed in significant numbers by Soviet formations on the Central Front. This example is armed with unguided air-to-ground rockets. The fixed-geometry Su-7 eventually gave way to the Su-17 series, which featured a variable-geometry wing planform.

Specifications

Crew: 1

Powerplant: 1 x 103.4kN (23,353lb) Tumanskii
R-29B-300 turbojet

Maximum speed: 1885km/h (1170mph)

Range: 540km (335 miles)

Service ceiling: over 14,000m (45,900ft)

Dimensions: span 13.97m (45ft 10in) spread,
7.78m (25ft 6.25in) swept; length 17.07m
(56ft 0.75in); height 5m (16ft 5in)

Weight: 20,300kg (44,750lb) loaded

Armament: 1 x 23mm cannon, provision for up
to 4000kg (8818lb) of stores

▲ Mikoyan-Gurevich MiG-27

Soviet Frontal Aviation / mid-1980s

NATO's shift to the doctrine of 'flexible response' saw the increasing primacy of the fighter-bomber with the Soviet air arms, and introduction of ever more capable strike/attack assets. The MiG-27 was the backbone of the 16th Air Army strike force by the end of the Cold War, with four regiments in East Germany.

▲ Mil Mi-8T

Soviet Army Aviation / late 1970s

Both the Mi-8 and Mi-24 were flexible, agile, well armed and could deliver troops to the rear of the battlefield when needed. The example illustrated is of the Mi-8T version, and is shown armed with external packs of 57mm rockets. Assault regiments typically operated a mix of both Mi-8 and Mi-24 helicopters.

Specifications

Crew: 3

Powerplant: 2 x 1454kW (1950shp) Klimov
TV3-117Mt turboshafts

Maximum speed: 260km/h (162mph)

Range: 450km (280 miles)

Service ceiling: 4,500m (14,765ft)

Dimensions: rotor diameter 21.29m
(69ft 10in); length 18.17m (59ft 7in);
height 5.65m (18ft 6in)

Weight: 11,100kg (24,470lb)

Armament: up to 1500kg (3,300lb) of
disposable stores

▲ Mil Mi-24D
Soviet Army Aviation / early 1980s
The Mi-24 was especially feared in the West, carrying an eight-man infantry squad or armament that included anti-tank missiles and unguided rockets. This is an example of the Mi-24D, which introduced a re-profiled forward fuselage, with tandem seating under separate cockpit transparencies for the pilot and gunner.

Specifications
Crew: 2-3
Powerplant: 2 x 1600kW (2200hp) Isotov
  TV-3-117 turbines
Maximum speed: 335km/h (208mph)
Range: 450km (280 miles)
Service ceiling: 4500m (14,750ft)

Dimensions: rotor diameter 17.3m (56 ft 7in);
  length 17.5m (57ft 4in); height 6.5m (21ft 3in)
Weight: 12,000kg (26,500lb) loaded
Armament: 1 x 12.7mm Gatling type MG,
  57mm rockets, AT-2C/ SWATTER ATGMs; up to
  500kg (1,102lb) bomb load

Specifications
Crew: 2-3
Powerplant: 2 x 1600kW (2,200hp) Isotov
  TV-3-117 turbines
Maximum speed: 335km/h (208mph)
Range: 450km (280 miles)
Service ceiling: 4500m (14,750ft)

Dimensions: rotor diameter 17.3m (56 ft 7in);
  length 17.5m (57ft 4in); height 6.5m (21ft 3in)
Weight: 12,000kg (26,500lb) loaded
Armament: 1 x fixed 30mm twin gun on the
  right fuselage side, 57mm rockets, AT-6C/
  SPIRAL ATGMs

▲ Mil Mi-24P
Soviet Army Aviation / mid-1980s
The Mi-24P was a dedicated anti-armour version of the Mi-24, with a harder-hitting 30mm twin-barrel cannon replacing the previous 12.7mm four-barrel machine-gun. Known to NATO as 'Hind-F', the Mi-24P was developed on the basis of combat experience in Afghanistan.

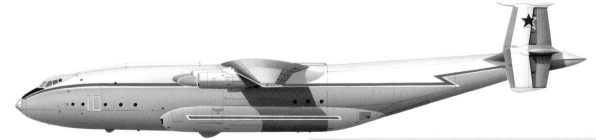

▲ Antonov An-22
Soviet Transport Aviation / 1970s
In the same way that USAFE and other European NATO forces relied upon strategic airlift capacity from the continental U.S., Soviet units forward-deployed in Eastern Europe were supplied by Soviet Transport Aviation. For much of the Cold War, the largest airlift asset available to the Soviets was the four-turboprop An-22.

Specifications
Crew: 5–6
Powerplant: 4 x 11,030kW (15,000hp)
  Kuznetsov NK-12MA turboprops
Maximum speed: 740km/h (460mph)
Range: 5000km (3100 miles)
Service ceiling: 8000m (26,240ft)

Dimensions: 64.4m (211ft 3in);
  length 57.9m (190ft 0in); height 12.53m
  (41ft 1in)
Weight: 250,000kg (551,000lb) loaded
Payload: 80,000kg (180,000lb)

SOVIET AF COMBAT UNITS IN GERMANY, 1990		
Aircraft	Unit	Base
MiG-29, MiG-23	33rd Fighter Regiment	Wittstock
MiG-29, MiG-23	733rd Fighter Regiment	Pütnitz
MiG-29, MiG-23	787th Fighter Regiment	Eberswalde
MiG-29, MiG-23	31st Fighter Regiment	Alt Lonnewitz
MiG-29, MiG-23	85th Fighter Regiment	Merseburg
MiG-29, MiG-23	968th Fighter Regiment	Nobitz
MiG-29, MiG-23	35th Fighter Regiment	Zerbst
MiG-29, MiG-23	73rd Fighter Regiment	Köthen
MiG-23	833rd Fighter Regiment	Altes Lager
MiG-27, MiG-23	559th Fighter-Bomber Regiment	Finsterwalde
MiG-27, MiG-23	296th Fighter-Bomber Regiment	Grossenhain
MiG-27, MiG-23	911th Fighter-Bomber Regiment	Brand
MiG-27, MiG-23	19th Fighter-Bomber Regiment	Mirow-Lärz
Su-17	20th Fighter-Bomber Regiment	Gross Dölln
Su-17	730th Fighter-Bomber Regiment	Neuruppin
Su-24	11th Reconnaissance Regiment	Welzow
Su-17	294th Reconnaissance Regiment	Allstedt
MiG-25	931st Reconnaissance Regiment	Werneuchen
Su-25	357th Combat Regiment	Brandis
Su-25	368th Combat Regiment	Tütow

Europe were integrated as a single defensive buffer zone, dissuading any future attack from the West.

By the mid-1980s, Warsaw Pact air power on the Central Front included around 2700 fixed-wing tactical aircraft, compared to 1300 in NATO's 2nd and 4th ATAFs. Total Warsaw Pact fixed-wing strength in Northern and Central Europe amounted to 4750 aircraft, against around 2000 for NATO. In the same way that home-based U.S. assets were available to reinforce NATO in wartime, additional Soviet air power could be provided by units normally based in the central and eastern USSR.

The Warsaw Pact was under Soviet control, with a Soviet commander-in-chief and chief-of-staff.

Advantages of this included a robust command structure and the potential for a high degree of standardization, while the major disadvantage remained Soviet misgivings concerning the reliability of satellite states. The latter were manifest during the Soviet military response to uprisings in Hungary in 1956 and Prague in 1968.

In peacetime, the USSR was divided into 16 Military Districts (MDs), plus four land/air Groups of Soviet Forces forward-deployed in satellite countries: the Group of Soviet Forces in Germany; Northern Group of Soviet Forces (in Poland); Central Group of Soviet Forces (Czechoslovakia); and Southern Group of Soviet Forces (Hungary). It was these four groupings that were arranged against NATO's forces on the Central Front. Soviet air power in Poland eventually amounted to around 300 aircraft. The Poland-based Soviet inventory included the Su-24 strike aircraft (introduced there in 1982) and Su-27 interceptors that were expected to counter NATO's advanced low-level strike aircraft. A further 200 Soviet combat aircraft were based in Czechoslovakia, but the major contribution was provided by the 16th Air Army, part of the Group of Soviet Forces in Germany. Headquartered at Zossen-Wünsdorf in East Germany, by 1989 this comprised around 1500 aircraft, including three fighter divisions and two fighter-bomber divisions (each of three regiments), two Shturmovik regiments, plus three reconnaissance regiments and two transport regiments.

When the last Soviet combat aircraft (MiG-29s of the 733rd Fighter Regiment) left the former East Germany in April 1994, they ended a process of withdrawal that had seen the eastward movement of almost 700 fixed-wing aircraft, 600 helicopters, 4000 tanks, 8000 armoured vehicles and 3500 artillery pieces. These had been maintained and operated by a force of around 338,000 troops.

Qualitative improvements

Soviet air arms on the Central Front were prioritized when it came to the receipt of new equipment. Some of the first MiG-15 operators were in East Germany, and units here also received early batches of Il-28s, MiG-17s, MiG-19s and MiG-21s. In the 1960s, the Su-7 and Yak-28 were introduced, with the MiG-23/27 and Su-17 arriving in the 1970s. By the early 1980s significant progress was being made in terms of advanced avionics and weaponry. The Su-24 was a major worry to NATO planners, but even the less advanced MiG-27 (exported to Warsaw Pact allies as the MiG-23BN) and, from 1977, the Su-17M (exported as the Su-22M) featured precision-guided weapons and all-weather capability. Tactics were based on wartime experience, with frontal fighters and ground-attack aircraft supporting a massive land assault, while maintaining battlefield air supremacy.

In response to the arrival in Europe of the F-15 and F-16, re-equipment with the MiG-29 assumed high priority, and the type went on to serve with eight of the nine fighter regiments in the 16th Air Army and was beginning to equip other Warsaw Pact units when the Cold War came to an end.

Within Frontal Aviation, reconnaissance was ultimately provided by the MiG-25R and Su-24MR, these types replacing the Yak-28R. Previously, reconnaissance-configured MiG-15s and MiG-17s had been employed, with MiG-21Rs arriving in the mid-1970s. The last of the Yak-28s were used for defence suppression until 1988–89, before MiG-25BM and Su-24MP aircraft replaced these.

Helicopters assumed an early importance in Warsaw Pact operations, with the initial Mi-4 being superseded by the versatile Mi-8 in the 1970s. Mi-8s were supplied to most Warsaw Pact allies and were supplemented by the heavy-lift Mi-6, the Mi-24 assault helicopter and various specialized Mi-8 electronic-warfare and command-post variants.

Specifications

Crew: 1

Powerplant: 1x 60.8kN (14,550lb) thrust
Tumanskii R-13-300 afterburning turbojet

Maximum speed: 2229km/h (1385mph)

Range: 1160km (721 miles)

Service ceiling: 17,500m (57,400ft)

Dimensions: span 7.15m (23ft 5.5in) length

(including probe) 15.76m (51ft 8.5in);
height 4.1m (13ft 5.5in)

Weight: 10,400kg (22,925lb) loaded

Armament: 1 x 23mm cannon, provision for
about 1500kg (3307lb) of stores, including
air-to-air missiles, rocket pods, napalm tanks
(or drop tanks)

▲ Mikoyan-Gurevich MiG-21M

JG-7, East German AF, Drewitz / early 1980s

East Germany employed the MiG-21 for air defence, ground attack and reconnaissance and retained later versions of the type in front-line service until the fall of the Berlin Wall and subsequent German reunification. JG-7 operated this MiG-21M from Drewitz, near Cottbus. East Germany acquired just under 90 MiG-21Ms.

Specifications

Crew: 1

Powerplant: 1 x 98kN (22,046lb) Rumanskii
R-27F2M-300

Maximum speed: about 2445km/h (1520mph)

Range: 966km (600 miles)

Service ceiling: over 18,290m (60,000ft)

Dimensions: span 13.97m (45ft 10in) spread
and 7.78m (25ft 6.25in) swept; length 16.71m
(54ft 10in); height 4.82m (15ft 9.75in)

Weight: 18,145kg (40,000lb) loaded

Armament: 1 x 23mm GSh-23L cannon, AA-3,
AA-7 and/or AA-8 air-to-air missiles

▲ Mikoyan-Gurevich MiG-23MF

JG-3, East German AF, Peenemünde / mid-1980s

In the 1980s, the major Warsaw Pact interceptor on the Central Front was the MiG-23. In addition to six Soviet regiments, East Germany was also home to a single locally operated MiG-23 interceptor unit, JG-3 at Peenemünde, on the Baltic coast. The wing operated both MiG-23MF and the later MiG-23ML variants.

Specifications

Crew: 3

Powerplant: 2 x 903kW (1210hp) Klimov
    M-105PF piston engines

Maximum speed: 580km/h (360mph)

Range: 1160km (721 miles)

Service ceiling: 8800m (28,870ft)

Dimensions: span 17.16m (56ft 3in); length
    12.66m (41ft 6in); height 3.5m (11ft 6in)

Weight: 7563kg (16,639lb) loaded

Armament: 4 x 7.62mm ShKAS machine guns;
    1600kg (3520lb) of bombs

▲ Petlyakov Pe-2FT

Polish AF / late 1940s

A mainstay of the Red Army during World War II, the Pe-2 light bomber remained in use after VE-Day, and examples were also supplied to Soviet satellite states. This aircraft served with the Polish AF in the late 1940s, and is seen with its ventral gun position retracted.

Specifications

Crew: 2

Powerplant: 1 x 1320kW (1770hp) Mikulin
    AM-42 liquid-cooled V-12 engine

Maximum speed: 550km/h (342mph)

Range: 800km (550 miles)

Service ceiling: 4000m (13,123ft)

Dimensions: span 13.40m (44ft); length 11.12m

(36ft 6in); height 4.10m (13ft 5in)

Weight: 6,345kg (14,000lb) loaded

Armament: 2 x 23mm (0.9in) Nudelman-
    Suranov NS-23 cannons; 1 x 12.7mm (0.5in)
    UBST cannon in the BU-9 rear gunner station;
    up to 600kg (1320lb) bomb load

▲ Ilyushin Il-10

Polish AF / 1951

Operated by a Polish ground-attack regiment in 1951, this is an example of the Il-10 that replaced the classic wartime Il-2 Shturmovik and which remained in large-scale service with Eastern Bloc air arms well into the 1950s. Unlike the Il-2, the Il-10 was of all-metal construction, and had refined aerodynamics.

▲ Ilyushin Il-28

Polish AF / 1960s

The Il-28 tactical bomber served with both Soviet units in Eastern Europe, and with a number of Soviet client states. This example wears the markings of the Polish AF, which used the type both as a level bomber and as a reconnaissance aircraft. Il-28 production was also undertaken in Czechoslovakia, by Avia.

Specifications

Crew: 3

Powerplant: 2 x 26.3kN (5952lb) Klimov VK-1
    turbojets

Maximum speed: 902km/h (560mph)

Range: 2180km (1355 miles)

Service ceiling: 12,300m (40,355ft)

Dimensions: span 21.45m (70ft 4.5in); length

17.65m (57ft 10.75in); height 6.70m (21ft
11.8in)

Weight: 21,200kg (46,738lb) loaded

Armament: 4 x 23mm cannon; internal bomb
    capacity 1000kg (2205lb), max bomb
    capacity 3000kg (6614lb)

▲ Mil Mi-2

Polish AF / early 1980s

Widely used by Warsaw Pact air arms, the Mi-2 was first built in the USSR before production responsibility was assumed by PZL of Poland. The type saw service in a variety of combat support and second-line roles. This example is fitted with external rocket pods, for use in a light assault capacity.

Specifications

Crew: 1	Service ceiling: 4000m (13,120ft)
Powerplant: 2 x 298kW (400shp) PZL GTD-350 turboshafts	Dimensions: rotor diameter 14.6m (47ft 11in); length 11.9m (39ft 4in); height 3.7m (12ft 2in)
Maximum speed: 220km/h (138mph)	Weight: 3550kg (7810lb) loaded
Range: 340km (211 miles)	Armament: various

The basic Mi-24 entered service with Soviet forces in East Germany in 1974, replaced by the much improved Mi-24D from 1976, and the Mi-24V from 1979. By 1980, Soviet Army Aviation had been separated from Frontal Aviation, with the result that helicopters were directly controlled by ground forces' commanders, with each Army having an Army Aviation component.

After West Germany's admission to NATO, the Soviets adopted a similar re-armament policy in East Germany, and following its creation in 1956, the East German AF (officially known as the *Luftstreitkräfte und Luftverteidigung*, LSK/LV, or Air Forces and Air Defence) eventually incorporated almost 270 fixed-wing combat aircraft (65 with a nuclear capability), 75 combat helicopters and 25 naval combat aircraft. Divided along north-south geographical lines between 1st and 3rd Divisions, the primary air defence combat equipment was based around fleets of 60 MiG-23MF/ML and 100 MiG-21MF/bis fighters. Although the East German AF was smaller than the air arms of Czechoslovakia and Poland, it was viewed by the USSR as a staunch ally, and was the first Warsaw Pact operator to receive the advanced MiG-29, in 1988. For offensive missions, 28 MiG-23BN and 25 Su-22M-4 variable-geometry strike/attack aircraft were available to the air force by 1989, these replacing earlier MiG-17 fighters that had been re-roled as ground-attack aircraft. Smaller numbers of MiG-21Rs were used for reconnaissance duties, while the helicopter arm included 48 Mi-24s

SOVIET AF COMBAT UNITS IN POLAND, 1992

Aircraft	Unit	Base
Su-24	3rd Bomber Regiment	Krzywa
Su-24	42nd Bomber Regiment	Kopernia
Su-24	89th Bomber Regiment	Szprotawa
Su-27	159th Fighter Regiment	Kluczewo
Su-27	582nd Fighter Regiment	Chojna
MiG-25, Su-24	164th Reconnaissance Regiment	Krzywa

and 80 combat-assault-configured Mi-8s. Twenty-four standard Mi-8 transport helicopters were in use, together with a small fixed-wing transport arm, primary equipment of which was the An-26.

Polish air power

Although it shared no border with NATO territory, Poland was regarded as an important marshalling point for Soviet reserve formations, and the strike-tasked Su-24s based here would have been supplemented by theatre bombers deployed from Soviet 46th Strategic Air Army bases in times of tension. Soviet Northern Group of Forces air bases were mainly located near the western border with East Germany, from where they could best support a Central Front campaign. The Polish AF, meanwhile, was the largest of any Soviet satellite, with reported totals of 480 aircraft (108 being nuclear-capable) and 43 helicopters by the end of the Cold War. MiG-29s

Specifications

Crew: 1

Powerplant: 1 x 15.6kN (3500lbf) Klimov
RD-500 turbojet

Maximum speed: 923km/h (577mph)

Range: 1400km (875 miles)

Service ceiling: 14,800m (48,500ft)

Dimensions: span 8.73m (28 ft 8in);
length 8.12m (26ft 8in); height 3.31m
(10ft 10in)

Weight: 3384kg (7445lb) loaded

Armament: 2 x 23mm Nudelman-Rikhter
NR-23 cannon

▲ Yakovlev Yak-23

Czechoslovak AF / late 1940s

While most Warsaw Pact air arms entered the jet age on receipt of their first MiG-15 fighters, the rival Yak family of straight-wing jet fighters also saw limited service. The Yak-23 was the final production version of Yakovlev's single-seat jet fighters, and this example was operated by the Czech AF as interim equipment, pending the arrival of the MiG-15.

Specifications

Crew: 1

Powerplant: 1 x 26.5kN (5952lb) Klimov VK-1
turbojet

Maximum speed: 1100km/h (684mph)

Range: 1424km (885 miles)

Service ceiling:15,545m (51,000ft)

Dimensions: span 10.08m (33ft 0.75in); length

11.05m (36ft 3.75in); height 3.4m (11ft
1.75in);

Weight: 5700kg (12,566lb) loaded

Armament: 1 x 37mm N-37 cannon and 2 x
23mm NS-23 cannon, plus up to 500kg
(1102lb) of mixed stores on underwing pylons

▲ Mikoyan-Gurevich MiG-15bis

Czechoslovak AF / mid-1950s

The MiG-15 was built in large numbers in Czechoslovakia, both for home and export operators. The improved MiG-15bis variant carried the local designation S.103, superseding the earlier S.102 (MiG-15). The blue bands adorning this example were related to participation in a Warsaw Pact air defence exercise.

Specifications

Crew: 1

Powerplant: 1x 60.8kN (14,550lb) Tumanskii
R-13-300 afterburning turbojet

Maximum speed: 2229km/h (1385mph)

Range: 1160km (721 miles)

Service ceiling: 17,500m (57,400ft)

Dimensions: span 7.15m (23ft 5.5in) length

(including probe) 15.76m (51ft 8.5in); height
4.1m (13ft 5.5in)

Weight: 10,400kg (22,925lb) loaded

Armament: 1 x 23mm cannon, provision for
about 1500kg (3307lb) of stores, including
air-to-air missiles, rocket pods, napalm tanks,
or drop tanks)

▲ Mikoyan-Gurevich MiG-21MF

Czechoslovak AF / early 1980s

This Czech MiG-21MF survived in service until after the collapse of the Warsaw Pact. This aircraft is depicted carrying a mixed load of R-3 air-to-air missiles and unguided rockets underwing. Codenamed 'Fishbed-J' by NATO, the MiG-21MF was built in the first half of the 1970s, and was optimised for export.

began to arrive in 1989, at which time the service was based around 1, 2 and 3 Corps. Divided according to regional taskings, the three Polish AF corps were equipped with around 350 MiG-21PFM/M/MF/bis, and 45 MiG-23MFs for air defence. The Polish National Air Defence Force (*Wojska Oborony Powietrznej Kraju*) was previously an organic structure, before being integrated into the Polish AF (*Polskie Wojska Lotnicze*, PWL).

Strike/attack units were provided with 170 Su-20/22M-4s and 40 Lim-6 (licence-built MiG-17) fighter-bombers, while both MiG-21R and reconnaissance-configured Su-20s were also in use. Around 60 Mi-24s were flown by two regiments,

supported by around 30 Mi-8s and large numbers of Mi-2s (including locally built versions). Transport assets included 20 An-12 airlifters, as well as smaller numbers of An-24s and An-26s.

Czech military aviation

The Czech AF was among the first of Moscow's satellite air arms to be reformed, and was initially equipped with S.199, La-5 and La-7 fighters. After the events of 1968, the air arm was almost disbanded. Based on its important strategic position as a buffer to NATO in the southern part of West Germany, the regime regained a measure of trust from the USSR. As a result, a very different picture was presented by

Specifications

Crew: 1

Powerplant: 1 x 98kN (22,046lb) Tumanskii R-27F2M-300 turbojet

Maximum speed: about 2445km/h (1520mph)

Range: 966km (600 miles)

Service ceiling: over 18,290m (60,000ft)

Dimensions: span 13.97m (45ft 10in) spread, 7.78m (25ft 6.25in) swept; length 16.71m (54ft 10in); height 4.82m (15ft 9.75in)

Weight: 18,145kg (40,000lb) loaded

Armament: 1 x 23mm GSh-23L cannon, provision for 3000kg (6614lb) of stores

▲ **Mikoyan-Gurevich MiG-23BN**

Czechoslovak AF / mid-1980s

Developed as a ground-attack counterpart to the MiG-23 fighter, the MiG-23BN was optimized for export, and saw service with Bulgaria, Czechoslovakia and East Germany within Eastern Europe. In addition to free-fall bombs and unguided rockets, the MiG-23BN could launch Kh-23 air-to-surface missiles.

▲ **Mil Mi-24D**

Czechoslovak Army Aviation / Plzen, early 1980s

By 1989, Czechoslovak ground forces could call upon the support provided by Mi-24 'Hind-Ds', like this example, based at Plzen. Additional rotary-wing assets available at this time included Mi-8 transports, improved Mi-17 transports, EW-configured Mi-8s, and Mi-2s, which were assigned to either the 1st or 4th Armies.

Specifications

Crew: 2-3

Powerplant: 2 x 1600kW (2200hp) Isotov TV-3-117 turbines

Maximum speed: 335km/h (208mph)

Range: 450km (280 miles)

Service ceiling: 4500m (14,750ft)

Dimensions: rotor diameter 17.3m (56ft 7in); length 17.5m (57ft 4in); height 6.5m (21ft 3in)

Weight: 12,000kg (26,500lb) loaded

Armament: 1 x 12.7mm Gatling type MG, 57mm rockets, AT-2C/ SWATTER ATGMs; up to 500kg (1102lb) bomb load the time of the fall of the iron curtain: among Soviet satellite states, the Czech AF (*Ceskoslovenské Letectvo*) ranked second only to Poland in terms of size, with a declared total of 407 aircraft (137 for strike/attack), in addition to 101 combat helicopters.

MiG-29s began to arrive with the Czech AF in 1989, joining the 7th Air Army, which was allocated the task of air defence. A total of some 305 MiG-21s of different subtypes were shared by the 7th Air Army and the 10th Air Army, the latter being responsible for strike/attack and battlefield support and additionally equipped with 35 Su-25s, 35 MiG-23BNs and 35 Su-22M-4s. The Su-22M-4 also had a reconnaissance

tasking. Helicopters included 45 Mi-24s, 45 Mi-8/17s, plus further examples for electronic warfare, and 32 Mi-2s. Airlift was undertaken by An-12, An-26 and An-24 transports, among others.

Hungary

With Bulgaria and Romania outside of the critical Central Front region, the final Warsaw Pact air arm in theatre, Hungary, was also the smallest. It was effectively disbanded in the wake of the 1956 Hungarian Uprising, and the air force (*Magyar Légierö*) re-emerged as a primarily defensive formation. In the meantime, Soviet air units were

Specifications

Crew: 1

Powerplant: 1 x 26.5kN (5952lb) Klimov VK-1 turbojet

Maximum speed: 1100km/h (684mph)

Range: 1424km (885 miles)

Service ceiling:15,545m (51,000ft)

Dimensions: span 10.08m (33ft 0.75in); length 11.05m (36ft 3.75in); height 3.4m (11ft 1.75in)

Weight: 5700kg (12,566lb) loaded

Armament: 1 x 37mm N-37 cannon and 2 x 23mm NS-23 cannon, plus up to 500kg (1102lb) of mixed stores on underwing pylons

▲ Mikoyan-Gurevich MiG-15bis

Hungarian AF / late 1960s

Smallest of the Warsaw Pact air arms available to support operations on the Central Front, the Hungarian AF included one air division (fighters, fighter-bombers and transport elements) and a single air defence division. The latter maintained both interceptors and surface-to-air missile units.

▲ Mikoyan-Gurevich MiG-17PF

Hungarian AF / early 1960s

The MiG-17PF was a minimum-change conversion of the basic MiG-17, incorporating a radar and an afterburning engine. Addition of the radar altered the nose profile, with a scanning antenna in the upper part of the engine air intake, and a tracking/ranging antenna in a radome in the middle of the intake.

Specifications

Crew: 1

Powerplant: 1 x 33.1kN (7452lb) thrust Klimov VK-1F afterburning turbojet

Maximum speed: 1480km/h (920mph)

Range: 2200km (1367 miles)

Service ceiling: 17,900m (58,725ft)

Dimensions: span 9m (29ft 6.5in); length 11.68m (38ft 4in); height 4.02m (13ft 2.25in)

Weight: 6350kg (14,000lb) loaded

Armament: 3 x 23mm NS-23 cannon; up to 500kg (1102lb) of bombs or rockets assembled in the country in support of the Southern Group of Forces, with their headquarters at Tokol, Hungary. By 1991, Soviet aviation in Hungary included three interceptor regiments (with MiG-29s and MiG-23s), an attack regiment (Su-17s), an electronic warfare squadron, a tactical reconnaissance squadron (again with Su-17s) and two helicopter regiments.

At the end of the Cold War, official strength comprised 113 fixed-wing combat aircraft and 96 combat helicopters. With air defence as its main role, three squadrons of interceptors under the authority of the National Air Defence Command were

supported by just one ground-attack unit. The latter was assigned to the Troop Air Command and was primarily responsible for support of the Hungarian Army. Hungary's interceptors comprised one squadron of 10 MiG-23MFs and two of MiG-21bis at Pápa airbase, and two further MiG-21MF/bis squadrons each at Kecskemet and Taszar. Around 65 MiG-21s were available in total, while 10 Su-22M-3 ground-attack aircraft were operated by a single unit at Taszar. Helicopter support for Hungarian ground forces was handled by 50 Mi-8/17s, 26 Mi-24s and 25 Mi-2s. A small transport capability existed in the form of An-24s, An-26s and L-410s.

▲ **Ilyushin Il-10**

Hungarian AF / early 1950s

Initially serving alongside Tu-2 bombers in four ground-assault and attack bomber regiments, Hungarian Il-10s remained in use into the late 1950s. The Il-10s were built under licence in Czechoslovakia, as Avia B-33s. Once favourably regarded, the Hungarian AF suffered in the wake of the 1956 uprising.

Specifications	
Crew: 2	Dimensions: span 13.40m (44ft);
Powerplant: 1 x 1320kW (1770hp) Mikulin	length 11.12m (36ft 6in); height 4.10m (13ft 5in)
AM-42 liquid-cooled V-12 engine	Weight: 6345kg (14,000lb) loaded
Maximum speed: 550km/h (342mph)	Armament: 2 x 23mm Nudelman-Suranov
Range: 800km (500 miles)	NS-23 cannons, 1x 12.7mm UBST cannon; up
Service ceiling: 4000m (13,123ft)	to 600kg (1320lb) of various weapons

Europe's Northern Front
1949–1989

A highly militarized zone, the Baltic Sea was crucial for both NATO and the Warsaw Pact, and both Alliances would have attempted to secure their flanks here in time of conflict.

THE COMPLEX GEOGRAPHY of NATO's exposed Northern Front was dictated by the Baltic Sea, including the Jutland peninsula and Denmark, the vital Skaggerak strait and Norway. While both Denmark and Norway were NATO members, their

Baltic neighbours, Finland and Sweden, were neutral. In peacetime, the Baltic Sea and Gulf of Bothnia were the front lines in the north, and the area hosted routine intelligence-gathering and military exercises by NATO and Warsaw Pact forces.

The geography of the region meant there was no possibility of a Soviet forward defence zone, as in Eastern Europe, and the value of the area was increased by the close proximity of the USSR's Baltic republics and Leningrad.

The Soviet Baltic Fleet was charged with securing the waters, with 550 combat vessels supported by the mid-1980s by a naval air arm with 275 strike/attack and reconnaissance aircraft. NATO expected that the Soviet war plan would involve an advance through Finland and Sweden to reach Norway. The Baltic

Fleet may also have attempted to break out into the North Sea, through the narrow channels at the entrance to the Baltic.

NATO's wartime tasking would have involved closing the Baltic approaches to shipping, intercepting Warsaw Pact reinforcements headed to the Central Front and controlling the air. The latter was necessary to prevent Warsaw Pact aircraft attempting a 'right hook' manoeuvre against NATO rear areas, or prosecuting an attack on the UK from across the North Sea. Denmark was of particular

Specifications

Crew: 1

Powerplant: 1 x 45kN (10,200lbf) Pratt & Whitney J57-P-21/21A turbojet

Maximum speed: 1380km/h (864mph)

Range: 3210km (1995 miles)

Service ceiling: 15,000m (50,000ft)

Dimensions: span 11.8m (38ft 9in); length 15.2m (50ft); height 4.95m (16ft 3in)

Weight: 13,085kg (28.847lb) loaded

Armament: 4 x 20mm (0.79in) M39 cannon, 4 x AIM-9 Sidewinder missiles, provision for 3190kg (7040lb) nuclear bombs

▲ **North American F-100D Super Sabre**

Eskadrille 730, Royal Danish AF / Skrydstrup, late 1970s

A former USAF aircraft, this F-100 served with Eskadrille 730, based at Skrydstrup. Deliveries of the F-100 to Denmark began in 1959, and the final Danish Super Sabres were retired in 1982, being replaced by F-16s. In total, three Danish squadrons operated the type in the fighter-bomber role.

Specifications

Crew: 1

Powerplant: 1 x 32.3kN (7275lb) thrust Avro Orenda Mark 14 turbojet engine

Maximum speed: 965km/h (600mph)

Range: 530km (329 miles)

Service ceiling: 14,600m (48,000ft)

Dimensions: span 11.58m (39ft); length 11.4m (37ft 6in); height 4.4m (14ft 8in)

Weight: 6628kg (14,613lb) loaded

Armament: 6 x .5in (12.7mm) machine guns

▲ **North American F-86F Sabre**

336 Sqn, Royal Norwegian AF / Rygge, 1960

This F-86F served with the Royal Norwegian AF in 1960. Primarily tasked with air defence against marauding Soviet bombers, the F-86F was supported by radar-equipped F-86Ks. The F-86F day fighter served at Bodo, Rygge and Orland. The last Norwegian squadron operating the F-86F converted to the F-5 in 1967.

importance to NATO and the Warsaw Pact, because it could be used to assemble forces in order to launch a counter-attack or open a second front. If NATO could secure Denmark, it could then launch forces to sever any attempted Warsaw Pact drive across the North German Plain.

Allied Forces Northern Europe

NATO's defence of the north was the job of Allied Forces Northern Europe (AFNORTH), with headquarters at Kolsaas, Norway, and responsible for Denmark, Norway and the northern part of West Germany. Norway was divided along a north-south axis, with zones administered by Commander South Norway (COMSOR) and Commander North Norway (COMNON).

The task of sealing off access to the Baltic was handled by HQ Allied Forces Baltic Approaches (BALTAP), headquartered at Karup in Denmark, and under the command of AFNORTH. BALTAP was divided into four operational commands, which included Danish and West German land forces and navies, the West German naval air arm (Marineflieger), Danish air force and northern-based elements of the Luftwaffe, the latter ultimately including a light attack wing (Alpha Jets) and a reconnaissance wing (RF-4Es).

Additional support in the Baltic was also available from NATO Allied Command Europe Mobile Force (AMF). This was a multi-national, variable-content rapid reaction force that could be deployed to

Denmark or Norway as required, bolstering the two countries' relatively small, defensively configured air arms, both of which were eventually based around a nucleus of four squadrons of F-16s. Further assets could be provided by the UK Mobile Force (one Jaguar wing, and one Harrier squadron), the U.S. Marine Corps, the Netherlands-UK amphibious force, the U.S. Army and USAF. By the 1980s, a forward operating location for NATO E-3 AWACS aircraft had been established at Ørland, Norway.

Like Denmark, Norway was equally vital to NATO and the Warsaw Pact. For NATO, Norway offered a platform from which to attack the Soviet Northern Fleet, including its ballistic missile submarines. Control of Norway also aided closing down the Baltic approaches. Sharing a land border with the USSR, Norway was threatened by direct invasion, or an amphibious assault directed against the north. For the Soviets, control of Norway would have assisted in closing the Norwegian Sea to NATO reinforcements, with a submarine barrier extending between Norway and Iceland.

In time of war, Norway would have been rapidly reinforced by NATO units, including ground forces. U.S. carrier battle groups regularly deployed to the Norwegian Sea, and the UK's 3rd Commando Brigade and Dutch Marines were also active in the area. Air support was made available via AMF, as well as Canada's Air-Sea Transportable Brigade Group, including two squadrons of CF-5As normally based in Canada, but with wartime duties in Norway.

Specifications

Crew: 1

Powerplant: 2 x 32.5kN (7305lb) Rolls-Royce/Turbomeca Adour Mk 102 turbofans

Maximum speed: 1593km/h (990mph)

Range: 557km (357 miles)

Service ceiling: 14,020m (45,997ft)

Dimensions: span 8.69m (28ft 6in); length 16.83m (55ft 2.5in); height 4.89m (16ft 0.5in)

Weight: 15,500kg (34,172lb) loaded

Armament: 2 x 30mm DEFA cannon; provision for 4536kg (10,000lb) of stores, including a nuclear weapon or conventional loads

▲ **SEPECAT Jaguar GR.Mk 1**

54 Sqn, RAF Coltishall / early 1980s

Based at Coltishall during peacetime, the RAF's three home-based Jaguar units could have been committed to the Northern Front during wartime as part of NATO's strategic reserve, and RAF Jaguars regularly undertook deployments to gain experience operating in the harsh conditions encountered in northern Norway.

Chapter 2

Air Power at Sea

Control of the sea became a vital facet of the Cold War, and aircraft were deployed for both offensive and defensive purposes. While carrier-based air power was one of the more visible indicators of naval prowess, equally important were shore-based patrol and strike aircraft. These, together with shipborne and land-based helicopters, were intended to complement navies in the protection of sea lanes and maritime resources, to protect the fleet and to challenge hostile surface vessels and submarine threats.

◀ **USS** *Carl Vinson*

Representing the unrivalled maritime might of the US Navy carrier force, the nuclear-powered USS Carl Vinson displays a 1980s air wing that includes F-14s, A-6s, A-7s, EA-6s, E-2s and an A-3. After World War II, air power ensured that the carrier assumed the role of capital ship in the US Navy.

U.S. Carrier Air Power
1945–1989

After its decisive showing during the war in the Pacific, the aircraft carrier took over from the battleship as the pre-eminent arbiter of naval warfare, with the U.S. Navy its leading exponent.

ALTHOUGH THE CARRIER had demonstrated its value during World War II, after VJ-Day the U.S. Navy carrier fleet was run down, and by 1950 only 15 carriers remained in commission. In addition, a projected new 'super-carrier' design, the USS *United States*, had been cancelled in 1948.

Completed too late to see service in World War II, later 'Essex'-class carriers served in a new 'power-projection' role in Korea, while the larger 'Midway' battle carriers were the first to support carrier-capable, nuclear-armed U.S. Navy bombers, the AJ-1 Savage being the first of this type to enter service.

Jet-age carriers

The arrival of the jet placed new demands on carriers, initially met though a modernization programme for 13 of the 'Essex' class, with reconfigured decks and elevators to better suit operations by jet aircraft. The revised 'Essex' design was available for deployment to Korea, by which time the U.S. Navy was increasingly concerned by the development of the Soviet submarine arm. In order to address the threat, new classes of light carrier (as well as converted escort

carriers) and aircraft configured for anti-submarine warfare (ASW) were fielded. At the same time, the U.S. was scheming a new type of carrier that could launch nuclear-armed bombers from their stations in the Atlantic against targets in the Soviet Union. Successor to the 'Midways' to prosecute this role was the first of a new class of 'super-carrier', the USS *Forrestal*, commissioned in 1955 as the first carrier purpose-built for jet operations. Most important of its revolutionary features were two British innovations: the angled deck and steam catapult.

A new 'super-carrier' was ordered each year between 1953–58, before the arrival of USS *Enterprise*, the first nuclear-powered aircraft carrier, commissioned in 1961. A nuclear powerplant allowed operations without refuelling, meaning that only the ship's stores and aviation fuel and ordnance needed to be replenished. *Enterprise*, the 'Forrestals' and surviving 'Essex'-class vessels (subject to a further upgrade, with angled decks and other improvements) were all active off the coast of Vietnam.

By now, the light carriers serving in the ASW role were proving too small, and it was the versatile 'Essex'

Specifications

Crew: 1	Dimensions: span 10.92m (35ft 10in); length
Powerplant: 1 x 156kW (2100hp) Pratt &	8.61m (28ft 3in); height 4.21m (13ft 9in)
Whitney R-2800-34W Double Wasp radial	Weight: 5873kg (12,947lb) loaded
piston engine	Armament: 4 x 12.7mm (0.5in) M2 machine
Maximum speed: 678km/h (421mph)	guns; up to 454kg (1000lb) of bombs or four
Range: 1778km (1105 miles)	5in (127mm) rockets)
Service ceiling: 11,796m (38,700ft)	

▲ Grumman F8F-1 Bearcat
VF-72, U.S. Navy / USS Leyte, *1949–50*

Appearing too late to see combat in World War II, the F8F was regarded as one of the finest piston-engined fighters, but the arrival of the jet saw it serve principally with the U.S. Naval Reserve. This F8F-1, among the last of the 770 of this version built, was embarked aboard the carrier USS *Leyte* in 1949-50.

Specifications

Crew: 1

Powerplant: 2 x 7.1kN (1600lb thrust)
   Westinghouse J30-WE-20 turbojets

Maximum speed: 771km/h (479mph)

Range: 1120km (695 miles)

Service ceiling: 12,525m (41,100ft)

Dimensions: span 12.42m (40ft 9in);
   length 11.35m (37ft 3in); height 4.32m
   (14ft 2in)

Weight: 4552kg (10,035lb) loaded

Armament: 4 x 12.7mm (0.50in) MGs

▲ McDonnell FH-1 Phantom

VF-171, U.S. Navy / Quonset Point, late 1940s

The first all-jet aircraft to be ordered into production by the U.S. Navy, the FH-1 entered squadron service July 1947. This aircraft served with VF-171 (the former VF-17A), the only U.S. Navy unit to take the aircraft aboard carriers, before the Phantom was demoted to Reserve and Marine Corps service.

Specifications

Crew: 1

Powerplant: 1 x 17.8kN (4000lb) Allison J35-
   A-2 turbojet

Maximum speed: 880km/h (547mph)

Range: 2414km (1500 miles)

Service ceiling: 9754m (32,000ft)

Dimensions: span 9.8m (38ft 2in); length
   10.5m (34ft 5in); height 4.5m (14ft 10in)

Weight: 7076kg (15,600lb) loaded

Armament: 6 x .5in machine guns

▲ North American FJ-1 Fury

VF-5A, U.S. Navy / San Diego, late 1940s

Only 30 production examples of the straight-wing FJ-1 were built, before North American switched to the swept-wing FJ-2 Fury and its successors, which were based on the F-86 Sabre. The FJ-1 served with a single fleet unit, VF-5A, home-based at San Diego, California. The unit was the first U.S. Navy jet squadron to go to sea under operational conditions, in March 1948.

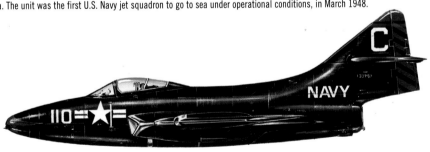

Specifications

Crew: 1

Powerplant: 1x 28.25kN (6354lb thrust)
   Allison J33 engine

Maximum speed: 1041km/h (647mph)

Range: 2111km (1312 miles)

Service ceiling: 12,800m (42,000ft)

Dimensions: span 10.5m (34ft 6in); length
   12.9m (42ft 2in); height 3.7m (12ft 3in)

Weight: 9116kg (20,098lb) loaded

Armament: 4 x 20mm (0.79in) M2 cannon; 6 x
   127mm (5in) rockets; 4 x AIM-9 Sidewinder
   air-to-air missiles; 2 x 454kg (1000lb) bombs

▲ Grumman F9F-7 Cougar

VF-21, U.S. Navy / Oceana, 1953

A swept-wing follow-on to the F9F Panther that saw combat over Korea, the Cougar is seen here in the form of an Allison J33-powered F9F-7 serving at the end of the Korean War in 1953. The Cougar did not see action in this conflict, but became standard fleet fighter equipment in the mid-1950s.

class that was again modified for this role, deploying specialist aircraft in the form of the AF Guardian, and later the S2F Tracker. Known as CVS, these carriers operated within anti-submarine task groups, the first of which went to sea in 1958. Additional 'Essex'-class ships were converted to serve as helicopter carriers, these fulfilling an amphibious assault role.

After the 'Midway' class and the AJ-1 had proven the potential of carrier-based nuclear strike forces, the U.S. Navy introduced its first carrier-based nuclear-capable jet, the A3D Skywarrior, in the late 1950s.

The much smaller A4D Skyhawk was also nuclear-capable, but could operate from smaller carrier decks. The U.S. Navy's first Mach 2-capable fleet interceptors, the missile-armed F8U Crusader and F4H Phantom II, joined these attack aircraft.

Enter the 'Nimitz'

By the end of the Vietnam War, in which U.S. Navy carriers played a vital role, completing 71 cruises to the Western Pacific, the conventionally powered 'Kitty Hawk'-class carrier – effectively an improved

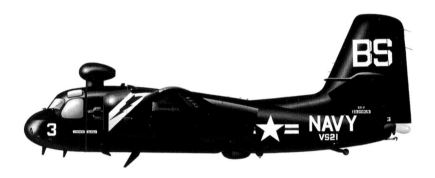

Specifications

Crew: 4	Dimensions: span 21m (69ft 8in); length 12.8m
Powerplant: 2 x 1135kW (1525hp) Wright	(42ft); height 4.9m (16ft 3in)
R-1820-82 radial piston engines	Weight: 11,069kg (24,408lb) loaded
Maximum speed: 438km/h (272mph)	Armament: torpedoes, rockets, depth charges or
Range: 1558km (968 miles)	1 x Mk 47 or Mk 101 nuclear depth bomb
Service ceiling: 6949m (22,800ft)	

▲ **Grumman S2F-2 Tracker**

VS-21, U.S. Navy / late 1950s

Backbone of the U.S. Navy's carrier-based anti-submarine fleet for much of the Cold War, the Tracker is seen here in the midnight-blue scheme in which it was originally delivered. The S2F-2 model featured an enlarged bomb bay and a wider span horizontal tail. The variant saw production between 1954-55.

Specifications

Crew: 2	(54ft 9in); height 4.93m (16ft 2in)
Powerplant: 2 x 41.4kN (9300lb) Pratt & Whitney	Weight: 26,581kg (58,600lb) loaded
J52-P-8A turbojets	Armament: five external hardpoints with
Maximum speed: 1043km/h (648mph)	provision for up to 8165kg (18,000lb)
Range: 1627km (1011 miles)	of stores, including nuclear weapons,
Service ceiling: 14,480m (47,500ft)	conventional and guided bombs, air-to-surface
Dimensions: span 16.15m (53ft); length 16.69m	missiles and drop tanks

▲ **Grumman A-6E Intruder**

VA-65, U.S. Navy / USS Independence, mid-1970s

A long-range all-weather strike aircraft, the A-6 entered operational service in 1964 and served until the end of the Cold War, seeing combat in Vietnam, Libya and elsewhere. This example of the definitive A-6E variant served with VA-65 'Tigers', part of Carrier Air Wing 7 (CVW-7) aboard USS *Independence*.

'Forrestal' design – was in service. The nuclear-powered 'Nimitz' class, the lead ship of which was commissioned in 1975, represented the next great technological advance. By now, the strategic nuclear tasking had passed over to the submarine force, and carriers were seen primarily as conventional tools for use in 'limited warfare' scenarios. The 'Nimitz' class, which began to be funded under the 1967 defence budget, remained the U.S. Navy's definitive carrier until the end of the Cold War, with five vessels in commission by 1989.

The 90,000-ton 'Nimitz' class were also the first of the truly multi-purpose carriers, combining attack and ASW functions in one hull. Each 'Nimitz' vessel could support an air wing of between 74–86 aircraft. By the time that offensive operations were launched against Libya in 1986, a typical U.S. Navy air wing included two squadrons of F-14A interceptors, a squadron of A-6E strike aircraft, two squadrons of A-7E attack aircraft and single squadrons each of EA-6B defence suppression aircraft, E-2C airborne early warning aircraft and SH-3H ASW helicopters.

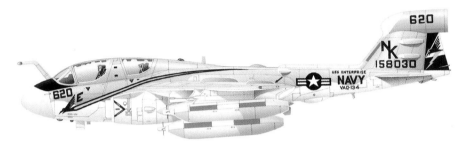

Specifications

Crew: 4	Dimensions: span 16.15m (53ft); length 18.24m
Powerplant: 2 x 49.8kN (11,200lb) Pratt &	(59ft 10in); height 4.95m (16ft 3in)
Whitney J52-P-408 turbojets	Weight: 29,484kg (65,000lb) loaded
Maximum speed: 982km/h (610mph)	Armament: none on early models, retrofitted
Range: 1769km (1099 miles)	with external hardpoints for four or six AGM-88
Service ceiling: 11,580m (38,000ft)	HARM air-to-surface anti-radar missiles

▲ **Grumman EA-6B Prowler**

VAQ-134, U.S. Navy / USS Enterprise, late 1970s

This EA-6B, which served aboard USS *Enterprise*, is depicted carrying the AN/ALQ-99 tactical jamming pods that formed the centrepiece of its electronic warfare suite. The EA-6B was developed from the EA-6A, itself an electronic warfare adaptation of the A-6A that was designed for the U.S. Marine Corps.

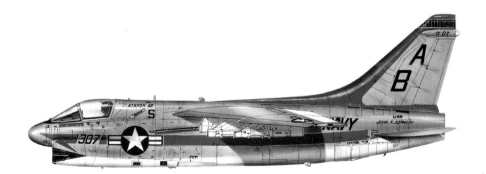

▲ **Vought A-7B Corsair II**

VA-46, U.S. Navy / USS John F. Kennedy, early 1970s

Operating from USS *John F. Kennedy*, this A-7B displays the vibrant markings prevalent in the earlier part of the Corsair II's fleet service. Developed as a successor to the A-4, the A-7 became standard equipment for U.S. Navy light-attack squadrons. This aircraft was part of CVW-1, assigned to the Atlantic Fleet.

Specifications

Crew: 1	Dimensions: span 11.8m (38ft 9in); length
Powerplant: 1 x 54.2kN (12,190lb) thrust Pratt &	14.06m (46ft 1.5in); height 4.9m (16ft 0.75in)
Whitney TF30-P-8 turbofan engine	Weight: 19,050kg (42,000lb) loaded
Maximum speed: 1123km/h (698mph)	Armament: 2 x 20mm Colt Mk 12 cannon; up to
Range: 1150km (4100 miles)	6804kg (15,000lb) of bombs, air-to-surface
Service ceiling: n/a	missiles or other stores

Specifications

Crew: 2

Powerplant: 2 x 92.9kN (20,900lb) Pratt &
  Whitney TF30-P-412A turbofans

Maximum speed: 2517km/h (1564mph)

Range: 3220km (2000 miles)

Service ceiling: 17,070m (56,000ft)

Dimensions: span 19.55m (64ft 1.5in) unswept;

11.65m (38ft 2.5in) swept; length 19.1m
(62ft 8in); height 4.88m (16ft)

Weight: 33,724kg (74,349lb) loaded

Armament: 1 x 20mm M61A1 Vulcan rotary
cannon; combination of AIM-7 Sparrow; AIM-9
medium range air-to-air missiles and AIM-54
Phoenix long range air-to-air missiles

▲ **Grumman F-14A Tomcat**

VF-14, U.S. Navy / USS **John F. Kennedy,** *mid-1970s*

The Tomcat was the definitive U.S. Navy interceptor fielded during the Cold War, based around the powerful AWG-9 radar system combined with AIM-54 Phoenix missiles. By the mid-1980s, a total of 22 front-line squadrons were equipped with the F-14, including VF-14, here serving CVW-1 aboard USS *John F. Kennedy.*

Specifications

Crew: 4

Powerplant: 2 x 41.26kN (9275lb) General
  Electric turbofans

Maximum speed: 828km/h (514mph)

Range: 5121km (2765 miles)

Service ceiling: 12,465m (40,900ft)

Dimensions: span (unfolded) 20.93m
(68ft 8in); (folded) 9m (29ft 6in); length
16.26m (53ft 4in); height 6.93m (22ft 9in)

Weight: 17,324kg (38,192lb) loaded

Armament: up to 2220kg (4900lb) bomb load

▲ **Lockheed S-3A Viking**

VS-24, U.S. Navy / USS **Nimitz,** *early 1980s*

In the latter half of the Cold War, U.S. Navy carrier-based anti-submarine capability was bolstered by the arrival of the S-3. Replacing the S-2, the Viking combined excellent range and a long loiter capability with advanced sensors and avionics. Operating from USS *Nimitz,* VS-24 was home-based at Oceana, Virginia.

British Carrier Air Power
1945–1989

Like the U.S. Navy, the Royal Navy had utilized the carrier with success in World War II, and carrier air power was to play an important role in British conflicts in the Cold War period.

T HE END OF World War II saw a number of Royal Navy carriers either cancelled or transferred to foreign navies. In the early 1950s, the carrier fleet was based around surviving wartime vessels, joined in the middle of that decade by the new 'Colossus' class.

Although carrier power had been reduced after the war, events in Korea would see Royal Navy carriers return to combat, with a Commonwealth carrier always on station to provide air support to the UN effort. Development of jet-capable carriers was slower

Specifications

Crew: 1	(47ft 7in); height 3.71m (12ft 2in);
Powerplant: 1 x 95.6kN (21,500lb) Rolls-Royce	Weight: 11,884kg (26,200lb) loaded
Pegasus vectored thrust turbofan	Armament: 2 x 30mm cannon, provision for AIM-
Maximum speed: 1110km/h (690mph)	9 Sidewinder or Matra Magic air-to-air
Range: 740km (460 miles)	missiles, and two Harpoon or Sea Eagle anti-
Service ceiling: 15,545m (51,000ft)	shipping missiles, up to a total of 3629kg
Dimensions: span 7.7m (25ft 3in); length 14.5m	(8000lb) bombs

▲ **British Aerospace Sea Harrier FRS.Mk 1**
800 NAS, Royal Navy / HMS Invincible, early 1980s
Illustrated by an example operating from HMS *Invincible*, the Sea Harrier FRS.Mk 1 was essentially similar to the RAF's Harrier GR.Mk 3, but the redesigned nose housed a Blue Fox radar and a raised cockpit was fitted. Typical air-to-air armament comprised a pair of Sidewinder missiles and 30mm cannon pods.

than that in the U.S., however, and throughout the Korean War the Fleet Air Arm relied on piston-engined Seafire, Firefly and Sea Fury aircraft. Korea began a period of significant activity for the British carrier force, and was followed by actions in Malaya and in response to the coup in Iraq. Most significant, however, was the Suez action of 1956, by which time Royal Navy carriers were operating jet equipment.

The first of the Fleet Air Arm's carrier jets was the Attacker, introduced in 1951, and events in Korea also promoted the construction of new carriers, notably the 'Centaur' class and HMS *Eagle*. While the Fleet Air Arm's jets – joined by the turboprop Wyvern strike fighter and the U.S.-supplied Skyraider airborne early warning platform – went to war in Suez, a new focus was being put on anti-submarine operations, evidenced by the introduction of dedicated carrierborne ASW aircraft.

The jet age
HMS *Ark Royal* was completed in 1955 as the world's first angled-deck carrier, while the arrival of steam catapults allowed heavier aircraft to be operated. The Royal Navy was also quick to recognize the value of carrier-based helicopters, with early operations by Dragonfly search-and-rescue helicopters in Korea. The use of the Whirlwind in Malaya starting in 1953 helped pioneer carrier-based heliborne assault operations, and the same type would serve in Suez, launching the first large-scale heliborne assault.

By the beginning of the 1960s, the last of the 'Centaur'-class carriers were in service, two of which were soon adapted for heliborne assault duties. A new generation of carrier aviation was in service, including the Buccaneer, which entered service in 1963, optimized for the low-level nuclear strike role.

During the 1960s, Royal Navy carrier air power saw action over Kuwait, Borneo, Aden, East Africa and Rhodesia. At the same time, the Admiralty was planning a new class of 'super-carrier', the CVA-01. This promising design was cancelled in 1966, when the UK announced it would withdraw all forces from 'east of Suez'. This decision also marked the end of the conventional carrier in Royal Navy service. The Fleet Air Arm introduced the Phantom carrierborne fighter, but this would only serve operationally from one carrier, HMS *Ark Royal*. This vessel, the last of its type, was finally decommissioned in 1978.

With the focus of operations now on the ASW mission in the Atlantic, the Royal Navy introduced a new type of carrier. The 'Invincible' class was primarily equipped with Sea King ASW helicopters, with vertical/short take-off and landing (V/STOL) Sea Harriers for air defence. The latter fighters were provided with a 'ski-jump' launch ramp, rather than catapults and arrestor gear. The first of these new vessels, HMS *Invincible*, was joined by the reconfigured HMS *Hermes*, now also featuring a 'ski-jump' for Sea Harrier operations. Both carriers would play a vital role in the Falklands campaign of 1982.

Soviet Carrier Air Power
1968–1989

Although the Soviet Navy never commissioned a conventional aircraft carrier during the Cold War, its activities in the field of ASW carriers reflected the USSR's growing maritime ambitions.

AT THE END of World War II, U.S. naval power was unchallenged; by the end of the Cold War, and based on the primacy of sea-based nuclear weapons, the Soviet Navy had grown immeasurably, and now presented a very real threat to the U.S. and its allies.

'The flag of the Soviet Navy now proudly flies over the oceans of the world. Sooner or later, the United States will have to understand that it no longer has mastery of the seas'. The words of Sergey Gorshkov, Admiral of the Fleet of the Soviet Union, in 1973, reflected the importance of naval warfare and the establishment of a 'blue-water navy' to Soviet strategic thinking. Earlier carrier studies, pursued by Stalin, had come to nought.

ASW carriers

Once a primarily defensive organization, the development of sea-based strategic missiles saw the Soviet Navy establish a powerful naval nuclear capability, ultimately expressed through the deployment of nuclear-powered ballistic missile submarines. As a result of the significance of the nuclear-armed submarine, ASW became a critical Cold War mission for the Soviet Navy.

Not a true aircraft carrier in the Western sense, the 14,600-ton 'Moskva' class was described as an 'anti-submarine cruiser with aircraft armament'. Its air wing comprised Ka-25 ASW helicopters, and the first of two vessels put to sea in 1968, both serving with the Black Sea Fleet.

The altogether more capable 'Kiev' class, four of which were completed, followed the 'Moskva' design. A true aircraft carrier – although classed as a 'heavy aircraft-carrying cruiser' by the Soviets – the 'Kiev' air wing could include Yak-38 V/STOL fighters or Ka-25 (and later Ka-27) ASW helicopters. The lead ship of the class entered service in 1975, and the vessels were divided between the Northern and Pacific Fleets. As the Cold War drew to a close, the Soviets were working on a new design of conventional aircraft carrier, although this was destined never to see service under a Soviet flag.

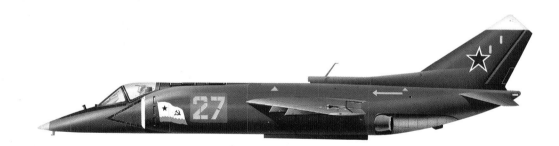

▲ **Yakovlev Yak-38**

AVMF / early 1980s

Although its capabilities were strictly limited, the Yak-38 provided the Soviet Navy with an entirely new ship-based, fixed-wing dimension. The aircraft's primary mission was light attack, but it could theoretically carry free-fall nuclear weapons. The Yak-38 made its first operational deployment aboard *Kiev* in 1975.

Specifications

Crew: 1

Powerplant: 2 x 29.9kN (6724lb) Rybinsk RD-36-
35VFR lift turbojets; 1 x 6950kg (15,322lb)
Tumanskii R-27V-300 vectored-thrust turbojet

Maximum speed: 1009km/h (627mph)

Range: 370km (230 miles)

Service ceiling: 12,000m (39,370ft)

Dimensions: span 7.32m (24ft); length 15.5m
(50ft 10in); height 4.37m (14ft 4in)

Weight: 11,700kg (25,795lb) loaded

Armament: provision for 2000kg (4409lb)
of stores

▲ **Kamov Ka-27**

AVMF / early 1980s

Developed as a successor to the Ka-25, the ship-based Ka-27, codenamed 'Helix' by NATO, initially appeared in anti-submarine warfare and utility/search and rescue variants. The basic design was later used as the basis for the Ka-29 assault transport, used from amphibious warships from the mid-1980s.

Specifications

Crew: 1-3

Powerplant: 2 x 1660kW (2225shp) Isotov turboshaft engines

Maximum speed: 270km/h (166mph)

Range: 980km (605miles)

Service ceiling: 5000m (16,400ft)

Dimensions: rotor diameter 15.80m (51ft 10in); length 11.30m (37ft1in); height 5.50m (18ft 1in)

Weight: 11,000kg (24,200lb) loaded

Armament: 1 x torpedoes or 36 RGB-NM & RGB-NM-1 sonobouys

Soviet Maritime Strike
1955–1989

The power of the U.S. Navy's carrier fleet dictated a response in kind by the USSR, which established the most powerful arm of maritime strike aircraft assembled during the Cold War.

THE SOVIET NAVY'S missile-armed strike aircraft were effectively in a class of their own during the Cold War. Based on land, these long-range aircraft were adaptations of air force strategic or theatre bombers, armed with dedicated anti-ship missiles.

The wartime targets of these aircraft, which included missile-carrying variants of the Tu-16, Tu-22 and Tu-22M bombers, included not only U.S. Navy carrier battle groups, but also the U.S. Navy fleet train that would have supplied Europe with vital supplies and reinforcements.

Anti-carrier doctrine

In the late 1960s, Marshal Vasily Sokolovsky noted the importance of 'attempting to destroy the attack carriers before they can launch their planes'. This was a mission that would have been carried out not only by missile-carrying naval aircraft but also by a series of submarines, surface warships and even ICBMs.

▲ **Tupolev Tu-16**

A mainstay of the Soviet Navy through most of the Cold War, the Tu-16 was deployed in a variety of roles, including missile-carrier, as illustrated.

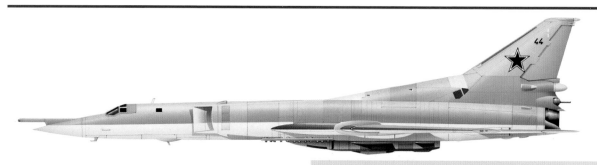

▲ **Tupolev Tu-22M-2**

AVMF / early 1980s

The Tu-22M served both with the Soviet AF and the Navy, the latter employing the aircraft for long-range maritime strike, armed with Kh-22 anti-ship missiles. Naval Tu-22s were operated by the Black Sea, Northern and Pacific Fleets, with almost 150 examples in service by 1988. Eight regiments were equipped by 1991.

Specifications

Crew: 4
Powerplant: 2 x 196kN (44,090lb thrust) Kuznetsov NK-22 turbojet engines
Maximum speed: 1800km/h (1118mph)
Range: 5100km (3169 miles)
Service ceiling: 13,000m (42,651ft)

Dimensions: span (spread) 34.28m (112ft 6in), (swept) 23.3m (76ft 5in); length 41.46m (136ft); height 11.05m (36ft 3in)
Weight: 122,000kg (268,964lb) loaded
Armament: 2 x 23mm (0.9in) GSH-23 guns; up to 3 KH-22 air-to-surface missiles

Maritime Patrol
1946–1989

The vital maritime patrol mission took on a new resonance in the Cold War era, as development of the nuclear-powered submarine demanded the deployment of specialist air power.

THE USE OF maritime patrol aircraft had effectively countered the submarine menace by the end of World War II, although the tables would be turned by submarine developments in the 1950s. There now began to appear faster and more agile submarines, and ultimately nuclear-powered submarines of almost unlimited endurance. The latter were soon armed with nuclear missiles and became critical elements in

▲ **Beriev Be-6**

AVMF / early 1970s

The Soviet Navy was unusual in retaining flying boats for maritime patrol operations until the end of the Cold War. Among the earliest equipment was the Be-6, with a prominent MAD 'stinger' carried in a rear fuselage boom. The Be-6 (NATO codename 'Madge') was retained in Soviet service into the early 1970s.

Specifications

Crew: 7
Powerplant: 2 x 1800kW (2400hp) Shvetsov ASh-73TK radial engines
Maximum speed: 414km/h (257mph)
Range: 5000km (3100 miles)
Service ceiling: 6100m (20,013ft)

Dimensions: span 33m (110ft); length 23.5m (77ft 1in); height 7.64m (25ft 1in)
Weight: 23,456kg (51,711lb) loaded
Armament: 5 x 23mm (0.91in) Nudelman-Rikhter NR-23 cannon; 2 x 1000kg (2205lb) torpedoes or 8 mines

the strategic balance. A measure of the neglect to which maritime patrol forces had been subject is seen in the fact that, by 1946, RAF Coastal Command was in possession of just 50 front-line aircraft.

Demise of the flying boat

Anti-submarine warfare (ASW) therefore returned to prominence, with long-range shore-based aircraft initially being supported by flying boats. The increased endurance offered by newly developed maritime patrol aircraft saw the flying boat discarded relatively quickly by most countries, although the

USSR was a notable exception, retaining amphibious aircraft until the end of the Cold War.

After the Korean War, NATO was subject to naval expansion, amid fears surrounding the growth of the Soviet submarine arm. The first postwar U.S. Navy patrol aircraft to see widespread service had been the P2V (later P-2) Neptune, which served with many NATO allies for at least three decades, until the arrival of more capable equipment, such as the P-3 Orion, the Canadian CL-28 Argus and the RAF's Nimrod. The particular importance assigned to the maritime patrol mission by Canada was reflected in

Specifications

Crew: 9

Powerplant: 4 x 2250kW (3017hp) General
  Electric T-64-IHI-10J turboprop engines

Maximum speed: 545km/h (339mph)

Range: 4700km (2921 miles)

Service ceiling: 9000m (29,550ft)

Dimensions: span 33.1m (108ft 7n); length
  33.5m (109ft 11in); height 9.7m (31ft 10in)

Weight: 43,000kg (94,799lb) maximum

Armament: bombs, torpedoes or depth charges

▲ **Shin Meiwa PS-1**

31st Kokutai, Japanese Maritime Self-Defence Force / early 1980s

As a maritime nation with close proximity to the USSR, Japan's defensive Cold War posture put an emphasis on anti-submarine warfare operations. Until replaced by US-provided P-3s, the indigenous PS-1 flying boat operated on patrol duty, with an endurance of up to 15 hours and a payload of ASW sensors and weapons.

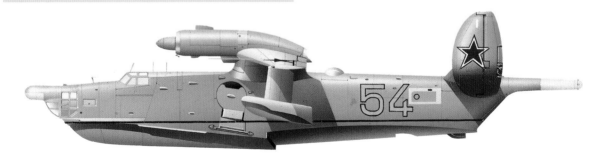

▲ **Beriev Be-12**

AVMF / late 1970s

The Be-12 was a dedicated maritime patrol and ASW amphibian, fitted with over-water sensors and equipment including a search radar and MAD boom. As the Be-12 began to be rendered obsolescent by submarine developments, examples were adapted for the transport and search-and-rescue roles.

Specifications

Crew: 4

Powerplant: 2 x 3864kW (5180hp) Ivchenko
  Progress AI-20D turboprop engines

Maximum speed: 530km/h (330mph)

Range: 3300km (2100 miles)

Service ceiling: 8000m (26,247ft)

Dimensions: span 29.84m (97ft 11in);
  length 30.11m (98ft 9in); height 7.94m
  (26ft 1in)

Weight: 36,000kg (79,200lb) loaded

Armament: 1500kg (3300lb) of bombs,
  depth-charges or torpedoes

that country's development of the Argus, later replaced by the CP-140 Aurora, a local development of the P-3, in the early 1980s. CP-140s were deployed on Canada's east and west coasts, supplemented by shorter-range S-2 Trackers.

A NATO requirement for a Neptune replacement led to the development of the Atlantic maritime patrol aircraft, an entirely new design that was first flown in 1961 and which was acquired by West Germany, France, the Netherlands and Italy.

Typically, Cold War maritime patrol aircraft were powered by efficient turboprop engines and their airframes were large enough to accommodate comprehensive sensors and offensive weaponry. The British Nimrod was somewhat unusual in being powered by jet engines, although it was, in common with the turboprop P-3 and Soviet Il-38, based on an existing airliner design. Mission equipment included radar, sonobuoys, magnetic anomaly detection (MAD) gear and other systems

Specifications

Crew: 9–11	Dimensions: span 30.4m (100ft);
Powerplant: 2 x 1715kW (2300hp) Wright	length 22.9m (75ft 4in); height 8.6m
R-3350-8A engines	(28ft 6in)
Maximum speed: 487km/h (303mph)	Weight: 26,3030kg (58,000lb) loaded
Range: 6618km (4110 miles)	Armament: 6 x 12.7mm (0.5in) MGs and
Service ceiling: 8230m (27,000ft)	capacity for 16 underwing rockets

▲ **Lockheed P2V-1 Neptune**

VP-8, U.S. Navy / late 1940s

The West's dominant land-based maritime air patrol platform for the first three decades after World War II, the first of the Neptunes to enter service was the P2V-1, from March 1947. The aircraft carried a crew of seven, a weapons bay for two torpedoes or up to 12 depth charges, and six defensive machine-guns.

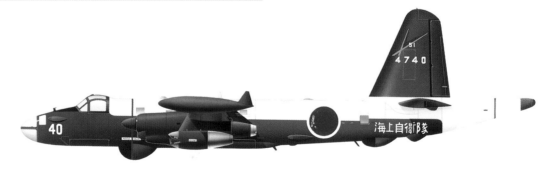

Specifications

Crew: 9	Dimensions: span 30.9m (101ft 4in); length
Powerplant: 2 x 2125kW (2850hp) General	27.9m (91ft 8in); height 8.9m (29ft 4in)
Electric T64-IHI-10 turboprop and 2 x 13.7kN	Weight: 34,020kg (75,000lb) maximum
(3081lb thrust) IHI-JE turbojet engines	Armament: up to 16 x 127mm (5in) rockets
Maximum speed: 650km/h (403mph)	and up to 3628kg (8000lb) of bombs, depth
Range: 5663km (3500 miles)	charges or torpedoes
Service ceiling: unknown	

▲ **Lockheed P-2J Neptune**

Japanese Maritime Self-Defence Force / mid-1970s

With increasing Soviet submarine activity in the seas surrounding its islands from the mid-1970s, Japan's ASW capacity rested with both fixed-wing and helicopter assets. Built by Kawasaki, the P-2J was an advanced local development of the Neptune, with a lengthened fuselage and a mixed turboprop/turbojet powerplant.

Specifications

Crew: 10

Powerplant: 4 x 1460kW (19600hp) Rolls-Royce
Griffon 57 liquid-cooled V12 engines

Maximum speed: 480km/h (300mph)

Range: 3620km (2250 miles)

Service ceiling: 6200m (20,200ft)

Dimensions: span 36.58m (120ft);
length 26.61m (87ft 4in); height 5.33m (17ft 6in)

Weight: 39,000kg (86,000lb) loaded

Armament: 2 x 20mm (0.8in) Hispano Mark V
cannon, 4536kg (10,000lb) bomb load

▲ Avro Shackleton MR.Mk 1A

120 Sqn, RAF / Aldergrove, 1959

Successor to the Neptune in RAF Coastal Command service was the Shackleton, which enjoyed a long career as a maritime patroller before being adapted to serve in the airborne early-warning role, which it fulfilled until the end of the Cold War. This example, from the third production batch of MR.Mk 1As, is seen in 1959.

Specifications

Crew: 4

Powerplant: 2 x 1137kW (1525hp) Wright R-
1820-82WA radial engines

Maximum speed: 450km/h (280mph)

Range: 2170km (1350 miles)

Service ceiling: 6700m (22,000ft)

Dimensions: span 22.12m (72ft 7in);
length 13.26m (43ft 6in); height 5.33m
(17ft 6in)

Weight: 11,860kg (26,147lb) loaded

Armament: 2 torpedoes

▲ Grumman S-2A Tracker

320 Sqn, Royal Netherlands Navy / Valkenburg, 1960s

Among Western Europe's NATO air arms, the Dutch Navy played an important Cold War maritime role over the North Sea. A total of 28 S2F-1s (S-2As) were delivered under MDAP in 1960-62, with a further 17 received from Canada in 1960-61. These served from land bases and from the Dutch carrier *Karel Doorman*.

Specifications

Crew: 11

Powerplant: 4 x 3356kW (4500hp) Allison T56-
A10W turboprop engines

Maximum speed: 766km/h (476mph)

Range: 4075km (2533 miles)

Service ceiling: 8625m (28,300ft)

Dimensions: span 30.37m (99ft 8in); length
35.61m (116ft 9in); height 10.27m (33ft 8in)

Weight: 60,780kg (134,000lb) loaded

Armament: up to 9070kg (20,000lb) of
ordnance, including bombs, mines and
torpedoes

▲ Lockheed P-3A Orion

VP-19, U.S. Navy / early 1960s

This Orion represents one of the very first examples to enter service with the U.S. Navy, and displays the midnight blue and white finish originally applied. The aircraft illustrated was part of the fourth production batch of P-3As, this variant entering service with VP-8 as a successor to the Neptune in mid-1962.

dedicated to the detection of surface and sub-surface threats. The search radar could detect surface contacts, or submarine periscopes, while MAD was also capable of uncovering a submerged target. Acoustic methods of detection employed were based on passive and active sonar, these being packaged as disposable sonobouys that could be dropped from the aircraft in patterns as it tracked its quarry, the onboard operators listening to the emitted signals via radio. As was the case with other maritime patrol aircraft in the latter half of the Cold War, data from the Nimrod's various mission sensors and navigation systems were brought together by a powerful data-processing computer that was designed to overcome potential electronic jamming and countermeasures. The resultant contacts were displayed on screens at the consoles of the radar operators, tactical navigators or plotters seated in the cabin and could also be transmitted to other air and surface assets using a secure radio link.

▲ Lockheed P-3B Orion

333 Sqn, Royal Norwegian AF / Andøya, early 1980s

Norway's extensive coastline and proximity to Soviet naval bases on the Kola Peninsula made the maritime patrol mission a vital component of the nation's defensive strategy. Based at Andøya in the north of the country, 333 Sqn was the first European operator of the Orion, the first five examples arriving in 1969.

Specifications

Crew: 11

Powerplant: 4 x 3700kW (4600hp) Allison T56-A-14 turboprop engines

Maximum speed: 766km/h (476mph)

Range: 4075km (2533 miles)

Service ceiling: 8625m (28,300ft)

Dimensions: span 30.37m (99ft 8in); length 35.61m (116ft 9in); height 10.27m (33ft 8in)

Weight: 60,780kg (134,000lb) loaded

Armament: up to 9070kg (20,000lb) of ordnance, including bombs, mines and torpedoes

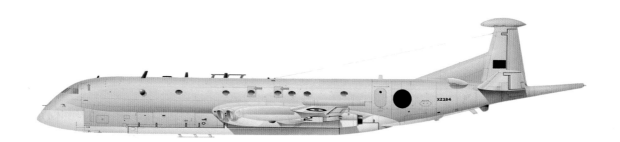

▲ British Aerospace Nimrod MR.Mk 2P

42 Sqn, RAF / Kinloss, early 1980s

The definitive RAF maritime patrol aircraft of the Cold War – and one of the most capable in its class – the Nimrod replaced the Shackleton MR variants. The MR.Mk 2P version of the Nimrod appeared during the Falklands campaign, and introduced an aerial refuelling capability, with a forward fuselage probe.

Specifications

Crew: 12

Powerplant: 4 x 53.98kN (12,140lb thrust) Rolls-Royce Spey Mk 250 turbofans

Maximum speed: 925km/h (575mph)

Range: 9265km (5755 miles) (on internal fuel only)

Service ceiling: 12,800m (41,995ft)

Dimensions: span 35m (114ft 10in); length 38.65m (126ft 9in); height 9.14m (31ft)

Weight: 87,090kg (192,000lb) loaded

Armament: provision for 6123kg (13,500lb) of dropped stores

Naval Helicopters
1948–1989

One of the answers to the ASW challenge during the Cold War was the deployment of the helicopter as an adjunct to surface warships, or as a coastal defensive asset.

THE HELICOPTER SAW only limited use in World War II, but it was already apparent that its capabilities suited it particularly to operations from warships. The first naval rotorcraft were handicapped by their limited range and payload, but as improved designs became available, the importance of the helicopter as a naval tool increased exponentially. Indeed, by the end of the Cold War, almost all of the world's navies deployed helicopters, while operators of fixed-wing maritime aircraft remained limited.

In addition to the ASW role, Cold War naval helicopters routinely undertook search and rescue (SAR), plane guard (aboard aircraft carriers), amphibious assault, mine countermeasures and vertical replenishment (Vertrep) tasks, as well as more mundane liaison and communications work. Towards the end of this period, the helicopter was being increasingly used as a weapon deployed against surface targets, primarily through the introduction of

anti-ship missiles. The USSR was unusual in deploying helicopters for targeting and mid-course guidance of land attack and anti-ship missiles launched from Soviet Navy warships.

Land-based designs

As well as the typically compact designs specifically intended for use from surface vessels, land-based maritime helicopters were also fielded, generally undertaking ASW and SAR missions in coastal areas.

In common with their fixed-wing counterparts, ASW helicopters relied upon sensors that included radar, MAD (normally a towed 'bird' sensor) and sonobuoys. A key advantage offered by the helicopter, however, was its ability to operate a dipping sonar in place of disposable sonobuoys. The number of sensor operators was clearly restricted by cabin dimensions, but the crew were provided with consoles similar to those found in fixed-wing maritime patrol aircraft.

Specifications

Crew: 4

Powerplant: 2 x 671kW (900shp) Glushnekov GTD-3 engines

Maximum speed: 220km/h (137mph)

Range: 400km (247 miles)

Service ceiling: 3500m (11,483ft)

Dimensions: rotor diameter 15.7m (51ft 8in); length 9.8m (32ft 3in); height 5.4m (17ft 7in)

Weight: 7100kg (16,100lb) loaded

Armament: none

▲ **Kamov Ka-25**

AVMF / mid-1970s

Serving both as a shipborne and land-based ASW helicopter, the Ka-25 featured a co-axial main rotor arrangement that made it notably compact. In addition to the ASW version depicted here, the Ka-25 was also fielded in utility/SAR and missile-targeting variants, the latter providing over-the-horizon guidance for missiles.

Weapons were similar too, but typically lighter, and chiefly comprised torpedoes and depth bombs.

For NATO, the 'standard' shipborne naval helicopters were successive Sikorsky designs, the maritime versions of the S-55 being followed by the S-58. The purpose-designed S-61 Sea King appeared in 1959, and was finally superseded by the S-70 Seahawk. The first three of these types were also built under licence in the UK and all were widely exported, with additional licence production undertaken elsewhere. The Lynx, a British design optimized for use from the decks of smaller warships, was also widely deployed towards the end of the Cold War.

▲ **Lynx HAS.Mk 2**

The British-designed Lynx was representative of the lighter ASW helicopters intended for operations from the flight decks of destroyers and frigates.

▲ **Mil Mi-14**

AVMF / mid-1970s

The Mi-14 was the primary Soviet shore-based ASW helicopter, and carried a useful load of ordnance that could include rocket-propelled torpedoes and nuclear depth charges. Illustrated is the ASW version (with MAD 'bird' stowed behind the rear fuselage), but mine countermeasures and SAR versions were also used.

Specifications

Crew: 4	Dimensions: rotor diameter 21.29m (69ft 10in);
Powerplant: 2 x 1400kW (1950shp) Klimov	length 18.38m (60ft 3in); height 6.93m (22ft 9in)
TV3-117MT turboshaft engines	Weight: 14,000kg (30,865lb) loaded
Maximum speed: 230km/h (143mph)	Armament: 1 x E45-75A torpedo or B-1 nuclear
Range: 1135km (705 miles)	depth bomb
Service ceiling: 3500m (11,500ft)	

U.S. Marine Air Power
1950–1989

While other Cold War protagonists also maintained an amphibious warfare capability, none was as powerful as that of the U.S. Marine Corps, which also boasted organic fixed-wing air power.

AMPHIBIOUS WARFARE HAD been a decisive factor in World War II, and the U.S. Marine Corps (USMC) retained this capability in the postwar period, with a powerful force of amphibious assault ships supported by both shipborne helicopters and fixed-wing aviation. Ultimately, the latter would also

include V/STOL AV-8 Harrier warplanes capable of operating from the decks of assault carriers.

Successive military actions in Korea and Suez during the 1950s reinforced the importance of amphibious assault, with the latter conflict also demonstrating the efficacy of the helicopter as an assault transport, replacing the landing craft employed in earlier conflicts. After Suez, the helicopter carrier came to prominence, able to deliver troops and equipment to the beachhead and beyond.

Marine Corps air assets

Typically, Cold War doctrine saw the USMC's amphibious capability expressed as a self-contained rapid-reaction force that could be deployed to trouble spots, from where they would stand just over the horizon, awaiting the call to action. Where U.S. Marines were fighting ground campaigns, as in both Korea and Vietnam, USMC air power was also on hand, operating from land bases alongside USAF warplanes. In a further measure of USMC air power versatility, its aircraft also routinely operated from

carrier decks, components within mixed air wings that also included U.S. Navy squadrons.

A prime example of the use of USMC amphibious forces as a tool for rapidly intervening in a global crisis was presented in Lebanon in August 1983, when the U.S. took action in support of a multinational stabilizing force in the country. The amphibious assault ship USS *Iwo Jima* and the embarked 24th Marine Expeditionary Unit were on station, standing off the coast, when two U.S. servicemen were killed in Beirut. The immediate response was conducted by AH-1T SeaCobra attack helicopters from the *Iwo Jima*, supported by a naval artillery bombardment.

By the mid-1980s, the USMC numbered almost 200,000 soldiers within three mobile divisions. Each

Specifications

Crew: 2	Service ceiling: 18,898m (62,000ft)
Powerplant: 2 x 75.5kN (17,000lb) General	Dimensions: span 11.7m (38ft 5in);
Electric J79-GE-8 engines	length 17.77m (58ft 3in); height 4.95m (16ft 3in)
Maximum speed: 2390km/h (1485mph)	Weight: 20,231kg (44,600lb) loaded
Range: 3701km (2300 miles)	Armament: none

▲ **McDonnell Douglas RF-4B Phantom II**

VMFP-3, USMC / El Toro, early 1980s

Wearing the low-visibility markings typical of the 1980s, this RF-4B was flown by the U.S. Marine Corps photo-reconnaissance squadron VMFP-3, based at El Toro, California. The RF-4B variant was developed specifically for the USMC and also provided a tactical reconnaissance capability for U.S. Navy Carrier Air Wings.

Specifications

Crew: 2	(54ft 9in); height 4.93m (16ft 2in)
Powerplant: 2 x 41.4kN (9300lb) Pratt & Whitney	Weight: 26,581kg (58,600lb) loaded
J52-P-8A turbojets	Armament: five external hardpoints with
Maximum speed: 1043km/h (648mph)	provision for up to 8165kg (18,000lb)
Range: 1627km (1011 miles)	of stores, including nuclear weapons,
Service ceiling: 14,480m (47,500ft)	conventional and guided bombs, air-to-surface
Dimensions: span 16.15m (53ft); length 16.69m	missiles and drop tanks

▲ **Grumman A-6E Intruder**

VMA(AW)-121, USMC / El Toro, early 1980s

The Intruder was the most capable strike asset deployed by the USMC during the Cold War, eventually equipping five squadrons. Key features of the A-6E model included a new multi-mode navigation radar and computerized nav/attack system. VMA(AW)-121 'Green Knights' was home-based at El Toro, California.

division was allocated a Marine Air Wing, operating around 315 aircraft. As well as the assault helicopters used to bring troops and stores ashore, the MAW also included fighters, strike/attack aircraft, close support aircraft and helicopters, reconnaissance and electronic warfare aircraft, plus forward air control and liaison assets. In total, around 60 amphibious warfare vessels were available to support USMC operations by 1987.

Combined, the three active force MAWs had a strength of around 35,600 personnel, 440 fixed-wing aircraft and 100 armed helicopters by the mid-1980s. In terms of air assets, 12 fighter squadrons were provided, most of these equipped with the F-4, although the F/A-18 began to enter service in the early 1980s. A total of 13 attack squadrons included three AV-8 units, while the remaining 10 were divided equally between the A-4M and the A-6E. Single squadrons operated the photo-reconnaissance RF-4B and the EA-6B electronic warfare platform. Both fighter and attack squadrons regularly embarked on carriers as part of the Carrier Air Wing.

In addition to the three active force Marine Air Wings, the U.S. Marine Air Reserve offered support in the shape of the 4th Marine Aircraft Wing, comprising four aviation groups. These maintained 11 squadrons, with F-4N/S, A-4E, A-4F/M, EA-6A, OV-10 and KC-130 aircraft on strength. The introduction of the KC-130 was spurred by the experience of Vietnam, when the USMC required an

aerial refuelling capability to deploy aircraft over long distances at short notice.

Support and second-line fixed-wing USMC air assets included the OV-10D (two squadrons for observation and forward air control), three assault transport/tanker squadrons with KC-130s, while TA-4J and OA-4M aircraft served with headquarters and maintenance units. A further 10 reserve squadrons operated helicopters, including the AH-1J, UH-1E/N, CH-53A and CH-46.

Rotary-wing fleet

Towards the end of the Cold War, the USMC operated 25 helicopter squadrons, eight of these equipped with the heavy-lift CH-53D/E. A further 11 front-line squadrons flew the medium-lift CH-46E/F. The UH-1N utility helicopter and the AH-1T attack helicopter were each flown by three squadrons.

In a European Cold War context, the USMC was expected to be active in Norway, in support of NATO's Northern Front. For this purpose, combat equipment was pre-positioned in Norway, with enough materiel to support a full USMC brigade. Had the Warsaw Pact launched an attack against Norway, up to three Marine Amphibious Brigades would have been on hand to counter it, supported by Norwegian forces, the Netherlands-UK Amphibious Group and a Canadian brigade, backed by air power.

The USMC's original helicopter carriers (LPHs) were the 'Essex' (modified fleet carriers) and 'Iwo

▲ McDonnell Douglas/BAe AV-8A Harrier
VMA-231, USMC / Cherry Point, late 1970s
The USMC's surviving force of Harriers had been upgraded from AV-8A to improved AV-8C standard by the mid-1980s, including improved defensive countermeasures systems. Armed with underwing rocket pods and cannon pods under the fuselage, this example, from VMA-231 'Ace of Spades', served at Cherry Point, North Carolina.

Specifications

Crew: 1	Dimensions: span 7.7m (25ft 3in); length
Powerplant: 1x 91.2kN (20,500lb) thrust Rolls-	13.87m (45ft 6in); height 3.45m (11ft 4in)
Royce Pegasus 10 vectored-thrust turbofan	Weight: 11,340kg (25,000lb) loaded
engine	Armament: maximum of 2268kg (5000lb) of
Maximum speed: 1186km/h (737mph)	stores on underfuselage and underwing points;
Range: 5560km (3455 miles)	one 30mm Aden gun or similar gun, with 150
Service ceiling: 15,240m (50,000ft)	rounds, rockets and bombs

Jima' classes. These were followed by altogether more capable vessels, the 'Tarawa' class, the first of which was commissioned in 1976. The final LPH was decommissioned in 1988, leaving the 'Tarawa' LHA as the primary base for USMC amphibious assault aviation. Each 'Tarawa' had a well deck to accommodate landing craft, amphibious assault vehicles and an assault hovercraft. The large flight deck could support any USMC helicopter, as well as the AV-8 Harrier and, when required, the OV-10 Bronco forward air control aircraft. The adoption of the British-designed Harrier by the USMC marked a

significant milestone, because high-speed air power could now be called upon over the beachhead, without the need for a local airfield or conventional carrier. USMC Harriers operated from shore bases, highways, beaches and a variety of warships, their typical mission being close air support, armed with rockets, guns and napalm. Further U.S. development of the basic design saw the fielding of the AV-8B Harrier II, a much improved aircraft with an entirely new wing of increased span and carbon-fibre construction, for additional fuel capacity and an increased payload.

Specifications

Crew: 1

Powerplant: 1 x 49.82kN (11,500lb) thrust Pratt
& Whitney J52-P408 turbojet engine

Maximum speed: 1083km/h (673mph)

Range: 3310km (2200 miles)

Service ceiling: 14,935m (49,000ft)

Dimensions: span 8.38m (27ft 6in); length

(excluding probe) 12.22m (40ft 1.5in);
height 4.66m (15ft 3in)

Weight: 12,437kg (27,420lb) loaded

Armament: 2 x 20mm Mk 12 cannon; provision
for 3720kg (8200lb) of stores, including AIM-
9G Sidewinder AAMs, rocket-launcher pods and
ECM pods

▲ **Douglas A-4M Skyhawk II**

VMA-324, USMC / Beaufort, early 1970s

The ultimate new-build, single-seat Skyhawk version was the A-4M, with numerous updates that included a reprofiled fin and canopy, a braking parachute and an uprated J52 engine, allowing operations from shorter airstrips. VMA-324 flew this aircraft from Beaufort, South Carolina, home of Marine Air Group 31.

▲ **AH-1J SeaCobra**

USMC / early 1980s

Developed specifically to meet USMC close-support requirements, the AH-1J introduced a twin-turboshaft powerplant to the AH-1 airframe, and its chin turret mounted a three-barrel M197 20mm cannon. USMC SeaCobras operated from ships and were used to support ground operations, particularly beach assaults.

Specifications

Crew: 2

Powerplant: 1 x 1342kW (1800shp) Pratt &
Whitney Canada T400-CP-400 turboshaft

Maximum speed: 352km/h (218mph)

Range: 571km (355 miles)

Service ceiling: 3475m (11,398ft)

Dimensions: rotor diameter 13.4m (43ft 11in);

length 13.5m (44ft 3in); height 4.1m (13ft 5in)

Weight: 4525kg (9979lb) loaded

Armament: 1 x 20mm (0.8in) M197 cannon;
14 x 70mm (2.75in) Mk 40 rockets;
8 x 127mm (5in) Zuni rockets; 2 AIM-9
anti-aircraft missiles

Chapter 3

Strategic Bombers and Air Defence

The dawn of the nuclear age and the destruction of the cities of Hiroshima and Nagasaki in August 1945 changed the face of aerial bombing immeasurably. Prior to the development of ICBMs, manned bombers remained the only nuclear-delivery platforms with intercontinental reach. Throughout the Cold War, nuclear-armed bombers would play a major role in the strategic balance, and the threat they posed demanded ever more advanced interceptors to be fielded for national defence.

◀ **Boeing B-52G Stratofortress**
One of the most potent symbols of the superpower standoff, the Stratofortress served with the USAF from 1955 until the end of the Cold War. Towards the end of this period, B-52Gs like this were armed with cruise missiles in order to strike from beyond the reach of hostile air defences.

U.S. Bombers
1946–1989

Created in 1946, Strategic Air Command (SAC) would eventually provide two elements of the U.S. strategic nuclear triad: intercontinental ballistic missiles (ICBMs) and manned bombers.

THROUGHOUT THE COLD War, SAC aircraft stood on alert at their bases in the U.S., and made frequent forward deployments to locations including the UK, Guam and Okinawa. Prior to the fielding of land-based ICBMs and submarine-launched ballistic missiles, SAC's bomber fleet was the most visible – and viable – expression of U.S. nuclear power.

SAC's original equipment was based around the wartime B-29 and its improved development, the B-50. The formidable B-36 arrived in service in 1948, providing intercontinental range for the first time. The arrival of the jet engine meant the B-36 would remain interim equipment, however, and SAC's first all-jet bomber, the B-47, entered service in 1950, and

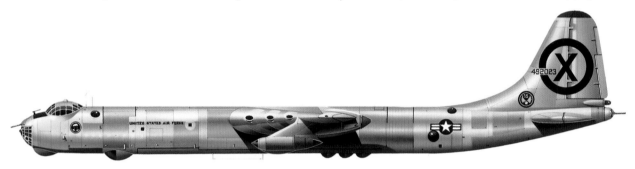

Specifications

Crew: 15	Dimensions: span 70.10m (230ft);
Powerplant: 6 x 2610kW (3500hp) Pratt &	length 49.39m (162ft 1in); height 14.24m
Whitney R-4360-41 engines	(46ft 8in)
Maximum speed: 613km/h (381mph)	Weight: 148,778kg (328,000lb) loaded
Range: 13,156km (8175 miles) (with bomb load)	Armament: 16 x 20mm (0.8in) cannon;
Service ceiling: 12,954m (42,000ft)	32,659kg (72,000lb) bomb load

▲ **Convair RB-36D Peacemaker**
72nd Bomb Squadron (Heavy), SAC / Travis AFB, 1950s
A force of almost 400 B-36s formed the backbone of SAC between 1948-59. The type was the largest bomber to serve with USAF, the RB-36D illustrated being a strategic reconnaissance version, with a forward bomb bay adapted to carry 14 cameras. The aircraft's crew was increased from 15 to 22.

Specifications

Crew: 3	Dimensions: span 35.4m (116ft);
Powerplant: 6 x 26.54kW (5970lb thrust)	length 32.56m (106ft 10in); height
General Electric J47-GE-23 turbojets	8.51m (27ft 11in)
Maximum speed: 978km/h (608mph)	Weight: 83,873kg (184,908lb) loaded
Combat radius: 3162km (1965 miles)	Armament: 2 x 12.7mm (0.5in) MGs; up to
Service ceiling: 10,333m (33,900ft)	8165kg (18,000lb) bombs

▲ **Boeing B-47B Stratojet**
SAC / 1950s
The B-47B was the first true production version of the Stratojet and entered service in 1951, with 399 examples being built. This version introduced an in-flight refuelling capability, with uprated engines on later production machines. B-47 wings regularly deployed to bases in the Pacific, North Africa and UK.

equipped 28 bomb wings before the end of the decade. Using forward bases and aerial refuelling to extend its range, the B-47 was joined in 1955 by the B-52, which combined jet performance with intercontinental capability. Such was the value of the B-52 that it remained a front-line element of the U.S. nuclear deterrent until the end of the Cold War. In the mid-1980s, the B-52 was responsible for carrying 45 per cent of the total U.S. strategic megatonnage.

Advances in air defences threatened to render free-fall bombers obsolete by the early 1960s. Responses included a move to low-level operations and introduction of the Short-Range Attack Missile in 1972. This was followed in the early 1980s by cruise missiles carried by B-52s, and a corresponding switch in targets from cities and industry to high-priority military installations and 'counter-force' targets.

By the end of the Cold War, SAC's B-52 force was complemented by supersonic FB-111As, while the advanced B-1B was active in SAC from the mid-1980s, carrying a payload of free-fall bombs. In terms of numbers, SAC in the 1980s was responsible for around one-fifth of U.S. strategic weapons, but wielded almost half of the total megatonnage.

▲ **Boeing KC-97G**

SAC, 1950s

The availability of aerial refuelling was a critical aspect of SAC's nuclear deterrent, which originally kept nuclear-armed aircraft airborne on 24-hour alert, ready to launch an attack at the shortest notice. The KC-97G version, of which 592 were built, was equipped for tanking, troop transport and cargo freighting duties.

Specifications

Crew: 5

Powerplant: 4 x 2610kW (3500hp) Pratt & Whitney R-4360-59B Wasp Major engines

Maximum speed: 604km/h (375mph)

Range: 6920km (4300 miles)

Service ceiling: 9205m (30,200ft)

Dimensions: span 43.05m (141ft 2in); length 35.79m (117ft 5in); height 11.68m (38ft 4in)

Weight: 69,400kg (153,000lb) loaded

Armament: none

Specifications

Crew: 6

Powerplant: 8 x 46.68kN (10,500lb) thrust Pratt & Whitney J57-P-29WA engines

Maximum speed: 1027km/h (638mph)

Range: 13,419km (8338 miles)

Service ceiling: 14,082m (46,200ft)

Dimensions: span 56.39m (185ft); length 47.73m (156ft 7in); height 14.73m (48ft 4in)

Weight: 204,116kg (450,000lb) loaded

Armament: 4 x 12.7mm (0.5in) M-3 MGs; up to 19,504kg (43,000lb) of bombs

▲ **Boeing B-52C Stratofortress**

7th Bomb Wing, SAC / Carswell AFB, 1971

Displaying the white undersides intended to reflect nuclear flash, the B-52C offered much improved performance and equipment compared to its B-52B predecessor, and 35 examples were completed. This particular aircraft served at Carswell AFB, Fort Worth, as part of the 2nd AF, and was one of the last C-model aircraft in service.

Specifications

Crew: 6

Powerplant: 8 x 61.1kN (13,750lb) Pratt &
    Whitney J57-P-43W turbojets

Maximum speed: 1014km/h (630mph)

Range: 13,680km (8500 miles)

Service ceiling: 16,765m (55,000ft)

Dimensions: span 56.4m (185ft); length 48m

(157ft 7in); height 12.4m (40ft 8in)

Weight: 221,500kg (448,000lb) loaded

Armament: remotely controlled tail mounting
    with 4 x .5in MGs; normal internal bomb
    capacity 12,247kg (27,000lb), including all
    SAC special weapons; external pylons for
    2 x Hound Dog missiles

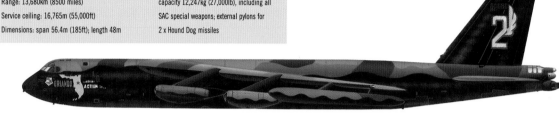

▲ **Boeing B-52G Stratofortress**

69th Bomb Squadron, 42nd Bomb Wing, SAC / Loring AFB, 1974

Penultimate model of the Stratofortress was the B-52G, this example being flown by the 69th BS during the 1974
Giant Voice bombing competition. The aircraft was home-based at Loring AFB, Maine. The B-52G introduced a
remote-controlled tail gun turret, with all six crew now grouped together in a single forward compartment.

Specifications

Crew: 2

Powerplant: 2 x 56kN (12,500lbf) dry thrust
    Pratt & Whitney TF30-P-7 engines

Maximum speed: 2338km/h (1452mph)

Range: 7242km (4500 miles)

Service ceiling: 17,373m (57,000ft)

Dimensions: span 21.33m (70ft); length 22.4m
    (73ft 6in); height 5.18m (17ft)

Weight: 54,105kg (119,250lb) loaded

Armament: 6 x AGM-69A SRAMs or up to
    16,100kg (35,500lb) bomb load

▲ **General Dynamics FB-111A**

380th Bomb Wing, SAC / Plattsburgh AFB, early 1980s

Just over 60 FB-111As were in use with SAC in the 1980s. The aircraft could be
armed with Short-Range Attack Missiles (SRAMs) as well as free-fall (gravity)
bombs. The FB-111A, a 'strategic' version of the basic F-111 strike aircraft,
served with two wings, at Pease, New Hampshire, and Plattsburgh, New York.

Soviet Bombers
1946–1989

**While the threat of Soviet bombers was taken extremely seriously in the West, the USSR
ultimately regarded manned bombers as a lower priority than ICBMs and missile submarines.**

IN THE EARLY 1950s, Soviet Long-Range Aviation
(DA) relied on the piston-engined Tu-4 bomber, a
copy of the American B-29. After a protracted
development, the Tu-4 entered service in 1949.
Theoretically nuclear capable, only a handful were
ever equipped to carry operational atomic weapons,
and the bomber's range was strictly limited.

The first modern Soviet bomber to enter service
was the Tu-16, which began to be delivered in 1954,
much to the consternation of Western defence
officials. The DA had entirely replaced the Tu-4 by
the early 1960s, by which time the Tu-16 was the
standard bomber type. Versions were developed to
undertake diverse roles including reconnaissance,

aerial refuelling, electronic intelligence (ELINT) and electronic countermeasures (ECM) support.

Long-range equipment

With few bases available in the Soviet Arctic, the mid-1950s saw the experimental use of Tu-16s from temporary airstrips on tundra or Arctic ice. These proved unsuitable for use by heavy bombers, but DA's reach was improved through the introduction of the Tu-95 bomber in 1956. The turboprop-powered Tu-95 proved far more durable than the jet-powered M-4 bomber, which was also intended to offer intercontinental range. Although it entered service as a free-fall bomber in 1954, the M-4 (and its upgraded 3M derivative) was never satisfactory in this role and was eventually relegated to tanking duties.

The 1960s saw the increasing use of missile-carrying bombers. The supersonic Tu-22 superseded the Tu-16 with a number of units starting in 1962, but never entirely replaced its predecessor.

The intermediate-range Tu-16 would remain in large-scale service into the mid-1980s, by which time it had been supplanted by the Tu-22M theatre bomber, which was first deployed in 1972. In 1979, DA still retained almost 500 Tu-16s of various types. Starting in the mid-1970s the USSR was working on the long-range Tu-160, a supersonic bomber with cruise missile armament. The Tu-160 was beginning to enter service as the Cold War came to an end, by which time DA's long-range backbone was provided by the Tu-95MS variant armed with up to 16 air-launched cruise missiles with nuclear warheads.

Specifications

Crew: 4

Powerplant: 2 x 93.2kN (20,900lbf) Mikulin AM-3 M-500 turbojets

Maximum speed:1050km/h (656mph)

Range: 7200km (4500 miles)

Service ceiling: 12,800m (42,000ft)

Dimensions: span 33m (108ft 3in); length 34.8m (114ft 2in); height 10.36m (34ft)

Weight: 76,000kg (168,00lb) loaded

Armament: 6–7 x 23mm (0.9in) Nudelman-Rikhter NR-23 cannons; 9000kg (20,000lb) bomb load or 1 x Kh-10 anti-ship missile and 1 x Kh-26 anti-ship missile

▲ **Tupolev Tu-16**

Soviet Long-Range Aviation / mid-1950s

Soviet bombers were organized into Heavy Bomber Air Divisions (TBAD), each of which normally contained two Heavy Bomber Air Regiments (TBAP). In the early part of its service, a typical Tu-16 regiment had three squadrons: one of missile-carriers and two of free-fall bombers. The type was also used as an in-flight refuelling tanker.

Specifications

Crew: 7

Powerplant: 4 x 11,000kW (14,800shp) Kuznetsov NK-12MV turboprops

Maximum speed: 920km/h (575mph)

Range: 15,000km (9,400miles)

Service ceiling: 13,716m (45,000ft)

Dimensions: span 51.10m (167ft 8in); length 49.50m (162ft 5in); height 12.12m (39ft 9in)

Weight: 171,000kg (376,200lb) loaded

Armament: 1 or 2 x 23mm AM-23 cannon in tail turret and up to 15,000kg (33,000lb) of bombs

▲ **Tupolev Tu-95**

Soviet Long-Range Aviation / mid-1950s

The Tu-95 was the first Soviet bomber with genuine intercontinental range and served as the mainstay of DA until the end of the Cold War, ultimately being armed with cruise missiles. Illustrated is one of the very first Tu-95s to be built. Production of the Tu-95MS version was still under way when the Cold War ended.

British Bombers
1946–1970

Serving from 1955 until 1968, the RAF's V-Force provided Britain's strategic nuclear deterrent until superseded by the Royal Navy's Polaris submarine-launched missiles.

IN 1946 BRITISH chiefs-of-staff requested government approval for the development of a nuclear weapon, with the go-ahead given in January 1947. A new bomber would be required to carry the weapon, and to replace the ageing Lancasters, Lincolns and Mosquitoes with Bomber Command.

In the interim, ex-USAF B-29s were supplied for RAF use as Washingtons, while Canberras provided the RAF's initial jet bomber equipment, entering service in May 1951. In August 1952 the Vulcan and Victor were ordered as part of a three-tier bomber programme, these two advanced designs being complemented by the more conventional Valiant.

Until the V-Bombers became available, Bomber Command continued to rely on Lincolns and (from March 1950) Washingtons, the bomb bay of the

Specifications

Crew: 11	length 30.20m (99ft); height 8.50m (29ft 7in)
Powerplant: 4 x 1640kW (2,200hp) Wright R-3350-23	Weight: 54,000kg (120,000lb) loaded
and 23A radial engines	Armament: 10 x 12.7mm (.50in) caliber
Maximum speed: 574km/h (357mph)	Browning M2/ANs, 2 x 12.7mm (.50in) and
Range: 9000km (5600 miles)	1 x 20mm (.79in) M2 cannon in tail position
Service ceiling: 10,200m (33,600ft)	plus bomb load of 9072kg (20,000lb)
Dimensions: span 43.10m (141ft 3in);	

▲ **Boeing Washington B.Mk 1**

90 Sqn, RAF / Marham, 1950–54

A total of 88 ex-USAAF Boeing B-29As were supplied to the RAF under MDAP as a stopgap between the Lincoln and the first jet bombers. The RAF's 90 Sqn operated the Washington (as the RAF's B-29 was known) from Marham and won trophies for visual bombing and gunnery excellence during 1952.

▲ **Vickers Valiant B.Mk 1**

7 Sqn, RAF / Honington, 1957–62

In October 1956 a Valiant dropped Britain's first air-launched nuclear weapon over southern Australia, and this was followed by a first British hydrogen bomb, dropped by another Valiant over Christmas Island in May 1957. Fatigue saw the Valiant prematurely withdrawn from service in 1964.

Specifications

Crew: 5	Dimensions: span 34.85m (114ft 4in);
Powerplant: 4 x 44.7kN (10,054lb)	length 32.99m (108ft 3in); height 9.8m (32ft 2in)
Rolls-Royce Avon RA.28 turbojets	Weight: 63,503kg (140,000lb) loaded
Maximum speed: 912km/h (576mph)	Armament: 1 x 4536kg (10,000lb) nuclear
Range: 7242km (4500 miles)	bomb or up to 9,525kg (21,000lb)
Service ceiling: 16,460m (54,000ft)	conventional bombs

Canberra being too small for the carriage of early nuclear weapons. In October 1952 Britain's first nuclear device was detonated in western Australia and this weapon was adapted for service as the Blue Danube, the UK's first air-launched nuclear weapon, deployed from November 1953.

First of the V-bombers

By the end of 1957 the Washington had been almost completely replaced by seven Valiant bomber squadrons, and the following year the first hydrogen bombs were deployed, in the form of Yellow Sun.

The Vulcan B.Mk 1 entered operational service in February 1957 and would equip six front-line units. In April 1958, the first of four front-line Victor B.Mk 1 squadrons was stood up. However, the 1957

Defence White Paper effectively reduced the V-Force to the status of a stopgap nuclear deterrent pending the arrival of long-range missiles.

Improved Mk 2 versions of the Vulcan and Victor entered service in 1960 and 1962 respectively. Vulcan B.Mk 2s were flown by nine units, and Victor B.Mk 2s by two units, while Victor B.Mk 1s were converted for use as tankers. The loss of Gary Powers' U-2 in May 1960 pre-empted a switch to the low-level role. Valiants had already assumed a tactical nuclear strike role, while Vulcans and Victors begin to transition to the low-level mission in 1963, some being armed with Blue Steel missiles. The V-Force was finally relieved of its strategic role in July 1969. Victor B.Mk 2s were converted as tankers, while the Vulcan continued to serve in the low-level tactical role.

Specifications

Crew: 5	Dimensions: span 33.83m (111ft); length
Powerplant: 4 x 88.9kN (20,000lb) Olympus	30.45m (99ft 11in); height 8.28m (27ft 2in);
Mk.301 turbojets	Weight: 113,398kg (250,000lb) loaded
Maximum speed: 1038km/h (645mph)	Armament: internal weapon bay for up to
Range: 7403km/h (4600 miles)	21,454kg (47,198lb) bombs, or Blue Steel
Service ceiling: 19,810m (65,000ft)	nuclear missile

▲ **Avro Vulcan B.Mk 2**

617 Sqn, RAF / Scampton, early 1960s

The definitive B.Mk 2 version of the Vulcan arrived in 1960, with more powerful engines, in-flight refuelling capability, and a considerably modified wing of increased area. The Vulcan B.Mk 2 could be armed with the Blue Steel missile, as seen on this example, from 617 Sqn, which is painted in anti-flash white.

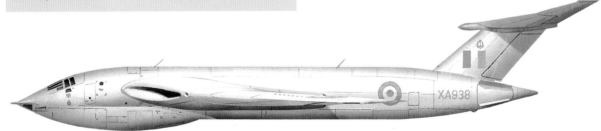

▲ **Handley Page Victor B.Mk 1**

10 Sqn, RAF / Cottesmore, early 1960s

Last of the three V-bombers to enter service, the crescent-winged Victor was first deployed by 10 Sqn at Cottesmore in April 1958. In common with many other B.Mk 1s, this aircraft, XA938, was later converted for use as an in-flight refuelling tanker. The first Victor tankers entered service with 55 Sqn in August 1965.

Specifications

Crew: 5	Dimensions: span 33.53m (110ft);
Powerplant: 4 x 49kN (11,050lbf) Armstrong	length 35.05m (114 ft 11in); height 8.15m
Siddeley Sapphire A.S.Sa.7 turbojets	(26ft 9in)
Maximum speed: 1,050km/h (650mph)	Weight: 75,000kg (165,000lb) loaded
Range: 4000km (2500 miles)	Armament: Up to 35 x 450kg (1,000lb) bombs
Service ceiling: 56,000ft (17,000m)	

U.S. Air Defence
1945–1989

Defence of the continental U.S. against a Soviet bomb or missile attack was entrusted starting in 1957 to North American Aerospace Defense Command (NORAD), covering the U.S. and Canada.

HEADQUARTERED AT CHEYENNE Mountain, Wyoming, NORAD consisted of both air and ground elements and provided early warning and defence against bombers and ICBMs. NORAD was in constant communication with SAC and the National Command Authorities, enabling the U.S. to launch a rapid nuclear counter-strike if required.

The limited reaction time in which to respond to a bomber attack from the USSR demanded the fielding of comprehensive interceptor defences. At the outset, the USAF's Air Defense Command (ADC) possessed over 50 interceptor squadrons, equipped with subsonic F-86D, F-89 and F-94 fighters, while Canada provided Sabres and CF-100s. After reaching a peak of around 1,000 interceptors, numbers were reduced in the 1960s as the true extent of the Soviet bomber threat was better understood.

By the mid-1970s ADC provided NORAD with just six F-106A squadrons, supported by Air National Guard (ANG) units operating F-101Bs, F-102s and F-106s, while Canada retained CF-101s. ADC was eventually disbanded, and its surviving units were passed on to SAC and Tactical Air Command (TAC), the latter being responsible for manned interceptors.

Early warning of bomber or missile attack was provided by a chain of radar stations including the Distant Early Warning Line, with important facilities in Alaska, Greenland and England in order to cover all lines of approach from the USSR and Asia.

Modernization

The 1980s saw improvements made to NORAD, in order to better counter the threat of low-level intruders and cruise missiles. F-15s began to replace F-106s in TAC, while ANG units received F-4s in order to allow F-101s and F-102s to be retired. As the Cold War came to an end, ANG F-106s had been withdrawn in favour of F-16s. Canada, meanwhile, introduced the CF-188 as a successor to its CF-101s in the early 1980s.

By the early 1980s, NORAD could also call upon TAC-operated E-3 AWACS, while the militarization of space saw the creation of Space Command specifically to defend against orbital threats.

Specifications

Crew: 1	Dimensions: span 11.81m (38ft 9in); length
Powerplant: 1 x 17.1kN (3850lb) General	10.49m (34ft 5in); height 3.43m (11ft 3in)
Electric J33-GE-11 or Allison J33-A-9	Weight: 6,350kg (14,000lb) loaded
Maximum speed: 792km/h (492mph)	Armament: 6 x 12.7mm (0.5in) MGs,
Range: 2317km (1440 miles)	10 x 127mm (5in) rockets or 907kg
Service ceiling: 13,716m (45,000ft)	(2000lb) bombs

▲ **Lockheed F-80A Shooting Star**
61st Fighter Squadron, 56th Fighter Group, USAF / Selfridge Field, 1948
Operating from Selfridge Field, Michigan, this F-80A was on strength with the 61st Fighter Squadron in summer 1948. The F-80 (previously P-80) was the first jet fighter to enter service in the U.S., and around a dozen squadrons were equipped with the type for homeland defence by the late 1940s.

Specifications

Crew: 2

Powerplant: 1 x 26.7kN (6000lb) Allison J33-A-
    33 turbojet

Maximum speed: 933km/h (580mph)

Range: 1850km/h (1150 miles)

Service ceiling: 14,630m (48,000ft)

Dimensions: span 11.85m (38ft 10.5in); length
    12.2m (40ft 1in); height 3.89m (12ft 8in)

Weight: 7125kg (15,710lb) loaded

Armament: 4 x .5in machine guns

▲ Lockheed F-94B Starfire

334th Fighter Interceptor Squadron, USAF / mid-1950s

Carrying AN/APG-33 radar in the nose, the F-94B two-seat all-weather interceptor
carried an armament of four machine-guns, although the subsequent F-94C
Starfire version introduced rocket armament. Over two dozen ADC squadrons flew
F-94s, including units based in Alaska.

Specifications

Crew: 1

Powerplant: 1 x 76.5kN (17,200lb) Pratt &
    Whitney J57-P-23 turbojet

Maximum speed: 1328km/h (825mph)

Range: 2172km (1350 miles)

Service ceiling: 16,460m (54,000ft)

Dimensions: span 11.62m (38ft 1.5in); length
    20.84m (68ft 4.5in); height 6.46m (21ft 2.5in)

Weight: 14,288kg (31,500lb) loaded

Armament: Various combinations of AIM
    missiles, some aircraft fitted with 12 x 70mm
    (2.75in) folding-fin rockets

▲ Convair F-106A Delta Dart

87th Fighter Interceptor Squadron, USAF / K. I. Sawyer AFB, 1968–85

A successor to the F-102, the F-106 offered much improved performance and an
armament that included Falcon guided missiles and the Genie nuclear rocket.
Seen here in service with an active-duty ADC unit at K. I. Sawyer AFB, Michigan,
the type continued in service with ANG units into the mid-1980s.

Specifications

Crew: 2

Powerplant: 2 x 75.6kN (17,000lb) General
    Electric J79-GE-15 turbojets

Maximum speed: 2414km/h (1500mph)

Range: 2817km (1750 miles)

Service ceiling: 18,300m (60,000ft)

Dimensions: span 11.7m (38ft 5in); length

17.76m (58ft 3in); height 4.96m (16ft 3in)

Weight: 26,308kg (58,000lb) loaded

Armament: 4 x AIM-7 Sparrow; two wing pylons
    for 2 x AIM-7, or 4 x AIM-9 Sidewinder,
    provision for 20mm M-61 cannon; provision
    for stores to a maximum weight of 6219kg
    (13,500lb)

▲ McDonnell Douglas F-4C Phantom II

*171st Fighter Interceptor Squadron / Selfridge ANGB, Michigan ANG,
1972–78*

The initial, minimum-change USAF version of the Phantom, the F-4C (originally
designated F-110) was passed on to ANG units once its active-duty days were
over. This example, which carries an infrared sensor under the nose, is seen in
service with an ANG squadron in 1980.

Specifications

Crew: 4

Powerplant: 4 x 93kN (21,000lb) Pratt & Whitney
TF33-PW-100A turbofan engines

Maximum speed: 855km/h (530mph)

Range: 7400km (4598 miles)

Service ceiling: 12,500m (41,000ft)

Dimensions: span 44.42m (145ft 9in); length
46.61m (152ft 11in); height 12.6m (41ft 4in)

Weight: 147,400kg (325,000lb) loaded

Armament: none

▲ **Boeing E-3A Sentry**

USAF, early 1980s

The first production E-3A Sentry was aircraft 73-1674, preceded by a pair of EC-137D test aircraft. The E-3A AWACS (Airborne Warning And Control System) was based around the AN/APY-1 radar, housed in a rotating radome. The radar could provide surveillance of the entire airspace out to a range of around 400km (250 miles).

Soviet Air Defence
1946–1989

The Air Defence Forces (PVO) existed as a separate branch of the Soviet military and was equipped with a succession of dedicated interceptors with which to tackle Western bombers.

TASKED WITH DEFENDING the USSR against bombers, and later also against missile strikes, the PVO was maintained on a high state of alert. Ultimately, its functions included providing warning of any attack and defeating bombers and missiles through the use of manned interceptors and successive layers of surface-to-air missiles (SAMs).

The PVO consisted of a number of commands,

Specifications

Crew: 2

Powerplant: 2 x 107.9kN (24,300lbf) Lyulka
AL-7F-2 turbojets

Maximum speed: 1740km/h (1089mph)

Range: 3200km (2000 miles)

Service ceiling: 18,000m (59,055ft)

Dimensions: span 18.10m (59ft 5in);
length 27.20m (89ft 4in); height 7m (23ft)

Weight: 40,000kg (88,185lb) loaded

Armament: 4 x Bisnovat R-4 air-to-air missiles

▲ **Tupolev Tu-128**

IA-PVO

The largest interceptor to enter service anywhere in the world, the Tu-128 was tailored for long-range patrol missions in defence of the USSR's vast and featureless northern and Arctic frontiers. The two-seat fighter was equipped with four R-4 series air-to-air missiles and a powerful interception radar.

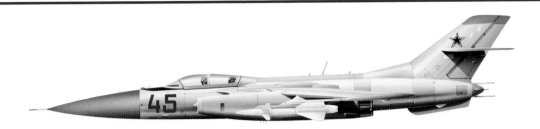

Specifications

Crew: 2

Powerplant: 2 x 66.8kN (13,669lb) Tumanskii
R-11 turbojets

Maximum speed: 1180km/h (733mph)

Maximum combat radius 925km (575 miles)

Service ceiling: 16,000m (52,495ft)

Dimensions: span 12.95m (42ft 6in); length
(long-nose late production) 23m (75ft 7.5in);
height 3.95m (12ft 11.5in)

Weight: 19,000kg (41,890lb) loaded

Armament: 4 x underwing pylons for two AA-2,
AA-2-2 or AA-3 air-to-air missiles

▲ Yakovlev Yak-28P

IA-PVO / mid-1960s

The Yak-28P was part of a family of twin-engined tactical jets that also included bomber and reconnaissance aircraft for Frontal Aviation use. The two-seat Yak-28P entered service with an IA-PVO unit defending the missile base at Semipalatinsk in November 1963. The last examples were finally retired in 1988.

▲ Sukhoi Su-15

IA-PVO / 1970s

The Su-15 gained notoriety for its role in the destruction of a Korean Airlines 747 airliner in September 1983. The twin-engined, all-weather interceptor was part of a new wave of equipment introduced by the IA-PVO in the 1970s, and could carry radar- and infrared-homing missiles as well as 23mm cannon pods.

Specifications

Crew: 1

Powerplant: 2 x 60.8kN (13,668lb) Tumanskii
R-11F2S-300 turbojets

Maximum speed: 2230km/h (1386mph)

Combat radius: 725km (450 miles)

Service ceiling: 20,000m (65,615ft)

Dimensions: span 8.61m (28ft 3in); length

21.33m (70ft); height 5.1m (16ft 8in)

Weight: 18,000kg (39,680lb) loaded

Armament: 4 x external pylons for two R8M
medium-range air-to-air missiles outboard and
2 x AA-8 'Aphid' short-range AAMs inboard,
plus 2 x pylons for 23mm UPK-23 cannon pods
or drop tank

including the Radio-Technical Troops (responsible for surveillance and control), SAM Troops, Missile and Space Defence Forces (including early warning and missile defence) and Fighter Aviation (IA-PVO).

The first postwar equipment for the IA-PVO included modifications of the initial generation of jet fighters, such as the MiG-9, MiG-15 and MiG-17.

Second generation

The IA-PVO entered the supersonic era through the introduction of dedicated interceptors, rather than adaptations of Frontal Aviation types. Typical of these new aircraft were missile-armed and all-weather aircraft including the Su-9, Su-11, Yak-25P, Yak-28P and Tu-128. These were complemented by MiG-21 variants optimized for point defence.

Starting in the late 1960s, new equipment arrived in the form of the MiG-25, Su-15 and MiG-23, while a basic airborne early warning (AEW)

▲ Mikoyan-Gurevich MiG-31

The MiG-31 was the first IA-PVO interceptor capable of tracking and engaging multiple targets. Up to 10 targets could be tracked, and four of these engaged.

capability was introduced through the Tu-126. By the mid-1980s, IA-PVO regiments were beginning to re-equip with MiG-31 and Su-27 interceptors with improved capability against low-flying targets. These fighters operated with a new AEW aircraft, the A-50.

Specifications

Crew: 1

Powerplant: 1 x 98kN (22,046lb) Rumanskii
   R-27F2M-300 turbojet

Maximum speed: 2445km/h (1520mph)

Range: 966km (600 miles)

Service ceiling: over 18,290m (60,000ft)

Dimensions: span 13.97m (45ft 10in) spread
and 7.78m (25ft 6.25in) swept; length 16.71m
(54ft 10in); height 4.82m (15ft 9.75in)

Weight: 18,145kg (40,000lb) loaded

Armament: 1 x 23mm GSh-23L cannon, AA-3,
AA-7 and/or AA-8 air-to-air missiles

▲ **Mikoyan-Gurevich MiG-23M**

IA-PVO

As well as equipping Frontal Aviation units in a tactical role, the MiG-23 was supplied to the PVO for homeland defence. The MiG-23M was the first major production version of the variable-geometry fighter and introduced a new radar capable of illuminating targets for semi-active radar-homing R-23 missiles.

British Air Defence
1946–1989

The experience of World War II meant the RAF was well aware of the importance of securing the UK's airspace, and powerful air defences were maintained throughout the Cold War.

BY 1946 THE RAF had reduced its fighter strength to 24 squadrons with which to defend the UK, these being equipped with Mosquito night-fighters, Hornet day fighters, as well as Meteor and Vampire jets. The burgeoning Soviet bomber threat and the detonation of the USSR's first nuclear device in September 1949 saw RAF Fighter Command re-equipped and expanded, with 45 squadrons available

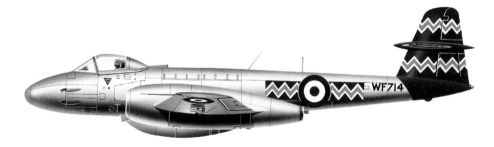

▲ **Gloster Meteor F.Mk 8**

500 Sqn, RAuxAF / West Malling, 1954

Flown by the commanding officer of 500 Sqn, this Meteor day fighter is typical of the type in service with the Royal Auxiliary Air Force. This particular aircraft flew from West Malling in 1954. The F.Mk 8 was the most numerous version of the Meteor and featured a revised canopy and an additional belly fuel tank.

Specifications

Crew: 1

Powerplant: 2 x 16.0kN (3600lb) Rolls-Royce
   Derwent 8 turbojets

Maximum speed: 962km/h (598mph)

Range: 1580km (980 miles)

Service ceiling: 13,106m (43,000ft)

Dimensions: span 11.32m (37ft 2in); length
   13.58m (44ft 7in); height 3.96m (13ft)

Weight: 8664kg (19,100lb) loaded

Armament: 4 x 20mm Hispano cannon

by the end of 1951. Twenty Royal Auxiliary Air Force squadrons backed up regular Fighter Command units, this force having been re-formed in 1946, and organized on a regional basis. Initially equipped with piston-engined fighters, the RAuxAF later received Meteors and Vampires.

Fighter Command, which had been lagging behind in the fielding of swept-wing, transonic equipment, felt the lessons of the Korean War keenly. In late 1951 Fighter Command maintained 402 aircraft, mainly obsolescent Meteor and Vampire day fighters, supported by Meteor, Vampire and Mosquito night-fighters. Modern equipment finally arrived in the form of the Hunter, ordered as a 'super-

priority' programme in 1950, together with the disappointing Swift, which served with just one fighter unit. Beginning in October 1951, 29 squadrons eventually re-equipped with Hunters in the UK and Germany over a period of four years. The Hunter continued in use as day fighter until 1960, when it was replaced by the supersonic Lightning.

Force reduction

Having attained a 50-squadron peak in January 1957, the Defence White Paper of that year saw significant cuts to Fighter Command, and just 11 squadrons were available to defend the UK by 1962. As well as promising to entrust the future defence of

Specifications

Crew: 2

Powerplant: 2 x 16.0kN (3600lb) Rolls-Royce
Derwent 8 turbojets

Maximum speed: 931km/h (579mph)

Range: 1580km (980 miles)

Service ceiling: 12,192m (40,000ft)

Dimensions: wingspan 13.1m (43ft); length
14.78m (48ft 6in); height 4.22m (13ft 10in)

Weight: 9979kg (22,000lb) loaded

Armament: 4 x 20mm Hispano cannon

▲ **Meteor NF.Mk 11**

29 Sqn, RAF / Tangmere, 1951–58

The Meteor was also fielded in a series of two-seat night-fighter versions, the first of which was the NF.Mk 11, with AI radar in a lengthened nose, and an armament of four 20mm cannon carried in the wing. First flown in 1950, the NF.Mk 11 flew with 14 RAF squadrons, including 29 Sqn, based at Tangmere.

▲ **Canadair Sabre F.Mk 4**

92 Sqn, RAF / Linton on Ouse, 1954–56

Acquired as an interim measure pending the arrival of indigenous swept-wing fighter equipment, a total of 430 Canadian-built Sabres were received by the RAF via MDAP channels. This aircraft served with 92 Sqn at Linton on Ouse. The Sabre F.Mk 4 was similar to the USAF F-86E and most featured slatted wings.

Specifications

Crew: 1

Powerplant: 1 x 32.35kW (7275lb) Avro Orenda
Mark 14 turbojet

Maximum speed: 1113km/h (692mph)

Range: 1930km (1200 miles)

Service ceiling: 14,935m (49,000ft)

Dimensions: span 11.29m (37ft 1in);
length 11.42m (37ft 6in); height 4.57m (15ft)

Weight: 6628kg (14.613lb) loaded

Armament: 6 x 12.7mm (0.50in) M2 Browning
machine guns; up to 1360kg (3000lb) of
payload

the UK to guided missiles (most of which never materialized), the 1957 Defence White Paper cancelled all manned fighter development with the exception of the Lightning. At the same time, budget cuts saw the dissolution of the RAuxAF squadrons in spring 1957.

After 1957, priority was placed on the point defence of V-bomber and Thor missile bases, in keeping with NATO 'tripwire' strategy. This doctrine proposed meeting Soviet aggression with an all-out nuclear attack, but this strategy began to be replaced by 'flexible response' beginning in the late 1960s. With a return to limited nuclear warfare options and the use of conventional arms, the manned interceptor returned to the fore. Moreover, the UK's Cold War status as a 'rear depot' from where troops and materiel could be assembled in time of war, made it a prime target for Warsaw Pact air attack.

Starting in the mid-1970s, the RAF's interceptor arm was subject to improvement, with particular emphasis on countering low-level attack aircraft and cruise missiles. The two key aircraft projects for the

▲ Hawker Hunter F.Mk 5
1 Sqn, RAF / Tangmere, 1956-58
Powered by a Sapphire engine, the Hunter F.Mk 5 was otherwise similar to the F.Mk 4 (with an Avon engine) and was equipped with a pair of underwing pylons for drop tanks and also carried additional fuel in the wing leading edge. Based at Tangmere, 1 Sqn replaced its Meteor F.Mk 8s with Hunters in 1955.

Specifications
Crew: 1
Powerplant: 1 x 35.59kN (8000lb) Armstrong-
    Siddeley Sapphire turbojet engine
Maximum speed: 144km/h (710mph)
Range: 689km (490 miles)
Service ceiling: 15,240m (50,000ft)

Dimensions: span 10.26m (33ft 8in); length
    13.98m (45ft 10.5in); height 4.02m (13ft 2in)
Weight: 8501kg (18,742lb) loaded
Armament: 4 x 30mm Aden cannon; up to
    2722kg (6000lb) of bombs or rockets

▲ English Electric Lightning F.Mk 3
56 Sqn, RAF / Wattisham, 1965
Natural metal finish and striking markings were a feature of RAF Lightning units in the 1960s. Armed with a pair of Firestreak missiles, this F.Mk 3 was based at Wattisham in 1965. This variant introduced more powerful Avon engines, Red Top missile capability, an extended fin and improvements to the avionics suite.

Specifications
Crew: 1
Powerplant: 2 x 72.7kN (16,360lb) Rolls-Royce
    Avon 301R engines
Maximum speed: 2415km/h (1500mph)
Range: 1300km (800 miles)
Service ceiling: 18,000m (60,000ft)

Dimensions: span 10.62m (34ft 11in);
    length 16.84m (55ft 3in); height 5.97m
    (19ft 7in)
Weight: 18,900kg (41,700lb) loaded
Armament: 2 x 30mm ADEN cannon; up to
    2750kg (6000lb) of external ordnance

1980s were the Tornado F.Mk 2 interceptor and the Nimrod AEW.Mk 3 airborne early warning platform. The latter proved a failure, while the definitive Tornado F.Mk 3 was beginning to enter service towards the end of the Cold War, as a replacement for Lightning and Phantom interceptors.

Strike Command successor

Fighter Command was succeeded by No. 11 Group, part of RAF Strike Command, under permanent NATO control. Further upgrades saw the increased use of hardened aircraft shelters and command and control facilities, new surface-to-air missiles (SAMs),

mobile radars and armed Hawk trainers. In order to meet the Soviet bomber threat head on, most No. 11 Group airfields were located on the east coast, from where raiders could be met over the North Sea.

In the mid-1980s, the RAF maintained two interceptor quick reaction alert (QRA) facilities, each with two aircraft held on 10-minute readiness to cover northern (with a QRA based at Leuchars) and southern sectors (QRA shared by Wattisham, Coningsby and Binbrook). An interceptor force of mainly Lightnings and Phantoms was supported by a large tanker fleet of Victor, VC10 and Tristar aircraft, as well as Bloodhound and Rapier SAMs.

▲ Avro Shackleton AEW.Mk 2

8 Sqn, RAF / Lossiemouth, early 1980s

Until the end of the Cold War, the RAF's airborne early warning capability was entrusted to the veteran Shackleton AEW.Mk 2, based at Lossiemouth in Scotland. The U.S.-built AN/APS-20 surveillance radar was inherited from the Gannet AEW.Mk 3 aircraft that had once served aboard carriers of the Royal Navy.

Specifications

Crew: 8–10

Powerplant: 4 x 1831kW (2455hp) Rolls-Royce Griffon 57A V-12 piston engines

Maximum speed: 500km/h (311mph)

Range: 5440km (3380 miles)

Service ceiling: 6400m (21,000ft)

Dimensions: span 36.58m (120ft); length 26.59m (87ft 3in); height 5.1m (16ft 9in)

Weight: 39,010kg (86,000lb) loaded

Armament: none

Specifications

Crew: 2

Powerplant: 1 x 23.1kN (5200lb) Rolls-Royce/Turbomeca Adour Mk 151 turbofan

Maximum speed: 1038km/h (645mph)

Endurance: 4 hours

Service ceiling: 15,240m (50,000ft)

Dimensions: span 9.39m (30ft 9.75in); length

11.17m (36ft 7.75in); height 3.99m (13ft 1.75in)

Weight: 7750kg (17,085lb) loaded

Armament: underfuselage/wing hardpoints with provision for up to 2567kg (5660lb) of stores, wingtip mounted air-to-air missiles

▲ British Aerospace Hawk T.Mk 1A

151 Sqn, RAF / Chivenor, early 1980s

A total of 89 Hawk trainers were converted to T.Mk 1A standard from 1983, with Sidewinder missile interface, in order to provide a clear-weather point-defence capability. It was planned to use the T.Mk 1A as a wartime adjunct to the Tornado F.Mk 3, with the latter illuminating targets for the Hawk with its Foxhunter radar.

Chapter 4

Strategic Reconnaissance

Aircraft have long been used for the collection of intelligence, and great importance was attached to strategic aerial reconnaissance during the Cold War in order to keep track of military developments in 'areas of interest'. As well as intelligence gathering by optical or infrared means, the electromagnetic spectrum was exploited as a means of developing an electronic order of battle for opposition forces and potential enemies.

◄ **Lockheed SR-71 Blackbird**
Flying higher and faster than any other operational spyplane, the USAF's SR-71 was typical of Cold War strategic reconnaissance assets: developed in great secrecy, it was used to fly intelligence-gathering missions over some of the most hazardous areas on Earth.

Cold War aerial spies
1946–1989

Photo-reconnaissance, together with electronic intelligence (ELINT), were among the most important – and hazardous – missions flown during the Cold War.

THE PRACTICE OF undertaking reconnaissance from the air was not limited to manned platforms during the Cold War, with satellites, balloons and remotely piloted vehicles (RPVs) all being widely used for strategic intelligence gathering. Typically, Cold War strategic reconnaissance involved gathering information on military developments, classifying national-level command and communications networks, and monitoring bomber dispositions, ballistic missiles and other strategic capabilities.

In the early years of the Cold War, the hazardous nature of spyplane missions was reflected in a number of high-profile shoot-downs, culminating on 1 May 1960, when Soviet air defences downed a CIA-operated U-2C flown by Francis Gary Powers over Sverdlovsk. As well as highlighting the threat posed by SAMs, the loss of the U-2 effectively put an end to direct over-flights of Soviet and Warsaw Pact territory. This series of U-2 over-flights of the USSR had begun just a month earlier, and followed the earlier Soviet rejection of President Dwight D. Eisenhower's 'Open Skies' plan for arms-control over-

flights. U-2 units (operating under the guise of USAF Weather Reconnaissance Squadrons) had been deployed to bases in West Germany and Turkey since 1956, with photographic over-flights beginning in July that year. A third U-2 squadron was formed in Japan in 1957.

Early operations
While the exotic U-2 had been designed specifically for the high-altitude reconnaissance mission, other early Cold War intelligence-gatherers were based on existing airframes, typically bombers or patrol aircraft. The U.S. Navy operated modified P4M and P4Y aircraft, while key USAF assets included variants of the prolific B-47 and C-130, as well as the RB-45.

The first recorded Cold War spyplane shoot-down occurred in April 1950, when Soviet fighters attacked a U.S. Navy PB4Y over the Baltic Sea. Other shoot-downs involving USAF aircraft saw an RB-29 downed by MiGs in October 1952, an RB-50 shot down by MiGs over the Sea of Japan in July 1953, an C-130 shot down over Armenia in September 1958

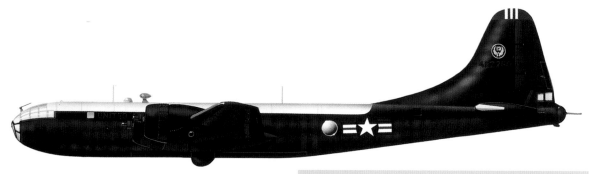

▲ **Boeing B-29A Superfortress**

55th Strategic Reconnaissance Wing, USAF / early 1950s

The B-29 remained in widespread service for a variety of duties after World War II, this example being a reconnaissance-configured B-29A-70-BN that operated on clandestine missions over Manchuria in 1953. RB-29A models were among the early equipment of the 55th SRW, the USAF's premier strategic recce wing.

Specifications

Crew: 11	length 30.2m (99ft); height 8.5m (29ft 7in)
Powerplant: 4 x 1640kW (2200hp) Wright R-3350-23	Weight: 54,000kg (120,000lb) loaded
and 23A turbosupercharged radial engines	Armament: 10 x 12.7mm (.50in) caliber
Maximum speed: 574km/h (357mph)	Browning M2/ANs, 2 x 12.7mm (.50in) and
Range: 9000km (5600 miles)	1 x 20mm (.79in) M2 cannon in tail position
Service ceiling: 10,200m (33,600ft)	
Dimensions: span 43.1m (141ft 3in);	

Specifications

Crew: 9

Powerplant: 2 x 20kN (4,600lbf) Allison J33-A-
23 turbojets and 2 x 2420kW (3250hp) Pratt &
Whitney R-4360 Wasp Major radial engines

Maximum speed: 660km/h (410mph)

Range: 4570km (2840 miles)

Service ceiling: 10,500m (34,600ft)

Dimensions: span 34.7m (114ft);
length 26m (85ft 2in); height 8m (26ft 1in)

Weight: 40,088kg (88,378lb) loaded

Armament: 4 x 20mm (.79in) cannons in nose
and tail turrets, 2 x 12.7mm (.50in) machine
guns in dorsal turret and up to 5400kg
(12,000lb) of bombs, mines, depth charges
or torpedoes

▼ Martin P4M-1 Mercator

VP-21, U.S. Navy / early 1950s

VP-21 replaced its PB4Y-2s with P4M-1s in June 1950 and deployed with the type
to the Mediterranean in 1951-52. A P4M-1Q of VQ-1 was lost over eastern China
in August 1956, and another example from the same unit was forced down by
North Korean MiG-17s in June 1959, while
engaged on an intelligence-gathering
mission.

Specifications

Crew: 3

Powerplant: 6 x 32kN (7,200lb) General Electric
J47 GE-25 turbojets

Maximum speed: 982km/h (610mph)

Range: 6437km (4000 miles)

Service ceiling: 11,826m (38,800ft)

Dimensions: span 35.36m (116ft);
length 32.92m (108ft); height 8.53m (28ft)

Weight: 56,699kg (125,000lb) loaded

Armament: 2 x 20mm (.79in) cannons in the
tail plus 9,072kg (20,000lb) internal
ordanance

▲ Boeing RB-47H Stratojet

55th Strategic Reconnaissance Wing, USAF / mid-1950s

Configured for ELINT, the RB-47H housed equipment and three systems operators (known as 'Crows') in the former bomb
bay, with additional sensors in the nose, under-fuselage and wing radomes. Active around the borders of the Eastern Bloc,
the RB-47Hs were charged with gathering intelligence on ground radar installations.

▲ Lockheed U-2C

100th Strategic Reconnaissance Wing, USAF, 1975

Built as a U-2A, the aircraft illustrated was later modified for high-altitude
atmospheric sampling as a WU-2A. The same aircraft was later converted to
become a U-2C, and served with the 100th SRW. It is seen here in 1975, with a
two-tone grey camouflage intended for operations in Europe.

Specifications

Crew: 1

Powerplant: 1 x 75.62kN (17,000lb) Pratt &
Whitney J75-P-13 turbojet

Maximum speed: 850km/h (530mph)

Range: 4830km (2610 miles)

Service ceiling: 25,930m (85,000ft)

Dimensions: span 24.30m (80ft);
length 15.1m (49ft 7in); height 3.9m (13ft)

Weight: 9523kg (21,000lb) loaded

Armament: none

while flying from Turkey, and a 55th SRW RB-47 flying from Brize Norton, England, that was downed over the Barents Sea in July 1960.

In the wake of the U-2 incident, the USAF and CIA continued to develop more advanced strategic reconnaissance aircraft, and the U.S. ultimately fielded the SR-71, the fastest and highest-flying air-breathing vehicle of its era, as well as increasingly advanced derivatives of the U-2, and the RC-135, the latter capable of carrying a plethora of ELINT sensors, side-looking airborne radar and other intelligence-gathering equipment capable of operating across a wide range of frequencies. Prolific development during the Cold War saw the USAF field 28 RC-135s in at least 12 different configurations, the ultimate versions being the RC-135V/W. The RC-135S version, operating from Shemya in the Aleutians, was tasked with intercepting telemetry intelligence (TELINT) from Soviet missile tests. The SR-71, U-2 and RC-135 were all active at the end of the Cold War, the information they gathered being of prime importance both to Strategic Air Command and the Pentagon. As well as

Specifications

Crew: 27

Powerplant: 4 x 80kN (18,000lb) Pratt & Whitney
   TF33-P-9 turbojets

Maximum speed: 991km/h (616mph)

Range: 4305km (2675 miles)

Service ceiling: 12,375m (40,600ft)

Dimensions: span 39.88m (130ft 10in); length
   41.53m (136ft 3in); height 12.7m (41ft 8in);

Weight: 124,965kg (275,500lb) loaded

Armament: 6 x 7.92mm (.3in) MGs; 1000kg
   (2205lb) bomb load

▲ Boeing RC-135V

55th Strategic Reconnaissance Wing, USAF / Offutt AFB, early 1980s

During the Cold War, USAF RC-135s could be found operating patrols lasting up to 10 hours over the Baltic, Barents and Black Seas in the west, and over the Bering and Siberian seas to the east. The aircraft carried a crew of around 16 specialist ELINT operators. The 55th SRW was based at Offutt, Nebraska.

Specifications

Crew: 1

Powerplant: 2 x 144.5kN (32,500lb) Pratt &
   Whitney JT11D-20B turbojets

Maximum speed: 3219km/h (2000mph)

Range: 4800km (2983 miles)

Service ceiling: 30,000m (100,000ft)

Dimensions: span 16.94m (55ft 7in);
   length 32.74m (107ft 5in); height 5.64m
   (18ft 6in)

Weight: 77,111kg (170,000lb) loaded

Armament: none

▲ Lockheed SR-71A

9th Strategic Reconnaissance Wing, USAF / early 1980s

Flying at speeds in excess of Mach 3 and at an altitude of almost 30,000m (100,000ft), the SR-71A, popularly known as 'Blackbird', was effectively immune to enemy air defences. The SR-71A operated along the borders of the USSR, China and the Eastern Bloc, as well as over Cuba, Nicaragua, North Korea and Vietnam.

monitoring Soviet activity, U.S. strategic reconnaissance assets were active over Korea, with aircraft including RC-135s and U-2s operating from Kadena to observe activity in the north.

The U.S. Navy also possessed a strategic reconnaissance capability, ultimately expressed through 12 examples of the EP-3E, an adaptation of the P-3 maritime patrol aircraft, outfitted with an Aries ELINT suite. Primary mission for the EP-3E involved gathering data on Soviet warships and their electronics and weapons systems. U.S. Navy EA-3Bs could undertake carrier-based ELINT missions. Both EP-3E and EA-3B aircraft were active over the Mediterranean, flying from Rota in Spain, with further EP-3Es stationed out of Guam.

Soviet capabilities

For the Soviets, the strategic aerial reconnaissance mission was assigned a lower priority, and focused on maritime intelligence-gathering, prosecuted by types based on the Tu-16 and Tu-95 bombers, as well as derivatives of the An-12 airlifter and the Il-20, an ELINT platform based on an airliner. These aircraft kept a close watch on NATO naval operations, and while the Tu-16 could frequently be found operating in the Baltic, North Sea and Mediterranean, the longer-range Tu-95 variants ventured as far as Angola, Cuba, South Yemen and Vietnam. Another important mission for adapted Soviet bombers was monitoring the reaction times and capabilities of

▲ **Tupolev Tu-16R**

A Soviet Navy Tu-16R 'Badger-F' reconnaissance aircraft swoops low over the North Sea while monitoring NATO maritime activity in the 1960s.

Western fighters, achieved by flying attack profiles against the coasts of the U.S. and UK.

The RAF maintained a strategic reconnaissance capability through the deployment of three Nimrod R.Mk 1s, supported by specially modified Canberras, and other nations also operated small fleets of strategic intelligence-gatherers, notably France, Israel and Sweden. These last three all operated dedicated reconnaissance adaptations of civilian airliners, comprising the DC-8, 707 and Caravelle, respectively. West Germany, meanwhile, fielded a small fleet of Atlantics adapted for signals intelligence (SIGINT) missions over the Baltic Sea.

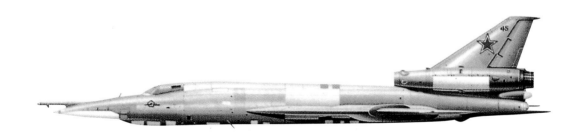

Specifications

Crew: 3	length 41.6m (136ft 5in); height 10.13m
Powerplant: 2 x 161.9kN (36,376lbf) Dobrynin	(33ft 3in)
RD-7M-2 turbojets	Weight: 85,000kg (187,390lb) loaded
Maximum speed: 1510km/h (938mph)	Armament: 1 x AM-23 23mm cannon in tail
Range: 4900km (3045 miles)	turret plus 9000kg (20,000lb) of bombs or
Service ceiling: 13,300m (40,540ft)	1 x Kh-22 cruise missile
Dimensions: span 23.17m (76ft);	

▲ **Tupolev Tu-22RD**

Soviet Long-Range Aviation, 1970s

Known to NATO as 'Blinder-C', the reconnaissance variant of the Tu-22 theatre bomber was flown by both Soviet AF and Navy units. For the DA Tu-22R units, areas of operation included tracking the U.S. Sixth Fleet in the Mediterranean, as well as wartime missions over central and southern Europe and the Baltic.

Chapter 5

The Middle East

Possessing wealth in the form of oil, commanding access to the Far East via the Suez Canal, and home to various opposing religious and political groups, the Eastern Mediterranean and Arabian Peninsula were long host to conflict and local rivalry. The escalation of the Cold War combined with the establishment of the state of Israel in 1948 to increase tensions. Now, the 'new' superpowers fought to fill the vacuum left in the wake of the departure of the former European powers, with the U.S. and Soviet Union battling for influence in this strategically vital region.

◀ **Sikorsky S-58**
The creation of Israel in 1948 precipitated a series of conflicts that would last the duration of the Cold War. Much of the battle lines of the Middle East were redrawn following the Six-Day War, illustrated here by a pair of Israeli Defence Force soldiers hunkering down in the desert as an Israeli S-58 passes overhead.

Britain in Arabia
1946–1967

Once the dominant power on the Arabian Peninsula, Britain's interests were based on the oilfields of Iraq and Persia, with Iraq, Transjordan and Palestine all governed by British mandate.

BRITAIN'S INFLUENCE OVER the Arabian Peninsula, Persia, Egypt and the Suez Canal Zone was expressed through a powerful military presence, including units of the RAF, which had been active since the start of the British mandates in the wake of World War I. The Arabian Peninsula saw a gradual reduction in British forces after World War II, in the midst of increasing Arab hostility towards the British.

Eventually the RAF withdrew entirely from its former stronghold in Iraq, as the focus increasingly shifted towards the Canal Zone. Nevertheless, Iraq remained home to a limited RAF presence, the primary role of which was to protect its vital oilfields. Into the mid-1950s, the British presence in Iraq included five squadrons variously equipped with Vampires, Beaufighters and Tempests, plus Valetta transports.

▲ **De Havilland Venom FB.Mk 4**

8 Sqn, RAF / Khormaksar, 1955–60

Operating from Khormaksar for over two decades starting in 1946, 8 Sqn flew the Venom FB.Mk 4 between 1955 and 1960. The FB.Mk 4 replaced the FB.Mk 1 in service with this unit, and the new version was in combat over South Arabia beginning in the summer of 1955, mostly launching strikes against dissident tribes.

Specifications

Crew: 1

Powerplant: 1 x 22.9kN (5150lb) de Havilland Ghost 105 turbojet

Maximum speed: 1030km/h (640mph)

Range: (with drop tanks) 1730km (1075 miles)

Service ceiling: 14,630m (48,000ft)

Dimensions: span (over tip tanks) 12.7m (41ft 8in);

length 9.71m (31ft 10in); height 1.88m (6ft 2in)

Weight: 6945kg (15,310lb) loaded

Armament: 4 x 20mm (.78in) Hispano cannon with 150 rounds, 2 x wing pylons capable of carrying either 2 x 454kg (1000lb) bombs or 2 x drop tanks; or 8 x 27.2kg (60lb) rocket projectiles carried on centre-section launchers

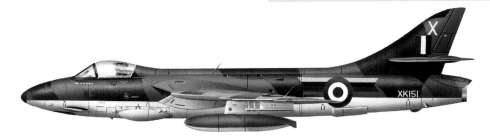

▲ **Hawker Hunter FGA.Mk 9**

8 Sqn, RAF / Khormaksar, 1955–60

Khormaksar-based 8 Sqn operated its Hunters on ground attack duties against Yemeni insurgents along the border with Aden during the final years of the British presence in South Arabia. The Hunter was therefore the final type to be employed by 8 Sqn in the colonial policing role that it undertook for almost 50 years.

Specifications

Crew: 1

Powerplant: 1 x 45.13kN (10,145lbf) Rolls-Royce Avon 207 turbojet

Maximum speed: 1,150km/h (715mph)

Range: 715km (445 miles)

Service ceiling: 15,240m (50,000ft)

Dimensions: span 10.26m (33ft 8in); length 14m (45ft 11in); height 4.01m (13ft 2in)

Weight: 8050kg (17,750lb) loaded

Armament: 4 x 30 mm (1.18 in) ADEN cannons, various rockets and missiles and up to 3357kg (7400lb) of payload

The most important focus for RAF operations in the Arabian Peninsula was Aden, and the major base at Khormaksar was home in the 1950s to Brigands, Vampires, Venoms and Meteors.

Maritime operations

Shackletons, tasked with protecting oil shipping between the Persian Gulf and the Red Sea, provided a maritime patrol presence out of Khormaksar. Lancasters, Valettas, Twin Pioneers and Pioneers provided transport capability.

Eventually the UK granted autonomy to the Aden states of Muscat and Oman, these following

the examples of Jordan, Kuwait, Qatar and the United Arab Emirates. In 1967 the UK had announced its intention to withdraw forces from territories 'east of Suez', however, the precarious security situation in Yemen meant that the RAF still had a role to play in the region. Until the final British withdrawal in 1969, RAF squadrons at Khormaksar were involved in combat operations in the wake of the October 1962 revolution in Yemen, after which hostile dissident tribes, incursions from Yemen and terrorist activity confronted security forces in South Arabia.

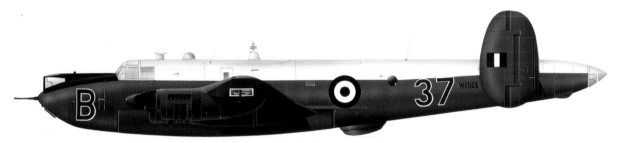

Specifications

Crew: 10

Powerplant: 4 x 1831kW (2455hp) Rolls-Royce
Griffon 57A V-12 piston engines

Maximum speed: 500km/h (311mph)

Range: 5440km (3380 miles)

Service ceiling: 6400m (21,000ft)

Dimensions: span 36.58m (120ft);
length 26.59m (87ft 3in); height 5.1m (16ft 9in)

Weight: 39,010kg (86,000lb) loaded

Armament: 2 x Hispano No. 1 Mk 5 20mm
(.79in) cannon in nose turret and up to
4536kg (10,000lb) of bombs

▲ Avro Shackleton MR.Mk 2

37 Sqn, RAF / Khormaksar, 1957–67

As well as ensuring the safe passage of oil from the Persian Gulf to the entrance of the Red Sea, 37 Sqn's Shackleton maritime reconnaissance aircraft were active countering various hostile Arab groups operating around Aden and the Gulf states. Khormaksar was home to 37 Sqn between 1957 and 1967.

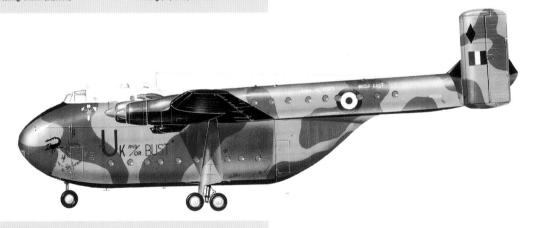

Specifications

Crew: 6

Powerplant: 4 x 2125kW (2850hp) Bristol
Centaurus 173 radial piston engines

Maximum speed: 383km/h (238mph)

Range: 5938km (3690 miles)

Service ceiling: 4875m (16,000ft)

Dimensions: span 49.38m (162ft); length 30.3m
(99ft 5in); height 11.81m (38ft 9in)

Weight: 64,864kg (143,000lb) loaded

Armament: none

▲ Bristol Beverley C.Mk 1

84 Sqn, RAF / Khormaksar, 1958–67

Bearing the legend 'UK and/or bust' on the fuselage, this Beverley was operated by 84 Sqn in the mid-1960s. Capable of operating from small desert strips, the Beverley provided vital tactical support for Army actions in the Middle East, including operations in the Aden Emergency, based out of Khormaksar.

Oman
1952–1976

Britain's departure from the Gulf did not put an end to the region's troubles, and Oman in particular was subject to inter-factional hostilities starting in the late 1960s.

POSSESSING BOTH OIL reserves and overseeing access to strategically important waterways, Oman was of long-term interest to the UK.

In the early 1950s, RAF Vampires were deployed from Iraq to conduct shows of force in response to Saudi Arabia's claims on Omani oilfields. With the Saudis refusing to back down, Vampires and Meteor FR.Mk 9s were deployed to Sharjah in 1953 in support of a blockade, before being replaced by Lancasters and Valettas, and later Ansons. Continued operations were staged from 1955 in response to further disputes and incursions by Saudi Arabia, with RAF Lincolns and Valettas engaged on reconnaissance missions, with support from Venom fighter-bombers and various transport types.

Confronting the OLA

Operations were stepped up in 1957 when Saudi-backed Omani Liberation Army (OLA) troops occupied villages in Oman. Venoms were soon in action, attacking ground targets, while Shackletons dropped leaflets, and Beverley and Valetta transports provided airlift support. Sorties were flown from Sharjah and Bahrain. Canberras and Meteors flew reconnaissance missions, before ground troops were deployed in force from August 1957. While the OLA was removed from Omani villages it was not extinguished, and began operating from the safety of more remote locations.

When the rebels threatened to regain the initiative and take more territory, the British established a blockade, launched in earnest in 1958 and undertaken in conjunction with the Sultan's Armed Forces. With the OLA continuing to receive arms, the RAF returned to offensive operations, with Shackletons being used for bombing raids in autumn 1958, supported by Fleet Air Arm Sea Hawk and Sea Venom fighter-bombers operating from the carrier HMS *Bulwark*. A final, successful, assault on OLA positions was launched by SAS troops in January 1959, and the vast majority of

RAF units began to be withdrawn from the region the following month.

Following the departure of UK forces from the region, the Sultan of Oman AF was established with British support, and began to receive combat aircraft in 1968. As well as equipment, the UK also provided personnel to fly and maintain Omani aircraft. Between 1968 and 1976 Soviet-supported Popular Front for the Liberation of Oman guerrillas were active on the border between Oman and South Yemen and in Dhofar, while Oman received military backing from the UK, India, Iran, Jordan, Pakistan and Saudi Arabia.

RAF IN OMAN, 1952–59		
Aircraft	**Unit**	**Base**
Lincoln B.Mk 2	7 Sqn (det)	Khormaksar
Lincoln B.Mk 2	1426 Flt (det)	Sharjah
Venom FB.Mk 4	249 Sqn (det)	Sharjah
Venom FB.Mk 4	8 Sqn (det)	Sharjah
Vampire FB.Mk 5, Venom FB.Mk 1	6 Sqn	Sharjah
Meteor FR.Mk 9	208 Sqn (det)	Sharjah
Canberra PR.Mk 7	58 Sqn (det)	Bahrain
Lancaster GR.Mk 3	37 Sqn	Sharjah
Lancaster GR.Mk 3	38 Sqn	Sharjah
Lancaster PR.Mk 1	683 Sqn (det)	Sharjah
Shackleton MR.Mk 2	37 Sqn (det)	Masirah
Shackleton MR.Mk 2	42 Sqn (det)	Masirah
Shackleton MR.Mk 2	224 Sqn (det)	Masirah
Shackleton MR.Mk 2	228 Sqn (det)	Masirah
Valetta C.Mk 1	ACF	Sharjah
Valetta C.Mk 1, Beverley C.Mk 1	84 Sqn	Sharjah, Bahrain
Anson C.Mk 19, Pembroke C.Mk 1	1417 Flt	Sharjah
Pembroke C.Mk 1, Twin Pioneer CC.Mk 1	152 Sqn	Sharjah
Sycamore HR.Mk 14	SAR Flt (det)	Sharjah

▲ Short Skyvan 3M

2 Sqn, Sultan of Oman AF / 1970s

Employed on light transport duties, the robust Skyvan was supplied by the UK between 1970 and 1975 and proved suitable for operations from rough desert airstrips. Major dissident groups had been contained by the early 1970s, and infiltration by guerrilla forces originating in South Yemen was also countered.

Specifications

Crew: 1-2

Powerplant: 2 x 533kW (715hp) Garrett
AiResearch TPE-331-201 Turboprops

Maximum speed: 324km/h (202mph)

Range: 1200km (694 miles)

Service ceiling: 6858m (22,500ft)

Dimensions: span 19.79m (64ft 11in);
length 12.21m (40ft 1in); height 4.6m (15ft 1in)

Weight: 5670kg (12,500lb) loaded

Armament: none

Iran–Iraq War
1980–1988

Widely misunderstood in the West, the prolonged 'Holy War' saw extensive and sophisticated use of air power, with Iran, once a staunch ally of the West, clashing with its neighbour Iraq.

PRO-WESTERN UNTIL THE Islamic revolution of 1979, Iran's air arms were previously primarily equipped by the U.S., which sought a strong ally in the Middle East and signed orders worth around $20 billion in the late 1970s, including advanced F-14A interceptors. The Iraqi AF, which was previously equipped with Western equipment, was turning increasingly towards the USSR for aircraft, but also fielded French equipment, such as Mirage F1s, outfitted as fighter-bombers or for reconnaissance.

The military potential of post-revolution Iran was underestimated both in the West and by Iraq, which chose to reignite a long-running border dispute after Iranian shelling of frontier positions in early September 1980. After a series of small-scale clashes, major fighting broke out on 22 September, and this included pre-emptive air strikes by the Iraqi AF against Iranian airfields Other early targets for the

Iraqi AF included Tehran and air raids, some of which were prosecuted by Tu-22 bombers, were followed almost immediately by troops crossing the border into Iran. Both air arms also attacked oil installations, and the campaign to target opposition oil industry would continue throughout the conflict.

Iraqi forces crossed the border in several locations, with the primary drive focused on Abadan and the southern end of the vital Shatt al-Arab waterway.

Helicopter warfare

The initial Iraqi drive was soon blunted by Iranian ground forces, supported by air power that included armed helicopters – Iraqi Mi-8s and Gazelles and Iranian AH-1Js. The latter type primarily saw action in the north, and confronted Iraqi forces around Dezful. With the Iraqi advance on the ground stalled, the Islamic Republic of Iran AF (IRIAF) was able to

Specifications

Crew: 2

Powerplant: 2 x 92.9kN (20,900lb) Pratt &
Whitney TF30-P-412A turbofans

Maximum speed: 2517km/h (1564mph)

Range: 3220km (2000 miles)

Service ceiling: 17,070m (56,000ft)

Dimensions: span 19.55m (64ft 1.5in) unswept;

11.65m (38ft 2.5in) swept; length 19.1m
(62ft 8in); height 4.88m (16ft)

Weight: 33,724kg (74,349lb) loaded

Armament: 1 x 20mm M61A1 Vulcan rotary
cannon; combination of AIM-7 Sparrow; AIM-9
medium range air-to-air missiles, and AIM-54
Phoenix long range air-to-air missiles

▲ Grumman F-14 Tomcat

Islamic Republic of Iran AF / 1980s

Among the huge numbers of aircraft acquired by Iran before the fall of the Shah, the F-14A proved highly successful during the war with Iraq, despite Western reports that serviceability was limited. A number of Iranian crews made 'ace' status on the F-14A, and the type scored aerial victories against MiG-25s.

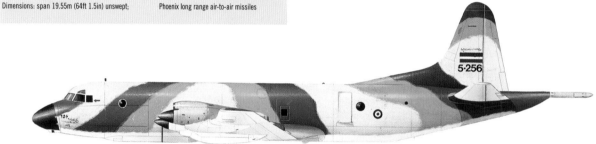

Specifications

Crew: 11

Powerplant: 4 x 3356kW (4500hp) Allison T56-
A10W turboprop engines

Maximum speed: 766km/h (476mph)

Range: 4075km (2533 miles)

Service ceiling: 8625m (28,300ft)

Dimensions: span 30.37m (99ft 8in); length
35.61m (116ft 9in); height 10.27m (33ft 8in)

Weight: 60,780kg (134,000lb) loaded

Armament: up to 9070kg (20,000lb) of
ordnance, including bombs, mines and
torpedoes

▲ Lockheed P-3F Orion

Islamic Republic of Iran AF / Bandar Abbas, 1980s

Iran acquired six examples of the P-3F variant of the Orion, which featured an in-flight refuelling capability. The first example was delivered in 1975. During the Iran-Iraq War, these maritime patrol aircraft flew from Bandar Abbas, and were active during the 'Tanker War' in the Persian Gulf.

Specifications

Crew: 2

Powerplant: 1 x 14.7kN (3308lbf) Ivchenko AI-
25T turbofan

Maximum speed: 635km/h (395mph)

Range: 1260km (783 miles)

Service ceiling: 13000m (42,650ft)

Dimensions: span 9.50m (31ft 2in);
length 12.30m (40ft 4in); height 4.70m (15ft 5in)

Weight: 2600kg (5732lb) loaded

Armament: 1 x 23mm cannon and up to
1100kg (2425lb) of weapons

▲ Aero L-39ZO

Iraqi AF / 1980s

Acquired by Iraq as an advanced trainer during the course of the 1980-88 conflict, the L-39 saw limited use in the light attack role during the Iran-Iraq War. Flying from bases at Mosul and Kirkuk, the primary role of the L-39 fleet was schooling prospective Iraqi AF combat aircrew, as well as weapons training.

make its mark, launching a series of reprisal strikes against the Iraqi capital, Baghdad. Aircraft involved included F-4s and F-5Es and the threat posed by IRIAF air strikes force Iraq to evacuate many of its aircraft to foreign bases. Periodic long-range attacks against the two countries' cities would remain a feature of the war, both sides incurring losses in the process, in air combat, and against increasingly sophisticated ground-based air defences.

Iraq had taken a risk in launching its offensive shortly before the onset of winter and the rainy season, with the aim of capturing territory that would then be denied to any Iranian counter-offensive by adverse weather. However, Iran was able to organize a response, which came in January 1981. The Iraqis contained the Iranian counter-thrust that came in the same month. Close support air power was utilized by both sides, Iraqi AF aircraft flying as many as 400-450 missions per day.

There followed a long period of stalemate, a war of attrition punctuated by limited, renewed ground offensives, while the opposing ground forces dug in across a front line of almost 1200 kilometres (750 miles). By September 1981, Iraqi gains were effectively limited to the town of Khorramshar. A return to strategic bombing missions came in September 1981, in the wake of abortive Iraqi attempts to capture the besieged town of Abadan. The renewed bombing campaign saw the Iraqi AF attack the oil pipeline at Gorreh at the end of September, this installation

being the last Iranian pipeline dedicated to export. The IRIAF response involved air strikes on a number of Iraqi power stations. For strikes against high-value targets, both sides used guided weaponry, typically employed by IRIAF F-4s and Iraqi AF Mirage F1s and Su-22s.

IRIAF F-14s, long thought by the West to have seen little in the way of combat, racked up an impressive tally of air-to-air victories, while the F-4 fleet undertook the bulk of IRIAF offensive missions. For air defence the Iraqi AF relied on MiG-25s and MiG-21s, the latter armed with Magic AAMs.

The 'Tanker War'

As the war expanded to the waters of the Persian Gulf, the Iraqi AF put to good use French-supplied Exocet anti-ship missiles against shipping and oil rigs. Exocets were launched by Super Frelon helicopters, Mirage F1EQ-5s and a handful of Super Etendards loaned from France in late 1983.

Early 1984 saw an Iranian attack against Majinoon Island in the Howizah marshes, aiming to sever the Iraqi front, and this was met by concerted Iraqi AF close air support. The 'Tanker War' escalated in 1984, with 51 sinkings, by both sides, Iran attacking tankers coming out of Iraq, Kuwaiti and Saudi ports.

In August 1990 the two nations agreed to a truce, which held despite some border incidents. By now, the Iraqi AF had received advanced new equipment – the MiG-29 fighter and Su-25 close support aircraft.

▲ **Mikoyan-Gurevich MiG-21MF**

Iraqi AF / 1980s

The most important air defence fighter of the Iraqi AF in the early part of the war, the MiG-21 was operated in a number of variants, ultimately supplemented by Chinese-built F-7 versions, used for training. The MiG-21MF variant was flown by two Iraqi AF units at the outbreak of fighting in September 1980.

Specifications

Crew: 1	length 15.76m (51ft 9in); height 4.1m (13ft 6in)
Powerplant: 1 x 60.8kN (14,550lb) thrust	Weight: 10,400kg (22,925lb) loaded
Tumanskii R-13-300 afterburning turbojet	Armament: 1 x 23mm (.91in) cannon, provision
Maximum speed: 2229km/h (1385mph)	for about 1500kg (3307lb) of stores,
Range: 1160km (721 miles)	including air-to-air missiles, rocket pods,
Service ceiling: 17,500m (57,400ft)	napalm tanks or drop tanks
Dimensions: span 7.15m (23ft 6in);	

Britain in Palestine
1945–1948

In British hands after World War I, Palestine was subject to increased attention after 1945, with local strife and Jewish resettlement combining with the struggle for control of the Suez Canal.

PALESTINE HAD BEEN host to a major RAF airfield-building programme in World War II as part of a general build-up of squadrons in the Middle East. Postwar, Britain decided to limit Jewish immigration into Palestine to 100,000, prompting additional settlers to enter Palestine illegally. At the same time, militant Jewish groups stepped up their campaign against the British occupiers, the assassination of a British Minister of State in Cairo in 1945 being followed by deployment of Hurricanes and Spitfires to Meggido and Ramat David. RAF Mustangs and Halifaxes carried out bombing sorties, and as the Jewish insurgents' campaign intensified, the RAF mounted standing fighter patrols.

In reaction to continued immigration, the Royal Navy began a blockade, which was supported from the air by RAF maritime reconnaissance and air-sea rescue units, flying from Ein Shemer and Aqir.

Israel established

In November 1946 the UN announced plans to partition Palestine west of Jordan. Britain's proposal to end land sales to the Jewish settlers led to a further decline in UK-Jewish relations before the British mandate finally ended, and the state of Israel was established on 15 May 1948. In the meantime, anti-immigration patrols continued, now prosecuted by RAF Lancasters.

Created in November 1947, the fledgling Israeli air arm was equipped with a handful of types, flown by both local Jewish pilots and former World War II servicemen from various Allied nations. The establishment of the Israeli AF prompted the RAF to deploy a squadron of Spitfires to Ein Shemer.

The RAF Spitfires were used against the Jewish settlement at Bat Yam in April 1948, part of an abortive British effort to prevent the Jewish militia from taking Arab Jaffa.

With the end of the British mandate, evacuation of British forces from the area was the responsibility of Halifax, Lancaster and Dakota transports. British

military units redeployed from Palestine to the Canal Zone. From their bases in Egypt, the British would now set about defending the Suez Canal, in order to ensure the safe passage of shipping to the Far East.

RAF IN PALESTINE, 1945–48		
Aircraft	**Unit**	**Base**
Spitfire Mk VC/IX/FR.Mk 18	32 Sqn	Ramat David, Petah Tiqva, Aqir, Ein Shemer, Nicosia
Spitfire Mk VC/IXC	208 Sqn	Ramat David, Petah Tiqva, Aqir
Spitfire FR.Mk 18E	208 Sqn	Ein Shemer, Nicosia
Hurricane Mk IV	6 Sqn	Meggido, Petah Tiqva, Ramat David
Spitfire Mk IX, Tempest F.Mk VI	6 Sqn	Ein Shemer, Nicosia
Mustang Mk III/V, Tempest F.Mk VI	213 Sqn	Ramat David, Nicosia
Mosquito Mk XVI/PR.Mk 34	680 Sqn	Aqir, Ein Shemer
Mosquito Mk XVI/PR.Mk 34	13 Sqn	Ein Shemer, Kabrit, Fayid
Auster AOP.Mk 5	651 Sqn	Haifa
Warwick GR.Mk 5, Lancaster GR.Mk 3	621 Sqn	Aqir, Ein Shemer
Halifax Mk VII/IX	644 Sqn	Quastina
Halifax Mk VII	620 Sqn	Aqir
Halifax Mk VII, Dakota C.Mk 4	113 Sqn	Aqir
Lancaster GR.Mk 3	37 Sqn	Ein Shemer
Lancaster GR.Mk 3	203 Sqn	Ein Shemer
Dakota C.Mk 4	78 Sqn	Kabrit, Aqir
Dakota C.Mk 4	216 Sqn	Kabrit, Fayid
Dakota C.Mk 4	215 Sqn	Kabrit
Dakota C.Mk 4	204 Sqn	Kabrit
Dakota C.Mk 4	114 Sqn	Kabrit

▲ **Hawker Tempest F.Mk 6**

213 Sqn, RAF / Nicosia, 1946–47

This Tempest was delivered to an RAF Maintenance Unit at Shurbra, Egypt, in 1946 before being put into service by 213 Sqn, based at Shallufa as part of the Middle East fighter force. Beginning in 1946 the unit operated from Nicosia, Cyprus, and replaced its Tempests with Vampires in 1950.

Specifications

Crew: 1

Powerplant: 1 x 2340hp (1745kW) Napier Sabre VA H-24 piston engine

Maximum speed: 686km/h (426mph)

Range: 2092km (1300 miles)

Service ceiling: 10,975m (36,000ft)

Dimensions: span 12.5m (41ft); length 10.26m (33ft 8in); height 4.9m (16ft 1in)

Weight: 6142kg (13,540lb) loaded

Armament: 4 x 20mm (.8in) Hispano cannon in wings, up to 907kg (2000lb) stores of either 2 bombs or 8 rockets for ground attack role

Early Israeli Air Wars
1948–49

As soon as the state of Israel declared its independence, the Jewish state was under attack by its Arab neighbours. Soon, however, it had assembled an air arm with which it could fight back.

INITIALLY EQUIPPED WITH mainly light aircraft, including Taylorcraft and Auster types, the Israeli AF was active on reconnaissance, communications and transport work during early fighting against Palestinian Arabs and their villages soon after its establishment in late 1947. By May 1948, the Israeli AF was in possession of 54 aircraft, while air power assembled in support of the Egyptian Expeditionary

Specifications

Crew: 1

Powerplant: 1 x 1170kW (1565hp) 12-cylinder Rolls-Royce Merlin 61 engine

Maximum speed: 642km/h (410mph)

Range: 698km (435 miles)

Service ceiling: 12,650m (41,500ft)

Dimensions: span 11.23m (36ft 10in); length 9.47m (31ft 1in); height 3.86m (12ft 8in)

Weight: 3343kg (7370lb) loaded

Armament: 4 x 7.7mm (.303in) MGs and 2 x 20mm (.8in) cannons

▲ **Supermarine Spitfire LF.Mk 9**

2 Sqn, Royal Egyptian AF / El Arish, 1948–49

In the early days of Jewish-Arab fighting in Palestine, the REAF operated 15 Spitfire Mk 9s in support of the Egyptian Expeditionary Force. The aircraft were acquired in 1946 and a REAF detachment operated from El Arish. Both Israel and Egypt made use of surplus RAF equipment during their early confrontations.

▲ Boeing B-17G Flying Fortress

69 Sqn, Israeli AF / Ramat David, 1948-49

By the time the second truce ended in October 1948, the Israeli AF was able to field three B-17s, which bombed Cairo on their delivery flight. Israel's acquisition of a dedicated bomber forced Egypt to obtain Stirling transports, which were in turn used for a handful of daylight bombing raids later in the conflict.

Specifications

Crew: 10

Powerplant: 4 x 895kW (1200hp) Wright R
Cyclone nine-cylinder radial engines

Maximum speed: 475km/h (295mph)

Range: 5085km (3160 miles)

Service ceiling: 10,850m (35,600ft)

Dimensions: span 31.62m (103ft 9in); length
22.8m (74ft 9in); height 5.85m (19ft 2in)

Weight: 29,710kg (65,500lb) loaded

Armament: 13 x 12.7mm (.5in) machine guns;
up to 6169kg (13,600lb) bomb load

Force in Palestine was based around Royal Egyptian AF Spitfires and Lysanders plus C-47s adapted for bombing. Additional support for the Arabs was provided by the Royal Iraqi AF, which sent Austers and Harvards. Further ground attack Harvards were made available by the recently established Syrian AF.

REAF Spitfires, Dakotas and Lysanders supported Egyptian ground forces in the attempt to put the Israeli AF out of action. On 15 May 1948, one day after the declaration of the state of Israel, two Egyptian AF Spitfires attacked Sde Dov. Combined with strikes on other airfields, many of Israel's aircraft were temporarily put out of action. Ramat David was also attacked by the REAF, apparently unaware that it was still occupied by the RAF, whose Spitfires in turn shot down four of the Egyptian attackers.

Starting on 18 May the REAF turned against strategic objectives, C-47s bombing targets around Tel Aviv. The Arab forces enjoyed success in June, with Spitfires assisting in taking the town of Nitzanin and in the defence of Isdud and Suweidan, both of which were kept in Arab hands.

With the receipt of new equipment, including Czech-built S.199 fighters in May, the Israeli AF was able to put up a better defence. Although losses were heavy, the S.199s helped limit C-47 raids.

The Israeli AF was also able to undertake bombing missions, striking Amman and Damascus in June with its own C-47s, and also raiding towns on the

West Bank. The Israeli AF met with less success in the support of ground forces, which suffered a major reverse at Jenin in May-June, while air assets proved increasingly vulnerable to Arab ground fire.

The Iraqi and Syrian air forces in the north were also involved in the support of ground operations. The Royal Iraqi AF participated in the action at Jenin, while Syrian AF Harvards first went into action in support of ground forces attacking Israeli positions near Lake Tiberias.

Ceasefire and rearmament

On 11 June a UN-engineered ceasefire came into being. Although brief, this allowed both Egypt and Israel to acquire new equipment and for the latter to send reinforcements to El Arish. From 9 July, combat resumed, with Israel attempting to take control of western Jerusalem, capture Arab territory in the north, and to break the Egyptian blockade of the Negev. S.199s provided close support while the Israeli AF resumed its bombing campaign. The initial ground operation was a major success, but a day later Syrian AF Harvards proved their worth in attacking Israeli infantry. Israeli AF B-17s then bombed Cairo on 14 July, although the air arm's primary mission remained ground support. A second truce was in place before the end of the month, allowing the Israeli AF to comprehensively re-equip. Sporadic fighting was followed by a renewed Israeli offensive beginning on 15 October. At this time the Israeli AF possessed numerical superiority, which was now focused against the Egyptians. Dispersal of REAF assets rendered their destruction on the ground difficult, although Beaufighters and Spitfires struck El Arish and other airfields. The Israeli AF continued to sustain losses, but the Egyptian forces on the ground were by now on the back foot, and the REAF was suffering the heavier losses both in the air and on the ground. Israeli AF operations in Galilee effectively concluded the campaign in the north before the end of October. By the end of December, El Arish was in Israeli hands, with the REAF forced out onto airstrips in the Sinai. British pressure forced Israel to give up some captured territory before a definitive ceasefire was agreed in January 1949.

ISRAELI AF, 1948–49		
Aircraft	Unit	Base
B-17	69 Sqn	Ramat David
Avia S.199, Spitfire Mk V/IX, P-51D	101 Sqn	Herzliya, Ekron
Avia S.199, Spitfire Mk IX	105 Sqn	Herzliya
C-46, C-47, Norseman	13 Sqn	Ekron
C-47, Beaufighter Mk X	103 Sqn	Sde Dov, Ramat David
Auster	1 Sqn	Sde Dov
Auster AOP.Mk 5	Judean Flt	Yavneel
Taylorcraft J-2	Negev Flt	Beit Daras
Harvard	35 Flt	
Autocrat, RWD-8/13/15	Tel Aviv Flt	Sde Dov

Sinai and Suez
1956

Linking Britain with the Middle East, East Africa and the Far East, the Suez Canal was assigned great strategic importance, but UK prestige would be seriously damaged by the Suez Crisis.

BRITAIN WAS LONG the dominant power in the Canal Zone region, and the waterway itself was a vital trade route. During World War II, numerous RAF airfields had been built or commandeered along the Canal, most of these being handed over to the REAF after the war. By the mid-1950s, RAF air power in the Mediterranean was centred on Cyprus and Malta, and the last of the bases in Egypt had been evacuated in 1955, with Britain the beneficiary of an agreement that ensured access to the Canal. Then, in July 1956, President Nasser nationalized the Canal.

Anglo-French response

As soon as Nasser announced the nationalization of the Canal, British Prime Minister Anthony Eden called on chiefs of staff to plan a military intervention in order to regain control of the waterway. The plan, codenamed Musketeer, emerged as a joint French-British operation. Air strikes on Egyptian AF airfields would aim to disable the recently modernized air arm that included Soviet-supplied Il-28 jet bombers and MiG-17 and MiG-15 jet fighters. Raids on airfields

would be followed by an airborne assault that would capture the Canal Zone.

In order to justify the operation, the Canal had to appear to be under threat, and the plan therefore also involved Israel. The latter hoped to defeat Egypt's military and occupy territory, notably the Gaza Strip. The war plan envisaged an Israeli paratroop raid against the Mitla Pass, in Sinai, as supposed retaliation for Palestinian terrorist actions that were being launched by the Fedayeen group, and others, out of Gaza. The Israeli assault would in turn provide Britain and France with a valid reason to issue Nasser an ultimatum concerning the Canal.

In addition to the RAF and Fleet Air Arm assets available for Musketeer, the French AF deployed four fighter-bomber units, three transport units and an aircraft carrier; three squadrons of French Mystère IVAs would be stationed in Israel to defend Tel Aviv against raids by EAF Il-28 bombers. Since the Israeli AF was lacking in terms of numbers, French Noratlas transports and F-84F fighter-bombers were also soon in Israel in order to support the

▲ De Havilland Mosquito FB.Mk 6

110 Sqn, Israeli AF / Ramat David, 1956

At the time of the Suez Crisis, Israel could call on around 70 jet fighters and 45 piston-engined warplanes. The latter included Mosquitoes operating in the ground attack role. Other Israeli AF assets comprised B-17s, Meteor F.Mk 8s and NF.Mk 13s, Mystère IVAs, Ouragans, P-51Ds, Harvards and assorted transports.

Specifications

Crew: 2

Powerplant: 2 x 1103kW (1480hp) Rolls-Royce
  Merlin 23 V-12 piston engines

Maximum speed: 612km/h (380mph)

Range: 2655km (1650 miles)

Service ceiling: 11,430m (37,500ft)

Dimensions: span 16.5m (54ft 2in); length
  12.47m (40ft 11in); height 4.65m (15ft 3in)

Weight: 10,569kg (22,300lb) loaded

Armament: 4 x .303in (7.7mm) Browning MGs
  and four 20mm Hispano MGs; up to 1361kg
  (3000lb) of bombs or eight rockets

▲ Dassault Ouragan

113 Sqn, Israeli AF / Hatzor, 1956

Operator of Israel's French-supplied Ouragan fighters during the Suez Crisis was 113 Sqn. While some Ouragans flew in bare metal, this example wears a pale sand/slate blue camouflage scheme. One unusual Ouragan action during the campaign was a successful attack against an Egyptian destroyer on 31 October.

Specifications

Crew: 1

Powerplant: 1 x 22.2kN (4990lbf) Rolls-Royce
  Nene 104B turbojet

Maximum speed: 940km/h (584mph)

Range: 920km (570 miles)

Service ceiling: 13,000m (42,650ft)

Dimensions: span 13.16m (43ft 2in);
  length 10.73m (35ft 2in); height 4.14m (13ft 7in)

Weight: 7404kg (16,323lb) loaded

Armament: 4 x 20mm (.787in) Hispano-Suiza
  HS.404 cannon, rockets and up to 2270kg
  (5000lb) of payload

forthcoming Israeli ground offensive in the Mitla Pass and Sinai. This began on 29 September, when the first Israeli paratroops landed on the Mitla Pass, the troop-carrying C-47s backed by close-support P-51s and escorted by Meteors and Ouragans. The French Noratlas force was used to deliver artillery, vehicles and ammunition. Despite the attentions of EAF MiG-15s, Meteors and Vampires near Mitla on 30 November, Israeli troops were soon in a strong position along the Canal, as protecting Mystères fought with MiGs in the skies overhead.

The expiry of the Anglo-French ultimatum (which called for Israeli and Egyptian forces to withdraw from a 16-kilometre (10-mile) zone either side of the Canal) on 31 October was the trigger for Musketeer to begin. Three waves of bombers, primarily RAF Valiants and Canberras flying from Malta and Cyprus, hit over a dozen Egyptian airfields the same evening, to destroy the EAF on the ground. The next day the RAF sent reconnaissance Canberra PR.Mk 7s over Egypt, one of these being damaged by an EAF MiG. The imagery obtained by the Canberras revealed the limited effects of the night's bombing,

▲ Republic F-84F Thunderstreak

EC 3/3, French AF / Akrotiri, 1956

Normally based at Rheims, this EC 3/3 F-84F fighter-bomber was one of those deployed to Akrotiri, Cyprus, for the Suez action. Also flying from Akrotiri were the French AF's EC 1/3 and EC 4/33, with the F-84F and the reconnaissance-configured RF-84F respectively. Further F-84Fs were based in Lydda, Israel.

Specifications	
Crew: 1	Dimensions: span 10.24m (33ft 7.25in); length
Powerplant: 1 x 32kN (7220lb) Wright J65-W-3	13.23m (43ft 4.75in); height 4.39m (14ft 4.75in)
turbojet	Weight: 12,701kg (28,000lb) loaded
Maximum speed: 1118km/h (695mph)	Armament: 6 x .5in Browning M3 machine-guns,
Combat radius (with drop tanks): 1304km (810 miles)	external hardpoints with provision for up to
Service ceiling: 14,020kg (46,000ft)	2722kg (6000lb) of stores

▲ Gloster Meteor NF.Mk 13

10 Sqn, Egyptian AF / Almaza, 1956

The EAF's Meteor night-fighters were not provided with early warning of the Anglo-French air attacks on 31 October, and were therefore of little value in defending Egyptian airbases, although one example reportedly fired on an RAF Valiant during the first night of Anglo-French bombing raids.

Specifications	
Crew: 2	Dimensions: span 13.11m (43ft); length
Powerplant: 2 x 17.48kN (3933lbf)	14.47m (47ft 6in); height 4.24m (13ft 11in)
TJE Rolls-Royce Derwent RD.8	Weight: 9979kg (22,000lb) loaded
Maximum speed: 931km/h (578mph)	Armament: 4 x 20mm (.787in) British Hispano
Range: 1580km (982 miles)	cannons
Service ceiling: 12200m (40,026ft)	

and tactics now switched to daylight raids launched from British and French carriers stationed in the Mediterranean, and by land-based fighter-bombers.

Therefore, 1 November saw attacks against all Egyptian airfields west of Sinai, offensive assets comprising RAF Canberras, Meteors and Venoms, FAA Sea Hawks, Sea Venoms and Wyverns, plus French AF F-84Fs and French Navy F4Us and F6Fs from the carrier *Arromanches*. Around 500 sorties were flown, without loss to the Allies. Despite the concerted attacks on airfields, the EAF Vampires in particular remained active, and were on hand to attack Israeli ground troops at Mitla on 1 November. As the EAF struggled to disperse its aircraft to safer locations, the attacks continued on 2-3 November, and were now extended to include military barracks, repair facilities and, starting on 6 November, air defence sites and railways. By targeting airfields near the port city of Alexandria, it was hoped that maximum surprise would be gained for the invasion of Port Said and Port Fuad in the Canal Zone.

Air war over Sinai

With the Anglo-French air effort tying up the EAF, the Israelis were able to launch a major armoured assault that precipitated the Egyptian withdrawal from Sinai. Following a bombing raid by B-17s, the Israelis occupied the Gaza Strip, leaving the Egyptian forces in retreat towards the Canal, which they duly crossed on 2 November. Although not all Israeli actions on the ground proceeded without loss, the Egyptians were rapidly leaving their positions, troops typically moving out at night to avoid air attack. The EAF was meanwhile limited since quantities of aircraft had either been destroyed or damaged on their airfields, or had fled to Saudi Arabia or Syria for their protection. The feared Il-28s that evacuated to the relative safety of Luxor were eventually discovered and attacked on the ground by F-84Fs.

With the Israelis in control on the ground, the Israeli AF clashed with the EAF over Sinai, while Egyptian aircraft continued to disperse to safer airfields. EAF Meteors and MiG-15s fought against

French AF Mystères over Sinai. Sharm el Sheikh was the last major Egyptian garrison standing in Sinai and was backdrop to intense fighting on 2 November, when Israeli paratroops continued their advance. For Israel, capture of this garrison was important as it had a commanding position over the port of Eilat. Israeli AF P-51s and B-17s were available to support the ground offensive on 3 November. Finally, on 4 November, Israeli troops entered Sharm el Sheikh. Aided by P-51s and Ouragans flying attack sorties armed with napalm and rockets, Sharm el Sheikh eventually fell to the Israelis on 5 November.

The Anglo-French airborne assault, meanwhile, began at dawn on 5 November. After carrier aircraft had 'softened up' Egyptian positions, British

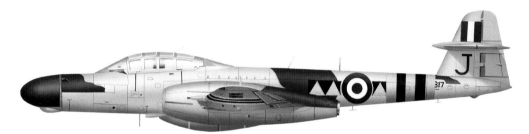

▲ **Gloster Meteor NF.Mk 13**

39 Sqn, RAF / Nicosia, 1956

The Meteor NF.Mk 13 was deployed by Egypt and Israel, as well as by the RAF, during the Suez campaign. This example wears the black and yellow 'Suez stripes' around the rear fuselage that served as identification during the operation. The semi-tropicalized Meteor NF.Mk 13 served with just two RAF units.

Specifications

Crew: 2	Dimensions: span 13.11m (43ft); length
Powerplant: 2 x 17.48kN (3933lbf)	14.47m (47ft 6in); height 4.24m (13ft 11in)
TJE Rolls-Royce Derwent RD.8	Weight: 9979kg (22,000lb) loaded
Maximum speed: 931km/h (578mph)	Armament: 4 x 20mm (.787in) British Hispano
Range: 1580km (982 miles)	cannons
Service ceiling: 12200m (40,026ft)	

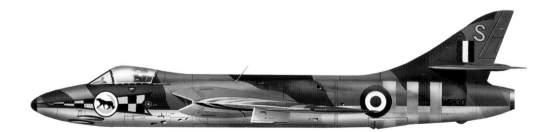

▲ **Hawker Hunter F.Mk 5**

34 Sqn, RAF / Nicosia, 1956

Home-based at Tangmere for UK air defence, RAF Hunters from 1 and 34 Sqns were mainly used for providing defensive top cover for the daylight strikes against Egyptian targets. Since their external fuel tanks had been damaged, their time on station was limited to around 10 minutes only. Note the incomplete 'Suez stripes'.

Specifications

Crew: 1	Dimensions: span 10.26m (33ft 8in); length
Powerplant: 1 x 35.59kN (8000lb) Armstrong-	13.98m (45ft 10.5in);height 4.02m (13ft 2in)
Siddeley Sapphire turbojet engine	Weight: 8501kg (18,742lb) loaded
Maximum speed: 144km/h (710mph)	Armament: 4 x 30mm Aden cannon; up to
Range: 689km (490 miles)	2722kg (6000lb) of bombs or rockets
Service ceiling: 15,240m (50,000ft)	

paratroops landed at Gamil airfield, near Port Said, having being conveyed to their objective by Hastings and Valetta transports flying from Nicosia. Despite some resistance, the British landings were successful. Minutes after the first British paratroops had touched down, their French counterparts landed near Port Fuad, delivered by Noratlas and C-47s flying from Tymbou, Cyprus. Again, the French paratroopers faced resistance, but completed their objectives.

Heliborne assault

The British planned to launch a heliborne assault against bridges along the Canal, using Fleet Air Arm and RAF Whirlwinds and RAF Sycamores flying from the carriers *Ocean* and *Theseus*. The assault was the first of its kind to be successfully carried out using helicopters, the hard-working rotorcraft making 200 deck landings in the course of the day's operations, and bringing casualties back to the carriers on the return journeys. Further reinforcements for the Anglo-French effort arrived in the Canal Zone in the form of amphibious landings, these beginning on 6 November. The landings were also preceded by air attack by carrier-based fighter-bombers, combined with naval bombardment, and carrier fighters remained on hand in 'cab rank' patrols. By 7 November, Anglo-French invasion forces had reached El Kap, and were making good progress despite having to contend with street fighting.

Ultimately it was international pressure that put an end to Musketeer, and the British and French agreed to a ceasefire on 7 November. For the British in particular, the Suez Crisis was a serious blow to the country's credibility on the world stage.

FLEET AIR ARM, SUEZ, 1956

Aircraft	Unit	Base
Sea Hawk FGA.Mk 4/6	800 NAS	HMS *Albion*
Sea Hawk FB.Mk 3	802 NAS	HMS *Albion*
Sea Hawk FGA.Mk 6	804 NAS	HMS *Bulwark*
Sea Hawk FGA.Mk 4	810 NAS	HMS *Bulwark*
Sea Hawk FB.Mk 3	895 NAS	HMS *Bulwark*
Sea Hawk FGA.Mk 6	897 NAS	HMS *Eagle*
Sea Hawk FGA.Mk 6	899 NAS	HMS *Eagle*
Sea Venom FAW.Mk 21	809 NAS	HMS *Albion*
Sea Venom FAW.Mk 21	892 NAS	HMS *Eagle*
Sea Venom FAW.Mk 21	893 NAS	HMS *Eagle*
Wyvern S.Mk 4	830 NAS	HMS *Eagle*
Skyraider AEW.Mk 1	849 NAS	HMS *Eagle* and *Albion*
Whirlwind HAS.Mk 22	845 NAS	HMS *Theseus*

RAF, SUEZ, 1956

Aircraft	Unit	Base
Valiant B.Mk 1	138 Sqn	Luqa
Valiant B.Mk 1	148 Sqn	Luqa
Valiant B.Mk 1	207 Sqn	Luqa
Valiant B.Mk 1	214 Sqn	Luqa
Canberra B.Mk 6	9 Sqn	Luqa, Hal Far
Canberra B.Mk 6	12 Sqn	Luqa, Hal Far
Canberra B.Mk 6	101 Sqn	Luqa
Canberra B.Mk 6	109 Sqn	Luqa
Canberra B.Mk 6	139 Sqn	Luqa
Canberra B.Mk 2	21 Sqn	Malta
Canberra B.Mk 2	10 Sqn	Nicosia
Canberra B.Mk 2	15 Sqn	Nicosia
Canberra B.Mk 2	27 Sqn	Nicosia
Canberra B.Mk 2	44 Sqn	Nicosia
Canberra B.Mk 2	18 Sqn	Nicosia
Canberra B.Mk 2	61 Sqn	Nicosia
Canberra B.Mk 2	35 Sqn (det)	Nicosia
Hunter F.Mk 5	1 Sqn	Nicosia
Hunter F.Mk 5	34 Sqn	Nicosia
Venom FB.Mk 4	6 Sqn	Akrotiri
Venom FB.Mk 4	8 Sqn	Akrotiri
Venom FB.Mk 4	249 Sqn	Akrotiri
Meteor NF.Mk 13	39 Sqn	Nicosia
Meteor FR.Mk 9	208 Sqn	Ta Kali
Canberra PR.Mk 7	13 Sqn	Akrotiri
Canberra PR.Mk 7	58 Sqn	Akrotiri
Shackleton MR.Mk 2	37 Sqn	Luqa
Hastings C.Mk 1	70 Sqn	Nicosia
Hastings C.Mk 1	99 Sqn	Nicosia
Hastings C.Mk 1	511 Sqn	Nicosia
Valetta C.Mk 1	30 Sqn	Nicosia
Valetta C.Mk 1	84 Sqn	Nicosia
Valetta C.Mk 1	114 Sqn	Nicosia
Whirlwind HAR.Mk 2, Sycamore HC.Mk 14	JHU	HMS Ocean

Specifications

Crew: 2

Powerplant: 2 x 28.9kN (6500lb) Rolls-Royce
 Avon Mk 101 turbojets

Maximum speed: 917km/h (570mph)

Range: 4274km (2656 miles)

Service ceiling: 14,630m (48,000ft)

Dimensions: span 29.49m (63ft 11in); length
 19.96m (65ft 6in); height 4.78m (15ft 8in)

Weight: 24,925kg (54,950lb) loaded

Armament: bomb bay with provision for up to
 2727kg (6000lb) of bombs, plus 909kg
 (2000lb) of underwing pylons

▲ **English Electric Canberra B.Mk 2**

10 Sqn, RAF / Nicosia, 1956

The Canberra bombers of 10 Sqn were normally based at Honington, as evidenced by the Honington Wing emblem on the fin. For the Suez operation, RAF Canberra B.Mk 2s and B.Mk 6s were based at Hal Far, Luqa and Nicosia and took part in the initial raids on Egyptian airfields, flown at high altitude.

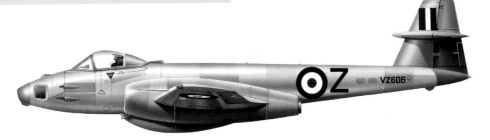

Specifications

Crew: 1

Powerplant: 2 x 16.0kN (3600lb) Rolls-Royce
 Derwent 8 turbojets

Maximum speed: 962km/h (598mph)

Range: 1580km (980 miles)

Service ceiling: 13,106m (43,000ft)

Dimensions: span 11.32m (37ft 2in);
 length 13.58m (44ft 7in); height 3.96m (13ft)

Weight: 8664kg (19,100lb) loaded

Armament: 4 x 20mm (.787in) Hispano
 cannon, 2 iron bombs or 8 rockets

▲ **Gloster Meteor FR.Mk 9**

208 Sqn, RAF / Ta Kali, 1956

The longest-serving RAF squadron in the Middle East, 208 Sqn operated from Egypt and Malta during 1951-58. As such, the unit was the primary tactical reconnaissance asset in the region. During the Suez Crisis, 208 Sqn operated the fighter-reconnaissance Meteor FR.Mk 9 variant from Ta Kali, Malta.

Specifications

Crew: 1

Powerplant: 1 x 24kN (5400lb) Rolls-Royce
 Nene 103 turbojet

Maximum speed: 969km/h (602mph)

Range: 370km (230 miles)

Service ceiling: 13,565m (44,500ft)

Dimensions: span 11.89m (39ft);

length 12.09m (39ft 8in); height 2.64m
 (8ft 8in)

Weight: 7348kg (16,200lb) loaded

Armament: 4 x 20mm Hispano cannon;
 provision for 4 x 227kg (500lb) bombs, or
 2 x 227kg (500lb) bombs and 20 x three-inch
 or 16 five-inch rockets

▲ **Hawker Sea Hawk FB.Mk 3**

802 NAS, Royal Navy / HMS Albion, 1956

The Sea Hawks of 802 NAS operated from the deck of HMS *Albion* for Operation Musketeer. The unit lost one Sea Hawk that was providing support during the Anglo-French landings on 5 November, with another example damaged by anti-aircraft artillery on 2 November, although this aircraft recovered to the carrier.

Six-Day War
1967

The destruction wrought on Arab air power by Israel's pre-emptive strike on opposition airbases in June 1967 was such that Operation Moked would serve as a template for future campaigns.

THE BUILD-UP TO the Six-Day War had seen increasing tensions since April 1967, culminating in an air battle over the Golan Heights involving Israeli AF Mystères and Syrian AF MiG-21s, while Israeli jets targeted artillery in the Golan Heights. Meanwhile, cross-border raids into Israel by Arab insurgents had been escalating in the wake of the 1956 war, these mainly originating in Jordan and Syria. After having been established in the Sinai to prevent such raids, a UN peacekeeping force departed in May 1967. In the same month, Egypt, Syria and Jordan formulated a new defence pact, while air assets began to be redeployed.

Although troops were mobilized in May, Nasser apparently did not expect another conflict against Israel so soon, and moved aircraft from Sinai to the Canal Zone. Meanwhile, United Arab AF MiG-17s and MiG-19s were deployed to Dumeyr, near Damascus, with other UARAF combat aircraft in Yemen or at Hurghada on the Red Sea. Egypt's force of Tu-16 bombers were also no longer kept on alert by June, although Egyptian troops were now in control of all posts in the Sinai after the UN withdrawal, and the Gulf of Aqba had been closed off to Israeli shipping.

The first day of the campaign, codenamed Moked, saw almost the entire strength of the Israeli AF attack airfields in Egypt, Syria and Jordan. Beginning in 1967, the Israelis had conducted regular air patrols over the Mediterranean, often in large formations, and at low level to avoid detection by radar. Therefore, the Israeli strike package that assembled on the morning of 5 June 1967 was not met with an appropriate response.

The first waves
Departing after dawn, the first package of Israeli AF strike aircraft heading west included Mirage IIIs and Mystères, with around 120 aircraft in three waves. These flew below Egyptian radar cover, then turned south towards the Egyptian coast and raided at least

10 airfields, including El Arish, Bir Gifgafa, Cairo West (home to Egypt's force of Tu-16 bombers), Fayid, Jebel Libni, Bir Thamada, Abu Sueir, Kabrit, Beni Sueif and Inchas. While Mirages and Super Mystères flew across the Mediterranean before turning to attack from the west, striking airbases in the Canal Zone and along the Nile, Mystère IVAs and Ouragans approached on a direct course from bases in southern Israel to raid airfields in Sinai. In most cases, 10 flights of four aircraft made a bombing run, followed by strafing. The second and third waves then arrived at 10-minute intervals.

After the initial eight waves had attacked their targets, the Israeli AF aircraft recovered to their airfields, before a further wave of strike aircraft set off for Egyptian airfields along the Nile.

Although claims were certainly exaggerated, Israel reported the destruction of 308 aircraft in total by the end of the assault on 5 June, of which 240 were Egyptian. The Israeli AF admitted losses amounting to 20 combat aircraft. In addition to the aircraft destroyed on the ground, the Israeli AF shot down a number of Egyptian aircraft, and others fell while attempting to scramble from their airfields during the course of the raids. Those Egyptian aircraft that did manage to take off – notably at Abu Sueir, where as many as 20 MiG-21s made it into the air – were generally only able to put up limited resistance, and sustained heavy losses in the process.

In response to the attack on Egypt, Jordan began an artillery bombardment of Israel, targeting Ramat David airfield. Air raids were then prosecuted against Israel by the Royal Jordanian AF, whose Hunter fighter-bombers struck Kfar Sirkin and Natanya, causing some damage to parked aircraft. The Iraqi AF, meanwhile, announced that it had attacked Lydda airfield, although this was denied by Israel.

With the war now opened up on the eastern front, Israel turned upon Egypt's allies. Operating MiG-17s, the Syrian AF had raided the oil installation at Haifa, and strafed Mahanyim airfield,

Specifications

Crew: 1

Powerplant: 1 x 27.9kN (6280lb) Hispano Suiza
Tay 250A turbojet; or 1 x 3500kg
(7716lb) Hispano Suiza Verdon 350 turbojet

Maximum speed: 1120km/h (696mph)

Range: unknown

Service ceiling: 13,750m (45,000ft)

Dimensions: span 11.1m (36ft 5.75in); length
12.9m (42ft 2in); height 4.4m (14ft 5in)

Weight: 9500kg (20,950lb) loaded

Armament: internal bomb bay with provision for
up to 10 bombs, underwing pylons
for two bombs up to 450kg (992lb), or two drop
tanks

▲ Dassault Mystère IVA

116 Sqn, Israeli AF / Tel Nov, 1967

Just over 30 serviceable Mystère IVA jets were available to the Israeli AF at the
beginning of the offensive. These were operated by 109 and 116 Sqns, In one of
the more notorious incidents of the war, Israeli AF Mystère IVAs were involved in
an attack on the U.S. intelligence vessel *Liberty*, sailing off El Arish.

Specifications

Crew: 1

Powerplant: 1 x 44.1kN (9920lbf) SNECMA Atar
101G-2 turbojet

Maximum speed: 1195km/h (743mph)

Range: 870km (540 miles)

Service ceiling: 17,000m (56,000ft)

Dimensions: span 10.51m (34ft 6in); length
14.13m (46ft 4in); height 4.60m (15ft 1in)

Weight: 9000kg (20,000lb) loaded

Armament: 2 x 30mm (1.18in) DEFA 552
cannons, rockets, missiles and up to
2680kg (5000lb) of payload

▲ Dassault Super Mystère B2

105 Sqn, Israeli AF / Hatzor, 1967

Israel possessed just under 40 Mystère B2s in June 1967, these being operated by
105 Sqn, the largest combat unit within the Israeli AF. Despite relatively heavy
losses, the Mystère B2 fleet was instrumental in the initial strikes against Arab
airfields, with all available aircraft being sent within the first wave.

and Israel responded with strikes against airbases at
Damascus, Dumayr, Marj Rial and Seikal. Later in
the afternoon the Israeli AF turned its attentions to
the Syrian base at T4, and H3 in Iraq.

The eastern front

After attacking Syria, Jordan was next to receive the
attentions of the Israeli AF on 5 June. In the
afternoon, the Israeli AF attacked Mafraq and
Amman airbases in Jordan, together with an early
warning radar station, a command centre, as well as

troops moving westwards. The almost total
destruction of the RJAF Hunter force meant that
Jordanian pilots were now seconded to the Iraqi AF.

The afternoon of 5 June saw the Israeli AF return
to Egypt, hitting Cairo International and airfields at
Al Minya, Bilbeis, Helwan, Hurghada, Luxor and Ras
Banas, as well as a number of radar installations.
Cairo International was assigned particular
importance, because a number of Egyptian Tu-16s
had fled here and thereby avoided destruction on
the ground at Cairo West. The attacking force now

Specifications

Crew: 1

Powerplant: 1 x 58.72kN (13,200lb) thrust
SNECMA Atar 09B-3 afterburning turbojet
engine and one 16.46kN (3700lb) thrust
auxiliary SEFR 841 rocket motor

Maximum speed: 2350km/h (1460mph)

Range: 2012km (1250 miles)

Service ceiling: 17,000m (55,755 ft)

Dimensions: span 8.26m (27ft 2in); length
14.91m (48ft 10in); height 4.6m (14ft 10in)

Weight: 11,676kg (25,740lb) loaded

Armament: 2 x 30mm DEFA cannon;
1 x Matra R.511 or R.530 AAM, up to
2295kg (5060lb) of bombs

▲ **Dassault Mirage IIICJ**

119 Sqn, Israeli AF / Tel Nov, 1967

From an Israeli perspective, one of the undoubted 'stars' of the 1967 war was the
Mirage III, with 70 Mirage IIICJ single-seat fighters having been received by 1964,
together with a pair of photo-reconnaissance versions. As well as assembling an
enviable record in aerial combat, Mirages were used for ground attack.

also included Vautour bombers flying from their bases at Hatzerim and Ramat David.

After the 'lightning' attacks on Arab airfields, which dominated the first day of operations, 6 June saw the Israeli AF used increasingly in support of the offensive on the ground. Helicopters began to be used on the night of 5/6 June, with a party of commandos being delivered behind Jordanian lines by S-58. With Israeli troops having made a break through the Egyptian lines near Rafah, under the support of artillery, Israeli aircraft were active in support of troops in Sinai and on the West Bank.

Helicopters once again played a vital role in Israel's capture of Abu Agheila, a key position near the Sinai border. In the face of Israeli AF ground support missions flown over Gaza and Bir Lahfan, the Egyptian Army was in retreat, and rapidly moving out of Sinai. Resistance by Arab air power was limited, although two MiG-21s did attack Israeli troops near Bir Lahfan on 6 June, both reportedly being shot down in the process. A pair of Egyptian Su-7s also made it as far as El Arish, while several attempts were made by Arab fighters to destroy Israeli helicopters. RJAF personnel were now at H3, where they were operating alongside the Iraqi AF. The latter force managed to bomb industry in Natanya with a single Tu-16 on 6 June. The lone raider was shot down by air defences, but it prompted an Israeli AF response, and fighter-bombers were duly sent against H3, where they clashed with both Iraqi and

Jordanian defenders. Further aerial battles were reported over H3 in the days that followed.

Israel on the offensive

While the Israeli AF kept up its attacks on Jordanian positions on the West Bank, in Sinai the Egyptians were apparently in disarray. Israel therefore took the opportunity to capture the Mitla and Giddi Passes. This had the effect of encircling Egyptian units east of the mountains in Sinai. Here, they were left to the mercy of the Israeli AF, which set about destroying Egyptian vehicles in the Mitla Pass. Magister trainers, equipped with rockets, proved especially useful in the close support role, and operated in concert with Israeli armoured formations. Indeed, the massed tank battles fought during the Six-Day War were the largest witnessed since World War II.

With the Mitla and Giddi Passes now in Israeli hands, the Arab air forces assembled their remaining equipment for an attempt to drive out the Israelis. Around 50 Arab aircraft were available for the attacks, which began at dawn on 7 June. In order for the attacks to be staged, airfields and aircraft had been repaired, and pilots had been redeployed where necessary to make good losses; before the war was over, Algerian pilots were also fighting alongside the Egyptians. Although the pace of the Israeli advance was slowed by the attentions of Arab air power, sporadic ground attack sorties were not enough to alter the course of the war in

Sinai. Arab aircraft also had to contend with standing air patrols mounted by the Israeli AF in defence of the troops below.

Bolstered by UARAF personnel, the Egyptians were able to mount more concerted air attacks against the Israeli ground forces by 8 June. Despite some success by Arab pilots, the outcome of the Sinai ground war had effectively been decided, and although an increasing number of Arab air force sorties were being made, it was the Israeli AF that was in a position to mount a more telling new campaign. This was to be directed against Syria.

After Egypt had agreed to the terms of a UN ceasefire early on 9 June, and with Jordan also defeated, Syria was left to face Israel alone. After Israeli AF raids on the Golan Heights, Syria had accepted ceasefire terms on 8 June, but the next day Israel launched a full-scale attack against Golan. Syrian forces quickly retreated to defensive positions around Damascus, while air combat saw Israeli AF jets clash with both UARAF and Syrian AF assets. Finally, a UN ceasefire came into force on 10 June, by which time Israel had captured the Golan Heights and the town of Qunaytra. Spearheaded by air power, Israel had achieved a decisive victory over its Arab neighbours.

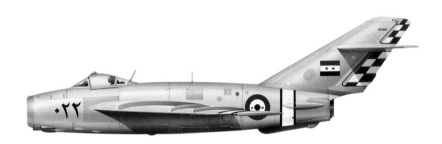

Specifications

Crew: 1	Dimensions: span 9.45m (31ft); length 11.05m
Powerplant: 1 x 33kN (7452lb) Klimov VK-1F	(36ft 3.75in); height 3.35m (11ft)
turbojet	Weight: 600kg (14,770lb) loaded
Maximum speed: 1145km/h (711mph)	Armament: 1 x 37mm N-37 cannon and
Range: 1470km (913 miles)	2 x 23mm NS-23 cannon, plus up to 500kg
Service ceiling: 16,600m (54,560ft)	(1102lb) of mixed stores on underwing pylons

▲ **Mikoyan-Gurevich MiG-17F**

20th Brigade, Egyptian AF, El Arish

The most numerous combat aircraft in the Arab inventory, the MiG-17 was used for both air defence and for ground attack duties in 1967. Towards the end of the fighting, surviving MiG-17s were active on offensive missions over the Mitla Pass and in southern Sinai, suffering a number of losses in the process.

Specifications

Crew: 3	17.65m (57ft 10.75in); height 6.70m (21ft
Powerplant: 2 x 26.3kN (5952lb) Klimov VK-1	11.8in)
turbojets	Weight: 21,200kg (46,738lb) loaded
Maximum speed: 902km/h (560mph)	Armament: 4 x 23mm cannon; internal bomb
Range: 2180km (1355 miles)	capacity 1000kg (2205lb), max bomb
Service ceiling: 12,300m (40,355ft)	capacity 3000kg (6614lb); torpedo version:
Dimensions: span 21.45m (70ft 4.5in); length	provision for two 400mm light torpedoes

▲ **Ilyushin Il-28**

61st Brigade, Egyptian AF

The efficiency of Israel's pre-emptive strikes meant that the Egyptian bomber force had little role to play in the subsequent fighting. Tu-16s and Il-28s suffered heavily on the ground at Cairo West, although at least one Il-28, escorted by MiGs, managed to launch a raid against Israeli aircraft at El Arish on 7 June.

▲ Sukhoi Su-7BMK

1st Brigade, Egyptian AF

Despite its limited range and payload, the Su-7 could have played a more significant role in the Six-Day War, but suffered heavily on the ground. By June 1967 the Egyptian AF had received 64 examples, but only a single unit, based at Fayid, had converted to the type, and just 15 examples were declared operational.

Specifications

Crew: 1	17.37m (57ft); height 4.7m (15ft 5in)
Powerplant: 1 x 88.2kN (19,842lb) Lyulka AL-7F	Weight: 13,500kg (29,750lb) loaded
turbojet	Armament: 2 x 30mm NR-30 cannon; four
Maximum speed: 1700km/h (1056mph)	external pylons for 2 x 750kg (1653lb) and
Range: 320km (199 miles)	2 x 500kg (1102lb) bombs, but with two
Service ceiling: 15,150m (49,700ft)	tanks on fuselage pylons, total external
Dimensions: span 8.93m (29ft 3.5in); length	weapon load is reduced to 1000kg (2205lb)

War of Attrition
1969–1970

Despite Israel's resounding victory in the Six-Day War, the fighting did not end with the UN-backed ceasefire. Instead there began a War of Attrition, in which air power played a key role.

THE CEASEFIRE OF June 1967 did not hold long, and on 1 July an Israeli patrol was ambushed by Egyptian troops on the eastern side of the Suez Canal. This was the catalyst for Israeli and Egyptian forces to begin a campaign of shelling across the Canal, which would in turn lead to the deployment of air power.

While the Israeli AF clashed with Arab MiGs over the Canal Zone, the Syrian AF launched longer-range raids into Israeli territory, losing a number of aircraft in the process. In October, for instance, Israeli air defences claimed the destruction of four Syrian AF MiG-19s. The same month saw the fighting escalate to include naval warfare, and the sinking of the Israeli destroyer *Eilat* by Egyptian gunboats.

Re-equipment programme

On the back of the losses sustained in the Six-Day War, Israel took the opportunity presented by the sporadic fighting that followed to re-equip its air arm. Most importantly, an order was placed in 1969 for 50 F-4E fighter-bombers and six RF-4E reconnaissance

aircraft, and the Israeli AF Phantom II fleet would go on to play a central role in the years to come. The Israelis also began to receive large numbers of A-4 attack aircraft, including examples delivered from U.S. Navy surplus, while renewal of the helicopter arm saw the S-58 progressively replaced by the S-65 and the Bell 205. At the same time Egypt was re-equipping its air force, with more advanced MiG-21PF/PFM variants delivered by the USSR.

The Egyptians deployed additional troops to the Canal Zone, and in September 1968 there began a major artillery battle fought across the waterway. From the following month, Israel stepped up its commando raids that ventured deep into Egyptian territory, often targeting air defence sites. The Israeli completion of the defensive Bar Lev Line along the Canal in March 1969 was the signal for Nasser to announce a war of attrition, which would be waged primarily by artillery and air power.

With the Egyptians possessing superior artillery, the Israeli AF was called into action, attacking

Egyptian troops along the West Bank starting in July 1969, knocking out radar sites in addition to artillery. In September the Israelis launched a large-scale raid against an Egyptian military complex at Ras Abu-Daraj, accompanied by air strikes. Meanwhile, the Israelis were also extracting a heavy toll on the EAF, through the use of both standing air patrols and surface-to-air missiles (SAMs).

With the Israeli AF able to operate over Egypt unscathed, Soviet advisors began to arrive in increasing numbers, manning air defence sites and flying MiGs on behalf of the Egyptians. After the Israeli AF hit targets around Cairo in early 1970, the Soviets sent additional air defence equipment, including squadrons of advanced MiG-21MFs.

Despite increasingly powerful Egyptian air defences organized along the Canal, the West Bank, and around major cities, the Israeli AF intensified its efforts, with numerous sorties flown over Egypt in the first quarter of 1970. The presence of Soviet 'advisors' was a concern, however, and Israel began to decrease its offensive operations as a result. This allowed the Egyptian AF to regain the initiative, with air strikes launched across the Canal. The Israeli bombing campaign was stepped up accordingly in May, with a considerable increase in air-to-air combat as a consequence. Although over-flights continued, both sides agreed to a ceasefire in August 1970.

Specifications

Crew: 1

Powerplant: 1 x 44.1kN (9920lbf) SNECMA Atar 101G-2 turbojet

Maximum speed: 1195km/h (743mph)

Range: 870km (540 miles)

Service ceiling: 17,000m (56,000ft)

Dimensions: span 10.51m (34ft 6in); length 14.13m (46ft 4in); height 4.6m (15ft 1in)

Weight: 9000kg (20,000lb) loaded

Armament: 2 x 30mm (1.18in) DEFA 552 cannons, rockets, missiles and up to 2680kg (5000lb) of payload

▲ **Dassault Super Mystère B2**

Israeli AF / 1969–70

Although by now relegated to ground attack and close support duties, the Super Mystère B2 remained a useful asset to the Israeli AF at the time of the War of Attrition. At around the same time, the survivors were re-engined with the same J52 as used in the U.S.-supplied A-4 Skyhawk.

Specifications

Crew: 1

Powerplant: 1 x 60.8kN (13,668lb) thrust Tumanskii afterburning turbojet

Maximum speed: 2050km/h (1300mph)

Range: 1800km (1118 miles)

Service ceiling: 17,000m (57,750ft)

Dimensions: span 7.15m (23ft 5.5in);

length (including probe) 15.76m (51ft 8.5in); height 4.1m (13ft 5.5in)

Weight: 9400kg (20,723lb) loaded

Armament: 1 x 23mm cannon, provision for about 1500kg (3307lb) of stores, including air-to-air missiles, rocket pods, napalm tanks or drop tanks

▲ **Mikoyan-Gurevich MiG-21PF**

United Arab Republic AF/Egyptian AF / Mansourah, 1969

As part of its re-equipment programme in the wake of the Six-Day War, Egypt was the recipient of Soviet military materiel in the form of 70 MiG-21PFs and MiG-21PFMs, together with additional MiG-17Fs and Su-7s. Despite new aircraft, the Egyptian AF still suffered from shortages of trained aircrew, however.

Yom Kippur War
1973

Beginning on 6 October 1973, the Jewish Day of Atonement, the Yom Kippur War was launched by Israel's Arab neighbours in a bid to regain the territories that they had lost in 1967.

FOR THE ARAB forces, success relied on catching the Israelis off their guard. The objectives of a two-pronged attack included regaining the West Bank, Golan Heights and Sinai Peninsula, which had been lost so dramatically in 1967. In catching the Israelis by surprise, the Egyptian Army was successful. After artillery and air strikes against the Suez Canal, around 75,000 Egyptian troops and 400 tanks proved too strong for the Israeli defences on the eastern bank of the Canal. Using bridges to cross the Canal, the Egyptians pressed on into Sinai. At the same time, the Syrian Army began to attack

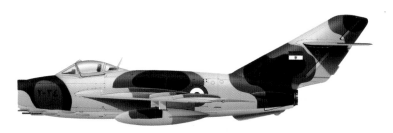

Specifications

Crew: 1

Powerplant: 1 x 33kN (7452lb) Klimov VK-1F turbojet

Maximum speed: 1145km/h (711mph)

Range: 1470km (913 miles)

Service ceiling: 16,600m (54,560ft)

Dimensions: span 9.45m (31ft); length 11.05m (36ft 3.75in); height 3.35m (11ft)

Weight: 6700kg (14,770lb) loaded

Armament: 1 x 37mm N-37 cannon and 2 x 23mm NS-23 cannon, plus up to 500kg (1102lb) of mixed stores on underwing pylons

▲ **Mikoyan-Gurevich MiG-17F**

Egyptian AF / 1970s

Approaching obsolescence by 1973, the MiG-17 remained in use with both Egypt and Syria, primarily for ground attack. However, MiG-21 losses meant that the MiG-17 was forced to undertake defensive missions, too. Together with Su-7s, MiG-17s played an important role during the Syrian advance on the Golan Heights.

▲ **Mil Mi-8**

Egyptian AF / 1970s

Helicopters played a vital role in the initial Egyptian assault across the Suez Canal, the Mi-8 being use to transport troops to their objectives both in Sinai and the Golan Heights. The Mi-8 was vulnerable to ground fire, however, and on 7 October alone Israel claimed no fewer than 10 Egyptian helicopters shot down.

Specifications

Crew: 3

Powerplant: 2 x 1454kW (1950shp) Klimov TV3-117Mt turboshafts

Maximum speed: 260km/h (162mph)

Range: 450km (280 miles)

Service ceiling: 4500m (14,765ft)

Dimensions: rotor diameter 21.29m (69ft 10in); length 18.17m (59ft 7in); height 5.65m (18ft 6in)

Weight: 11,100kg (24,470lb)

Armament: up to 1500kg (3300lb) of disposable stores

Israeli positions in the Golan Heights in the northeast, under the cover of air support provided by MiG-17 and Su-7 fighter-bombers.

Simultaneous with the land assault, Egyptian AF aircraft struck Israeli airfields, SAM sites, radar stations and other targets in Sinai. Targets deeper within Israel were attacked by Tu-16s launching standoff cruise missiles. Fighting a war on two fronts, the Israeli AF was required to launch air strikes against Egyptian and Syrian forward positions and rear areas, bringing to bear its F-4, A-4 and Mirage III and Nesher jets within 30 minutes of the invasion. In the first four days of the conflict, the Israeli AF launched 3555 sorties for the loss of 81 aircraft.

Having learned the lessons of 1967, the Arab forces were now much better protected against air attack. Egypt planned to occupy a narrow strip of Sinai desert, before a battle of attrition could begin. As well as defensive air patrols to defeat the Israeli AF in the air, the Arab forces were protected by Soviet-made SAMs and effective anti-aircraft artillery. Fixed SAM sites were deployed along the western bank of the Canal, while mobile and man-portable SAMs, together with self-propelled anti-aircraft artillery were deployed with the troops in the field.

The SAM threat

Operating in the face of modern ground-based air defences provided the Israeli AF with a steep learning curve, and initial electronic countermeasures (ECM) proved ineffective. From an estimated 120 Israeli aircraft lost during the conflict, around 90-100 of these were claimed by ground-based air defences.

Israel decided to focus on the northern front, and defeat the Syrians before becoming further involved in Sinai. After three days of fighting, including a tank battle, the Syrian Army was forced back, while the Israeli AF targeted the military HQ in Damascus and the Homs oil installation on 19 October.

Eventually, the Israeli loss rate was reduced to one aircraft for every 102 sorties, aided by the receipt of more advanced ECM equipment and guided weapons from the U.S., and through the use of revised tactics. In order to boost the Arab air forces' capabilities, Iraq provided a squadron of Hunters and one of MiG-21s, while Jordanian SAMs targeted any Israeli AF aircraft that were within range. The Syrians were pushed back in the north, with Israeli AF aircraft now ranging almost as far as the Turkish border. By mid-October the Arab air defences were in a state of disarray, and with the Syrian AF unable to defeat the Israelis in the air, the Israeli troops pressed on.

On the Sinai front, Egypt was in control of the eastern side of the Canal after two days. Numerous Israeli counter-attacks initially failed to make an impression, and Egypt was holding out for its planned war of attrition. Support for the Egyptian AF came in the form of Algerian Su-7s on 8 October, when both sides were engaged in attacking each other's airfields. From 14 October further back-up appeared in the form of Libyan AF Mirages. At the same time as the USSR was making good Arab aircraft losses, Israel was benefiting from huge

▲ **Mikoyan-Gurevich MiG-21PFM**

Egyptian AF / 1970s

The backbone of both the Egyptian and Syrian air arms in 1973 was provided by the MiG-21, in a number of different variants. In order to compensate for early losses to the Israeli AF the Soviets delivered additional MiG-21s later in the war, some of these being transferred from Warsaw Pact orders.

Specifications

Crew: 1	length (including probe) 15.76m (51ft 8.5in);
Powerplant: 1 x 60.8kN (13,668lb) thrust	height 4.1m (13ft 5.5in)
Tumanskii afterburning turbojet	Weight: 9400kg (20,723lb) loaded
Maximum speed: 2050km/h (1300mph)	Armament: 1 x 23mm cannon, provision for
Range: 1800km (1118 miles)	about 1500kg (3307lb) of stores, including
Service ceiling: 17,000m (57,750ft)	air-to-air missiles, rocket pods, napalm tanks
Dimensions: span 7.15m (23ft 5.5in);	or drop tanks

quantities of materiel delivered by air from the U.S., including additional A-4s and F-4s.

On 14 October Egyptian forces advanced without their air defence 'umbrella', playing into Israeli hands. After Israeli naval attacks on the Egyptian coast in the west, Israeli troops threatened the Egyptian flanks on both sides of the Canal. Israel established a bridgehead and began to take out Egyptian air defence sites, before Egypt requested a ceasefire on 20 October, although Israel continued to advance towards Suez. Ending with Israeli victory on 24 October, the war had been closely contested, and although the Arabs caught the Israelis off guard, their hopes of superpower intervention to force a ceasefire under favourable terms were not to be.

▲ **F-4E Phantom II**

A signature warplane of the Middle East wars, Israel began to receive the Phantom II in 1969. These 119 Sqn F-4Es are seen over Jerusalem.

Lebanon
1982

Having learned hard lessons during the October 1973 war, the Israeli AF was much better equipped when it took on the Syrian AF over Lebanon during the next major Middle East conflict.

AMID A BACKDROP of fighting between rival Palestinian and Christian factions, the Syrian Army intervened to bring a fragile peace to Lebanon. On the afternoon of 4 June, a day after an assassination attempt on the Israeli ambassador to the UK, Israel invaded Lebanon, sending seven waves of jets to attack Palestinian refugee camps and suspected terrorist strongholds located around the capital, Beirut. Also hit were the Palestine Liberation Organization (PLO) HQ and weapons dumps.

By now, the Israeli AF was better able to counter the SAM menace, using advanced ECM equipment

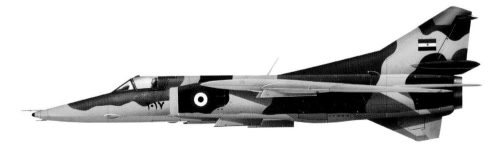

Specifications

Crew: 1

Powerplant: 1 x 98kN (22,046lb) Tumanskii R-27F2M-300 turbojet

Maximum speed: about 2445km/h (1520mph)

Range: 966km (600 miles)

Service ceiling: over 18,290m (60,000ft)

Dimensions: span 13.97m (45ft 10in) spread, 7.78m (25ft 6.25in) swept; length 16.71m (54ft 10in); height 4.82m (15ft 9.75in)

Weight: 18,145kg (40,000lb) loaded

Armament: 1 x 23mm GSh-23L cannon, provision for 3000kg (6614lb) of stores

▲ **Mikoyan-Gurevich MiG-23BN**

Syrian AF / early 1980s

The variable-geometry MiG-23BN was the most advanced offensive asset available to the Syrian AF at the time of the 1982 conflict. In fact, Syria had deployed its MiG-23BNs over Lebanon before the Israeli invasion, with two examples being claimed destroyed over Bekaa during an April 1982 raid.

and dedicated suppression of enemy air defence (SEAD) assets, including anti-radar missiles. The Israeli AF had been greatly improved through the induction of the F-15, widely used to provide defensive top cover over Lebanon, and the F-16. Between them, these two modern fighters were more than a match for the Syrian AF's fleet of MiGs, and Israel eventually posted claims for 85 aerial victories against the Syrian AF, 44 of these credited to F-16s.

Relentless campaign

After follow-up air raids on Palestinian targets in southern Lebanon, the Israeli AF carried out further air strikes on 5 June, these targeting Beirut, transport connections along the coast, and PLO positions. The

following day Israeli troops moved into Lebanon, a full-scale invasion being supported by helicopters, some of which were armed with anti-tank missiles to defeat Syrian armour. The Israelis' aim was to extinguish the fighting capability of the Palestinian militant groups in the south who had long been launching raids into Israeli-occupied territory, under the protection offered by the Syrian occupation.

In order to attempt to outflank PLO and Lebanese resistance, Israeli naval and airborne commando landings were conducted early in the campaign, supported by helicopters at Zahrani and Sidon. In the east, the ground campaign was fiercest in the Bekaa Valley, and here transport helicopters and helicopter gunships played a valuable role, under the cover of

Specifications

Crew: 1	Dimensions: span 13.05m (42ft 9.75in); length
Powerplant: 2 x 106kN (23,810lb) Pratt &	19.43in (63ft 9in); height 5.63m (18ft 5in)
Whitney F100-PW-100 turbofans	Weight: 25,424kg (56,000lb) loaded
Maximum speed: 2655km/h (1650mph)	Armament: 1 x 20mm M61A1 cannon, pylons
Range: 1930km (1200 miles)	with provision for up to 7620kg (16,800lb)
Service ceiling: 30,500m (100,000ft)	of stores

▲ McDonnell Douglas F-15A Eagle

133 Sqn, Israeli AF / Tel Nov, early 1980s

Delivered to Israel under the Peace Fox programme, the F-15 played a vital role in establishing Israeli AF air supremacy over Lebanon, and claimed significant numbers of Syrian AF aircraft destroyed. Prior to the conflict, F-15s claimed five out of 12 MiG-21s that were attacking an Israeli strike package on 27 June 1978.

Specifications

Crew: 1	15.65m (51ft 4.25in); height 4.55m (14ft 4.25in)
Powerplant: 1x 79.6kN (17,900lb) General	Weight: 16,200kg (35,715lb) loaded
Electric J79-J1E turbojet	Armament: 1 x IAI (DEFA) 30mm cannon;
Maximum speed: 2445km/h (1520mph)	provision for up to 5775kg (12,732lb) of
Range: 346km (215 miles)	stores; for interception duties AIM-9
Service ceiling: 17,680m (58,000ft)	Sidewinder air-to-air missiles, or indigenously
Dimensions: span 8.22m (26ft 11.5in); length	produced AAMs such as the Shafrir or Python

▲ IAI Kfir

144 Sqn, Israeli AF / Hatzor, early 1980s

Developed on the basis of the Mirage 5, delivery of which had been embargoed, the Kfir was a further improvement on the indigenous Nesher, and first saw significant combat usage over Lebanon. The aircraft flew defensive missions, as well as prosecuting attacks against Syrian radar stations and other targets.

Israeli AF air supremacy. With the Israelis threatening to cut off the Syrian ground forces, the Syrian AF was called into action in a close support capacity.

The majority of the aerial fighting over Lebanon was recorded between 9-11 June, with F-16s frequently clashing with Syrian MiGs over Beirut. As well as the deployment of the advanced F-15 and F-16 fighters (the former armed with beyond-visual-range AAMs) the conflict was notable for the successful employment of remotely piloted vehicles (RPVs) for reconnaissance and targeting, and Israeli AF E-2Cs, which were operated in an airborne early

warning and control capacity. Anti-armour helicopters would also prove their worth, Israel fielding the Hughes 500MD and AH-1G/S, while Syria deployed armed Gazelles, Mi-8s and Mi-25s.

Under the sheer weight of numbers, and bolstered by superior weaponry and tactics, the Israelis were able to overcome PLO forces, despite stiff resistance. A ceasefire came into force on 11 June, but the Israeli strikes against the PLO continued for another day until both sides agreed to put an end to the fighting. Although the Syrians had enjoyed some success on the ground, Israeli victory in the air was undisputed.

Specifications

Crew: 5
Powerplant: 2 x 3800kW (5100hp) Allison T56-A-427 turboprop engines
Maximum speed: 604km/h (375mph)
Range: 2583km (1605 miles)
Service ceiling: 10,210m (33,500ft)

Dimensions: span 24.6m (80ft 7in); length 17.56m (57ft 7in); height 5.58m (18ft 4in)
Weight: 24,655kg (60,000lb) loaded
Armament: none

▲ Douglas A-4N Skyhawk II
Israeli AF / early 1980s
Israeli AF Skyhawks had first seen combat during the War of Attrition, and remained in service in 1982, examples including the improved A-4N version. The extended tailpipe was an Israeli modification that was designed to defeat heat-seeking SAMs. Nevertheless, at least two examples were lost over Lebanon.

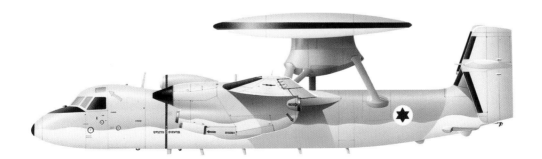

Specifications

Crew: 5
Powerplant: 2 x 3800kW (5096hp) Allison T56-A-425 or -427 turboprop
Maximum speed: 604km/h (375mph)
Range: 2583km (1605 miles)
Service ceiling: 9300m (30,800ft)

Dimensions: span 24.58m (80ft 7in); length 17.56m (57ft 7in); height 5.58m (18ft 4in)
Weight: 23,391kg (55,000lb) loaded
Armament: none

▲ Lockheed E-2C Hawkeye
Israeli AF / early 1980s
One of the decisive factors in the Israeli AF's aerial dominance over Lebanon was the presence of the E-2C. Carrying powerful surveillance radar, these were able to alert fighter assets of any incoming Syrian AF aircraft, and also coordinated defensive top cover (mainly F-15s and Kfirs) for Israeli offensive missions.

Chapter 6

Africa

In addition to a number of civil wars fought on the continent, the conflicts that afflicted Africa during the Cold War were typically colonial in origin. A result of the final break-up of empires after World War II, these conflicts frequently saw European powers attempt to extricate themselves from the continent in the face of local rebellion or insurgency. While well equipped Western powers clashed with rebel groups, the situation was made more complex by superpower rivalries, and attempts by eastern and western power blocs to influence politics on the African continent.

◀ **Aérospatiale SA 316B Alouette III**
Portuguese soldiers disembark from Alouette IIIs during operations in Mozambique. The 'Bush Wars' that afflicted Africa throughout the Cold War were typified by the use of helicopters to deliver troops across difficult terrain, and counter-insurgency tactics to put down guerrilla activity.

France in Algeria
1954–1962

In the early years of the Cold War France experienced the loss of its colonies in both Africa and Southeast Asia. In the former, Algeria's struggle for independence was most significant.

CONSIDERED PART OF metropolitan France, Algeria's Muslim community sought independence, while European settlers fought a civil war. In contrast to the former French colonies of Morocco and Tunisia, Algeria's road to independence would involve years of conflict, and French air power played an important role from the outset. Despite the involvement of over one million French troops, France failed to make a military breakthrough, and by 1958 a revolution was close. The fighting would continue until 1962, when Algerian independence was finally recognized.

The war broke out in 1954, with resistance from the Front de Libération Nationale (FLN) and its military Armée de Libération Nationale (ALN) wing. The French AF was initially unable to counter the guerrillas, with the only local combat aircraft being Mistral jets and F-47s. However, trainers were soon adapted for counter-insurgency (COIN) work.

France soon established a force of light COIN aircraft better able to tackle the insurrection. Closely integrated with the ground forces, three French AF tactical air groups (GATAC) were formed on a regional basis, conforming to Army deployment; the first light support squadrons became operational in 1955. Starting in 1956, squadrons (EALA) were reorganized within light aircraft groups (GALA), each assigned to a GATAC. A flexible, rapid-reaction force was created, with aircraft types including the M.S.500, M.S.733, the U.S.-supplied T-6, and SIPA S.111 and S.112. The major roles comprised ground support, reconnaissance and transport, and aircraft were also based in neighbouring Morocco and Tunisia. Light observation squadrons were fielded beginning in 1956, equipped with the Broussard, while French Army L-19s operated in a similar role.

In 1957-58 the French AF M.S.500 and M.S.733 were replaced by T-6s, while in 1959 the light aircraft groups were superseded by an *escadre/escadron* structure, and the light aircraft assets came under direct control of the GATAC, for increased flexibility. Improved COIN equipment then became available in the form of the T-28, which arrived in 1960, replacing the increasingly vulnerable T-6.

Specifications
Crew: 3
Powerplant: 2 x 1491kW (2000hp) Pratt & Whitney R-2800-79
Maximum speed: 571km/h (355mph)
Range: 2255km (1400 miles)
Service ceiling: 6735m (22,100ft)
Dimensions: span 21.30m (70ft); length 16.60m (51ft 3in); height 5.6m (18ft 6in)
Weight: 15,876kg (35,000lb) loaded
Armament: Various 12.7mm (0.50in) M2 Browning MGs and up to 2700kg (6000lb) bomb load

▲ **Douglas B-26C Invader**
EB 2/91, French AF / Oran, 1956–62
Among the 'heavy' offensive assets fielded by the French AF in Algeria was the B-26, deployed among bomber (B-26B/C/N) and reconnaissance units (RB-26P) based at Bone and Oran. EB 2/91 'Guyenne' was a bomber unit and served at Oran between 1956 and 1962.

Soon 26 light aircraft squadrons and three of liaison/observation aircraft were operational in Algeria, but arguably the most important development was France's use of military helicopters, deployed in their hundreds for assault transport and gunship missions. It was during the 250,000 (French AF) combat flying hours in Algeria that many of the initial tactics for rotary-winged warfare were developed. All three French armed forces deployed helicopters, primarily the Bell 47, H-21, S-55, S-58 and the Alouette II.

Helicopter war

Helicopters were active against the rebellion from the start, with a first French Army helicopter unit being established in 1954, and a first French AF unit following a year later. Capable of delivering commando raids or conducting casualty evacuation, observation and a range of other missions, the helicopters were ultimately used as an offensive tool against the ALN, armed with guns and rockets, as exemplified by the Pirate gunship conversion of the S-58. The arrival of this latter type in 1956 was critical in that it considerably increased troop-carrying capabilities and led to creation of French AF heavy helicopter *escadrons*. By late 1957 there were around 250 helicopters in Algeria, with all three services, including three active French AF escadres. Army strength included 32 flights by 1960, including 15 mixed units with helicopters and fixed-wing types.

After early French AF combat missions by the F-47, heavier fixed-wing assets appeared in the form of B-26s, deployed within two bomber groups. Almost certainly the most effective fixed-wing COIN type was, however, the AD-4, first joining EC 20 in early 1960. In many ways a template for later actions in Southeast Asia, the innovative use of air power in Algeria contained the rebels to an extent, but was not able to put an end to terrorist actions.

Morocco
1975–1989

After gaining independence from France in 1956, Morocco became involved in a long-running conflict fought against the Algerian-based guerrillas of the Polisario Front.

MOROCCO'S WAR AGAINST the Polisario Front began following the North African kingdom's annexation of the northern part of the former Spanish Sahara when the last Spanish colonial forces departed in early 1976. Mauritania occupied the southern part of the disputed area, and between them, the two nations took on the Polisario forces, which began attacking regular formations.

In July 1978 Mauritania signed a peace treaty and abandoned its claim to the territory, and Morocco was left to fight the guerrilla war alone, at this time with an air force that included F-5A jet fighters, RF-5As for reconnaissance, Magisters and C-130s. Early support was also provided by France, with French AF Jaguars involved in ground support missions, flown by EC 1/11 and EC 3/11 from Dakar in Senegal.

New combat aircraft equipment was soon ordered by Morocco, including Mirage F1s and Alpha Jets from France, and U.S.-supplied F-5Es and OV-10s.

Initially the U.S. was unwilling to allow its equipment to be used in the conflict zone, but attitudes changed when it became apparent to Washington that the Polisario Front was being supported by Algeria and Libya, two nations with pro-Soviet sympathies. The U.S. warplanes were delivered starting in 1981.

In its battle against the Polisario Front, the Royal Moroccan AF used its front-line aircraft for ground attack duties, with combat missions supported by CH-47 and AB.205 troop-transport helicopters. In a reflection of the improved weaponry available to the guerrillas, losses to man-portable SAMs began to be recorded in the early 1980s.

In late 1981 the conflict began to intensify, and Morocco increasingly struggled to finance its combat operations, despite funding from Saudi Arabia and military equipment received from both the U.S. and Israel. The construction of the Moroccan Wall in the mid-1980s finally led to a stalemate situation.

Specifications

Crew: 1-2

Powerplant: 1 x 1044kW (1400hp) Lycoming
T53-L-13B turboshaft

Maximum speed: 222km/h (138mph)

Range: 580km (360 miles)

Service ceiling: 4570m (15,000ft)

Dimensions: rotor diameter 14.63m (48ft);
length 12.69m (41ft 8in);
height 4.48m (14ft 8in)

Weight: 4309kg (9500lb) loaded

Armament: none

▲ **Agusta-Bell AB.205A**

Royal Moroccan AF / early 1980s

During the mid-1980s the Royal Moroccan AF operated 24 AB.205A helicopters, licence-built versions of the Bell 205 manufactured by Agusta in Italy. These were put to use in the campaign against the Polisario Front, conducting troop-transport missions in support of the larger CH-47s and fixed-wing C-130 airlifters.

Libya
1977–1986

Soon after assuming power in 1969, Libyan leader Muammar al-Gaddafi turned to the USSR for arms, and began to assume an increasingly belligerent stance on the world stage.

AFTER PROVIDING EGYPT with Mirage fighters during the Yom Kippur War, Libya turned on its former ally in July 1977, when a border dispute between Egypt and Libya escalated into a brief air war. After Libya began an artillery assault, Egyptian AF MiG-21s and Su-20s attacked Libyan radar sites, and ground-based air defences claimed a Libyan MiG and a Mirage. Fighting continued for some days, during which time the Egyptian AF bombed the Libyan airbase at El Adem and Libyan warplanes attacked Egyptian border settlements.

U.S. Navy involvement

After the action against Egypt, and intervention in regional conflicts in Uganda and Chad, Libya took on the might of the U.S. Navy. Behind this move was Libya's claim to the entire Gulf of Sidra as territorial waters. This was enforced through regular air patrols and harassment of U.S. Navy Sixth Fleet aircraft and

warships. Events came to a head in August 1981 when a pair of Libyan AF Su-22s were shot down by U.S. Navy F-14As from the carrier USS *Nimitz*.

Hostility between Libya and the U.S. increased, particularly because of Libya's sponsorship of terrorist acts by the PLO and other groups. Relations became especially strained in March 1986, when a number of Libyan SAMs were fired at U.S. Navy aircraft after a pair of F-14s turned away an intercepting Libyan AF MiG-25. In response, A-7Es from USS *Saratoga* launched anti-radar missiles against Libyan SAM sites. A-6Es from the USS *America* and *Saratoga* then sunk three Libyan patrol craft.

The April 1986 bombing of a discotheque in West Berlin was the trigger for the U.S. to launch a large-scale air offensive against Libya. This was spearheaded by USAF F-111s flying from bases in England, together with tanker support. Intelligence-gathering prior to the raids was conducted by USAF RC-135s

Specifications

Crew: 4

Powerplant: 2 x 2535kW (3400hp) General
Electric T64-GE-P4D turboprops

Maximum speed: 540km/h (336mph)

Range: 1371km (852 miles)

Service ceiling: 7620m (25,000ft)

Dimensions: span 28.70m (94ft 2in);
length 22.7m (74ft 6in); height 9.8m
(32ft 2in)

Weight: 28,000kg (61,730lb) loaded

Armament: none

▲ Aeritalia G.222

Libyan AF / early 1980s

Although Libya was a major customer of Soviet aircraft during the 1970s and 1980s, the country's oil wealth enabled it to purchase equipment from France and Italy, too. Mk 82 227-kg (500-lb) conventional bombs dropped by USAF F-111Fs destroyed at least one Italian-supplied G222 transport on the ground at Tripoli.

and by U.S Navy EP-3Es and EA-3Bs, while targets were reconnoitred by SR-71As, U-2Rs and TR-1As.

The 18-strong force of F-111Fs (plus six support aircraft) left the UK on the evening of 15 April, supported by EF-111A jamming aircraft. The plan, codenamed El Dorado Canyon, involved a joint USAF/U.S. Navy strike on targets that included Tripoli airport, Benina airbase, plus various training facilities, military barracks and command centres. U.S. Navy strike aircraft were launched by the carriers USS *Coral Sea* and *America*, and offensive assets comprised F/A-18s, A-6Es and A-7Es, supported by EA-6B jamming aircraft. For the loss of one F-111, the U.S. air arms claimed the destruction or damage of numerous Libyan aircraft and helicopters on the ground, and the operation was judged a success.

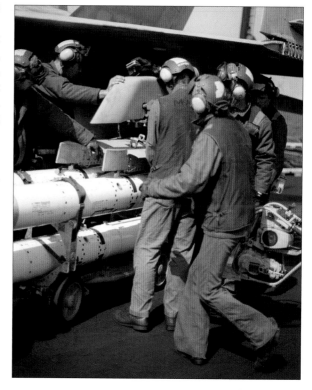

▲ F/A-18 Hornet

The U.S. attacks on Libya in 1986 marked the combat debut of the U.S Navy's F/A-18 Hornet attack fighter, launched from the USS *Coral Sea*. Here, aviation ordnancemen load AGM-88 missiles on one of the carrier's VFA-131 Hornets.

Aircraft	Unit	Base
F-111F	48 TFW	RAF Lakenheath
EF-111A	42 ECS	RAF Upper Heyford
U-2R, TR-1A	9 SRS (Det)	RAF Akrotiri
SR-71A	9 SRW (Det)	RAF Mildenhall
KC-10A	various units	RAF Mildenhall, RAF Fairford
KC-135A/E/Q	various units	RAF Mildenhall, RAF Fairford

USAF, LIBYA, 1986

Chad
1968–1987

Soon after it had gained independence from France in 1960, Chad began to be beset by internal strife, and the situation intensified when Libya intervened in the civil war in 1980.

AFTER ITS INDEPENDENCE, A French military presence remained in Chad in order to help the Christian administration counter Islamic anti-government rebels. Staring in 1968 French AF AD-4s were stationed N'Djamena, and within a year these COIN assets were supported by French military transports and helicopters. As the rebel offensive intensified, and threatened N'Djamena, additional French ground forces were deployed.

With the AD-4s flying numerous close support sorties, the French succeeded in pushing the rebels back to isolated pockets of resistance. In 1973 Libya intervened by taking control of the disputed Aouzou region in the north of Chad, and continued to provide support to the rebels. A French military presence remained in Chad in order to help preserve security until a military coup in 1975. After the last French troops left in October 1975, a handful of AD-4s were turned over for use by Chad for anti-guerrilla work in support of the now Muslim-led government.

The French military returned to Chad in April 1978, with Jaguars being deployed between April 1978 and January 1980 in support of a French Army presence. At least four Jaguars were lost during operations before the French departed again in mid-1980. By this stage it was apparent that the ceasefire between government and guerrilla forces could no longer be effectively enforced.

Libya strikes

Libya then intervened more directly in the civil war. In 1980, large numbers of Libyan troops were sent to Chad, and in October of that year Libyan AF Tu-22s bombed anti-government Forces Armées du Nord (FAN) rebel positions near N'Djamena. However, the most widely used Libyan AF type was the turboprop-powered SF.260W COIN aircraft.

International pressure prevented Libya from annexing Chad, and Libyan forces were encouraged to depart the country in late 1981. The presence of an African peacekeeping force thereafter was not enough to prevent FAN forces taking power in Chad. Libya then joined the ousted government forces, which had assembled in the north of the country, to wage a counter-attack. The Libyan AF employed MiG-23s, Su-22s and SF.260Ws in an operation

▲ **Dassault Mirage 5M**

21 Wing, Zairean AF / Kamina/N'Djamena, 1981–83

In addition to air power from Chad, France and Libya, the air force of Zaire was active during the fighting in Chad in the early 1980s. Initially deployed in support of the African peacekeeping force in Chad, Zairean AF Mirages and close-support M.B.326s were active against Libyan-backed rebels through much of the 1980s.

Specifications

Crew: 1	Service ceiling: 16,093m (52,800ft)
Powerplant: 1 x 58.72kN (13,200lb) thrust	Dimensions: span 8.26m (27ft 2in); length
SNECMA Atar 09C afterburning turbojet	15.65m (51ft 4in); height 4.51m (14ft 10in)
engine	Weight: 13,671kg (30,140lb) loaded
Maximum speed: 2350km/h (1460mph)	Armament: 2 x 30mm DEFA 552A cannon;
Range: 1307km (812 miles)	various AAMs, up to 3991kg (8800lb) of bombs

from June 1983, with aircraft forward deployed in Aouzou. The Libyan assault, which also involved the use of Mirage fighter-bombers and Mi-25 helicopter gunships, eventually forced the anti-government guerrillas to agree to a ceasefire and withdrawal.

A mutual treaty meant that France was compelled to intervene in support of Chad, and ground-attack Jaguars and air defence Mirage F1s went into action, again flying from N'Djamena, and supplemented by Puma and Gazelle helicopters. Additional support was provided by Zaire, with Mirage 5s and M.B.326s, while the U.S. delivered man-portable SAMs. Libyan AF attacks were halted as a result, but the Libyan-supported rebels remained in control of the north of the country, under an uneasy stalemate.

In autumn 1984 France and Libya agreed to withdraw from Chad, but hostilities resumed in 1986 with a new Libyan-backed rebel offensive and French air strikes against the Libyan base at Ouadi Doum. In response, Libyan air sorties were stepped up, with Tu-22 raids against N'Djamena. Finally in August 1987 government forces briefly held Aouzou before Chad attacked Libyan AF bases. A ceasefire was signed, and a stabilizing French AF presence remained in Chad.

FRENCH AF/FRENCH NAVAL AIR ARM/FRENCH ARMY, CHAD, 1968–88		
Aircraft	Unit	Base
AD-4 Skyraider	EAA 1/21	N'Djamena
AD-4 Skyraider	EAA 1/22	N'Djamena
Noratlas, Alouette II, Broussard	GMT 59	N'Djamena, Mongo
H-34	DPH 2/67	N'Djamena
Jaguar A/E	EC 11	N'Djamena, Bangui, Libreville
Jaguar A	EC 7	Bangui
Noratlas, Alouette II	ETOM 55	N'Djamena
Mirage F1C	EC 5	N'Djamena, Bangui
Mirage F1CR	ER 33	N'Djamena, Bangui
C.160NG Transall	ET 1/63	N'Djamena, Bangui
KC-135F	ERV 93	N'Djamena, Bangui
Atlantique	22F	N'Djamena, Bangui, Dakar
Gazelle	1 RHC	N'Djamena, Abeche
Gazelle	2 RHC	N'Djamena, Abeche
Puma	5 RHC	N'Djamena, Abeche

Portugal in Africa
1959–1975

Three Portuguese colonies in Africa – Angola, Mozambique and Portuguese Guinea – all waged campaigns for independence, during which major use was made of Portuguese air power.

FIRST OF PORTUGAL'S surviving African colonies to take up arms against its colonial occupier was Portuguese Guinea. In Portuguese Guinea, as in Angola and Mozambique, the Portuguese AF was widely used in the COIN role. The rebellion in Portuguese Guinea began in August 1959, at which time only a small number of Portuguese AF T-6s were available, although these were followed by F-84Gs from 1963. As rebel activity escalated, the Portuguese AF presence was strengthened from 1967, with the arrival of the first G.91s. The jungle and swamp typical of the country made operations especially difficult, although these problems were countered to an extent by the arrival of Alouette III helicopters

starting in 1968. The Portuguese military began to take a harder line from 1970, with extensive use of napalm and defoliants, with the rebels now receiving support from Nigerian AF MiG-17s based at Conakry, which were used for reconnaissance, as well as Soviet-supplied Mi-4 helicopters for transport. The rebels claimed 21 aircraft shot down in seven years, using man-portable SAMs and anti-aircraft artillery (AAA). Independence was declared by the rebels in 1973, before the Portuguese military coup in Lisbon saw independence granted in September 1974.

While Portugal became entrenched in a COIN campaign in Portuguese Guinea, trouble flared in Angola where the Movimento Popular de Libertação

Specifications

Crew: 2-6

Powerplant: 2 x 1490kW (2000hp) Pratt &
  Whitney R-2800-31 air-cooled radial engines

Maximum speed: 454km/h (282mph)

Range: 2880km (1790 miles)

Service ceiling: 7285m (23,900ft)

Dimensions: span 22.86m (75ft 0in);
  length 15.87m (52ft 1in); height 4.04m
  (13ft 3in)

Weight: 15,271kg (33,668lb) loaded

Armament: three fixed 0.50-inch machine
  guns, Eight 127mm (5in) HVAR rockets,
  1814kg (4000lb) bomb load

▲ Lockheed PV-2 Harpoon

Esq 91, Portuguese AF / BA9 (Luanda), 1962

The PV-2 played an important role early on in Angola's colonial conflicts in Africa, when dedicated COIN equipment was at a premium. This example of the veteran Lockheed design served at BA9 (Luanda) in Angola during 1962. Outfitted for bombing, the PV-2s were among the first combat aircraft available in Angola.

Specifications

Crew: 1

Powerplant: 1 x 24.7kN (5560lbf) Allison J35-
  A-29 turbojet

Maximum speed: 1000km/h (622mph)

Range: 1600km (1000 miles)

Service ceiling: 12,344m (40,500ft)

Dimensions: span 11.1m (36ft 5in); length
  11.6m (38ft 1in); height 3.84m (12ft 7in)

Weight: 8,200kg (18,080lb) loaded

Armament: 6 x 12.7mm (.50in) M3 Browning
  MGs, and up to 2020kg (4450lb) of rockets
  and bombs

▲ Republic F-84G Thunderjet

Esq 93, Portuguese AF / BA9 (Luanda), early 1960s

The F-84G saw action in Angola in the ground support role, although a number of losses were sustained – primarily due to operational accidents, which claimed at least five examples during the first three years of operations in Angola. Typical weapons for the Thunderjet included fragmentation bombs and napalm.

Specifications

Crew: 2

Powerplant: 1 x 450kW (600hp) Pratt &
  Whitney R-1340-AN-1 Wasp radial engine

Maximum speed: 335km/h (208mph)

Range: 1175km (730 miles)

Service ceiling: 7400m (24,200ft)

Dimensions: span 12.81m (42ft);
  length 8.84m (29ft); height 3.57m (11ft 8in)

Weight: 2548kg (5617lb) loaded

Armament: up to 3 x 7.62mm (.30in) MG, plus
  light bombs and rockets

▲ North American T-6G Texan

Portuguese AF / Sintra, Portugal

A widely used COIN type, the T-6G served in numerous post-colonial conflicts during the Cold War. This example was operated from Sintra, Portugal, but Portuguese AF Texans saw action in Guinea, Angola and Mozambique. The type proved well suited to attacks on guerrilla forces, using light bombs and rockets.

▲ Fiat G.91R/4

Esq 121, Portuguese AF / BA12 (Bissalanca), 1967-74

The most potent ground attack aircraft deployed by Portugal in Africa was the Fiat G.91R/4, which served in Portuguese Guinea, Angola and Mozambique. Esq 121 flew from BA12 Bissalanca in Portuguese Guinea, and was equipped with G.91s supplied by West Germany. Three examples fell to SAMs in spring 1973.

Specifications

Crew: 1

Powerplant: 1 x 22.2kN (5000lbf) Bristol-
Siddeley Orpheus 803 turbojet

Maximum speed: 1075km/h (668mph)

Range: 1150km (715 miles)

Service ceiling: 13,100m (43,000ft)

Dimensions: span 8.56m (28ft 1in);
length 10.3m (33ft 9in); height 4m (13ft 1in)

Weight: 5440kg (11,990lb) loaded

Armament: 4 x 12.7mm (0.5in M2 Browning
MGs, provision to carry up to 1814kg (4000lb)
bomb payload

▲ Aérospatiale Alouette III

Esq 121, Portuguese AF / BA12 (Bissalanca), 1971

Workhorse of the Portuguese military in its African colonial campaigns was the Alouette III. This example was based at BA12 Bissalanca in 1971, and was used to transport troops during operations against insurgents in Guinea-Bissau. The first 12 examples of the helicopter arrived in Guinea in 1969.

Specifications

Crew: 2

Powerplant: 1 x 649kW (870hp) Turbomeca
Artouste IIIB turboshaft

Maximum speed: 220km/h (137mph)

Range: 604km (375 miles)

Service ceiling: 3200m (10,500ft)

Dimensions: rotor diameter 11.02m (36ft 2in);
length 10.03m (32ft 11in);
height 3m (9ft 10in)

Weight: 2200kg (4950lb) loaded

Armament: 20mm cannons, carried in the rear
cabin and fired over the side

de Angola (MPLA) became increasingly active, and the local Portuguese Army units struggled to contain the rebellion. The Portuguese AF deployed PV-2s and C-47s to Luanda. These were supported by impressed civilian aircraft types used as transports to resupply military outposts, with DC-3s and Beech 18s converted into makeshift bombers.

Jets over Angola

F-84Gs were available to the Portuguese AF in Angola starting in June 1961, although these suffered a number of losses, mainly through accidents. In order to relieve besieged towns, paratroops were delivered by C-47, and later Noratlas. Despite a U.S. arms embargo, Portugal managed to obtain a number of B-26s, which were used to strike MPLA targets, supported by F-84Gs, T-6s and Do 27s.

As the USSR provided increasing support to the MPLA, from 1966 Portugal faced another insurgent group, União Nacional para a Independência Total de Angola (UNITA). Portuguese AF aircraft waged a constant COIN campaign. In both Angola and Guinea, as it had with the French in Algeria, the T-6 bore the brunt of anti-guerrilla operations.

With MPLA forces advancing towards the west, the Portuguese AF stationed G.91s in Angola from

▲ **Dornier Do 27A-4**

Portuguese AF

During the Portuguese operations in Angola, Do 27 liaison aircraft were operated from BA9 (Luanda), AB3 (Negage) and AB4 (Henriques de Carvalho), and were flown alongside Austers. Do 27s were also flown on COIN sorties, and an example was the first aircraft claimed shot down by the MPLA, in June 1967.

Specifications

Crew: 1-2

Powerplant: 1 x 201kW (270hp) Lycoming GO-480-B1A6 6-cylinder piston engine

Maximum speed: 232km/h (144mph)

Range: 1100km (684 miles)

Service ceiling: 3353m (11,000ft)

Dimensions: span 12m (39ft 4in); length 9.60m (31ft 5in); height 3.5m (11ft)

Weight: 1850kg (4079lb) loaded

Armament: none

PORTUGUESE AF, ANGOLA, 1961–75		
Aircraft	**Unit**	**Base**
G.91R/4	Esq 93	BA9
PV-2, B-26B/C	Esq 91	Luanda, BA9
T-6G	Esq 501	Luanda, Nacala
DC-6A/B, 707	Gr. Trans.	Lisbon
C-54, Noratlas	Esq 92	BA9, Maguela, BA4
C-47, Beech 18	Esq 801	Lorenco Marques
Auster, Do 27	n/a	BA9, AB3, AB4
Alouette II/III, Puma	Esq 94	BA9, Gago, Cuito and others

PORTUGUESE AF, MOZAMBIQUE, 1962–75		
Aircraft	**Unit**	**Base**
G.91R/4	Esq 502	Nacala
G.91R/4	Esq 702	Tete
PV-2, T-6G	Esq 101	Beira
T-6G, C-47, PV-2, Alouette III	BA10	Beira
T-6G, Auster, Do 27, Alouette III	AB5	Nacala, Mueda, Porto Amelia
T-6G, Auster, Do 27	AB6	Nova Freixo
T-6G, Auster, Do 27, Alouette III	AB7	Tete
Noratlas	Esq Trans	Beira
C-47	Esq 801	Lourenço Marques

PORTUGUESE AF, PORTUGUESE GUINEA, 1963–74		
Aircraft	**Unit**	**Base**
G.91R/4	Esq 121	Bissalanca
T-6G	n/a	Bissalanca
Do 27	Esq 121	Bissalanca
Noratlas	Esq 123	Bissalanca
Alouette III	Esq 122	Bissalanca

1972, while helicopters began to be used increasingly for troop transport. Angola was finally granted independence in November 1975, bringing Portugal's African operations to a close.

In Mozambique the Portuguese faced resistance from Frente da Libertação de Moçambique (FRELIMO) starting in 1962. As in Angola, the Portuguese AF in Mozambique was initially equipped only with C-47s and T-6s when major fighting began in 1964. Before long, troop numbers increased to 16,000, backed by further T-6s, PV-2s, Do 27s and Alouette IIIs. FRELIMO was operating from bases in Tanzania and Zambia, and eventually the Portuguese AF commitment in Mozambique was larger than that in either Angola or Guinea. Major air operations took place beginning in 1968, with FRELIMO increasing the intensity of its own campaign from 1970. With Portuguese forces struggling to make an impact, the G.91s returned home in 1974, before Mozambique was granted independence in June 1975.

Nigeria
1967–1970

Granted independence in 1960, Nigeria remained relatively peaceful until 1966, when the federal government collapsed, and the country descended into bloodshed.

AFTER MASSACRES OF the Ibom people in the north of the country, the military authorities in the east – homeland of the Ibo tribe – declared independence in turn in 1961. The result was brutal civil war fought between the federal government and the newly created state of Biafra. Initial equipment for the Nigerian AF was primarily supplied by the Eastern Bloc, and use was made of contract aircrew. These maintained a bombing campaign of Biafran villages in which, between May and October 1968, around 3000 people were killed.

Rebel air wing

In contrast, the Biafran air arm maintained an assortment of impressed, generally obsolete civilian aircraft that were mainly flown by mercenary pilots. The most potent aircraft available in 1967 included a pair of B-26s that were used in a daring raid on a Nigerian destroyer at Port Harcourt. More effective equipment arrived in the form of MFI-9B Minicoin light aircraft equipped with rockets for COIN work, and flown against the federal forces by mercenaries

including the Swedish Count Gustav von Rosen. The Minicoins were used primarily for attacks against the Nigerian oil industry, causing some damage.

The civil war ended in January 1970 with the collapse of the Biafran regime, and as a result its leader, Colonel Ojukwu, fled to Ivory Coast.

NIGERIAN AF, 1967–70	
Aircraft	**Base**
Il-28	Port Harcourt, Calabar, Benin City
MiG-17	Benin City, Lagos, Enugu, Kaduna, Port Harcourt
Jet Provost	Lagos, Benin City
L-29	Benin City, Kaduna
DC-3	Benin City
DC-4, Noratlas	Benin City, Lagos
Do 28	Benin City
Do 27	Benin City, Kaduna, Kano
Azec	Benin City
Whirlwind 2/3	Kaduna

▲ **Ilyushin-28**

Nigerian AF / Port Harcourt/Calabar/Benin City, 1967-70

Nigeria received six Il-28 bombers from Algeria and Egypt for use during the Biafran War of 1967-69. These were flown by Egyptian, mercenary and Nigerian pilots and were used to bomb Biafran villages. At least three Il-28s were claimed damaged or destroyed on the ground by the fleet of Biafran Minicoins.

Specifications

Crew: 3
Powerplant: 2 x 26.3kN (5952lb) Klimov VK-1 turbojets
Maximum speed: 902km/h (560mph)
Range: 2180km (1355 miles)
Service ceiling: 12,300m (40,355ft)
Dimensions: span 21.45m (70ft 4in); length

17.65m (57ft 10.75in); height 6.7m (21ft 11.8in)
Weight: 21,200kg (46,738lb) loaded
Armament: 4 x 23mm cannon; internal bomb capacity 1000kg (2205lb), maximum bomb capacity 3000kg (6614lb); torpedo version: provision for two 400mm light torpedoes

Specifications

Crew: 4

Powerplant: 4 x 2610kW (3500hp) Pratt &
  Whitney R-4360B Wasp Major radial engines

Maximum speed: 603km/h (375mph)

Range: 6920km (4300 miles)

Service ceiling: 10,670m (35,000ft)

Dimensions: span 43.1m (41ft 3in);
  length 33.7m (110ft 4in); height 11.7m
  (38ft 3in)

Weight: 54,420kg (120,000lb) loaded

Armament: none

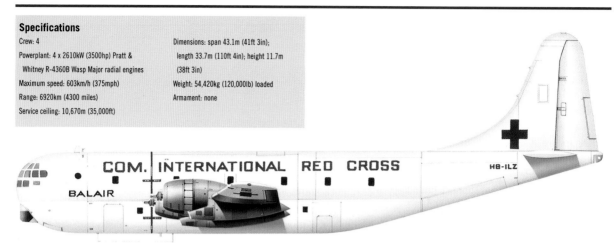

▲ **Boeing C-97G**

International Red Cross, Biafra, 1969–70

HB-ILZ, an ex-USAF C-97G, was one of three examples that were wet-leased to the International Red Cross in 1969-70 for relief missions to war-torn Biafra. Military equipment, including the aerial refuelling installation and underwing tank/jet pylons, was removed for humanitarian operations.

Congo
1960–1963

With little in the way of preparation, Belgium granted Congo independence in 1960 and the country was quickly sucked into a tribal civil war that would continue for seven years.

WHILE BELGIAN SETTLERS were subject to attack, a secessionist movement attempted to separate the Katanga region from the Congo Republic. The UN formulated a charter that established a peacekeeping force in the Congo, and air support was eventually provided by Canada, Ethiopia, India, Italy and Sweden. Among the most effective aircraft deployed by the Organization Nations-Unies au Congo

▲ **English Electric Canberra B(I).Mk 58**

Indian AF/ONUC / Luluabourg, 1961-62

Wearing ONUC titles, this Indian Canberra bomber-intruder was part of a small detachment of the type that was based at Luluabourg between 1961-62. While the Swedish AF Saab 29 excelled, the Canberra was found ill suited to low-level strike in the Congo, but still conducted a number of night raids against Elisabethville.

Specifications

Crew: 2

Powerplant: 2 x 28.9kN (6500lb) Rolls-Royce
  Avon Mk 101 turbojets

Maximum speed: 917km/h (570mph)

Range: 4274km (2656 miles)

Service ceiling: 14,630m (48,000ft)

Dimensions: span 29.49m (63ft 11in); length
  19.96m (65ft 6in); height 4.78m (15ft 8in)

Weight: 24,925kg (54,950lb) loaded

Armament: bomb bay with provision for up to
  2727kg (6000lb) of bombs, plus 909kg
  (2000lb) of underwing pylons

(ONUC) were volunteer-flown Swedish AF Saab 29 jets, armed with guns and rockets for ground attack against the Katangan separatists, but also used for reconnaissance (in the form of the S29C). These operated from 1961-63 and took part in surprise December 1962 and January 1963 raids on Kolwezi that succeeded in destroying most of the fledgling Katangan air arm on the ground.

The country, now known as Zaire, saw a further attempt at Katangan secession in 1977-78, leading to French and Moroccan military intervention, as well as the use of Zairean AF Mirage IIIs and M.B.326s.

ONUC, 1960–64		
Aircraft	Unit	Base
Canberra B(I). Mk 58	5 Sqn, Indian AF	Kamina
J29B, S29C	F22, Swedish AF	Luluabourg, Kamina
F-86F	Ethiopian AF	Luluabourg, Kamina
Sabre Mk 4	4 Aerobrigata, Italian AF	Leopoldville
C-119G	46 Aerobrigata, Italian AF	Leopoldville, Kamina

Rhodesia
1965–1979

When Ian Smith's white minority regime declared unilateral independence from Britain in 1965, an economic blockade was the result, involving the RAF and British aircraft carriers.

THE BLOCKADE AGAINST Rhodesia was imposed by the UN and involved RAF Shackletons based in Madagascar, as well as Royal Navy carriers. At the time, the Royal Rhodesian AF was spearheaded by Hunters and Canberras, but the measures against Rhodesia remained ecomomic rather than military.

After the blockade the Rhodesian AF was increasingly involved in fighting guerrillas both inside Rhodesia and outside its borders. Early tasks included air supply, patrol and reconnaissance, and a number of AL.60 transports were received by covert means in 1967. A republic was declared in 1969, and in 1972

▲ **Percival Provost T.Mk 52**

4 Sqn, Royal Rhodesian AF / Thornhill, mid-1960s

Operated in the mid-1960s, this Provost wears the insignia used before Rhodesia's declaration of unilateral independence. Among the first actions after the declaration of UDI saw Provosts relocate to form detachments at Wankie and Kariba, in order to defend against attacks by the insurgents.

Specifications

Crew: 2

Powerplant: 1 x 410kW (550hp) Alvis Leonides 126 9-cylinder radial engine

Maximum speed: 320km/h (200mph)

Range: 1020km (650 miles)

Service ceiling: 7620m (25,000ft)

Dimensions: span 10.7m (35ft 0in); length 8.73m (28ft 6in); height 3.70m (12ft 0in)

Weight: 1995kg (4399lb) loaded

Armament: no fixed armament

Rhodesia began to be infiltrated by groups based in Botswana, Mozambique and Zambia. Air power was used to counter the guerrillas, with airborne landings, commando raids and air strikes by Canberras and Hunters against terrorist bases. From 1976 new COIN types were deployed, including the Reims-Cessna 337 Lynx, Alouette III and SF.260W. Despite sanctions, Rhodesian kept up its COIN offensive until 1979, when an internal settlement was reached on majority rule and Rhodesia became Zimbabwe.

ROYAL RHODESIAN AF, 1965		
Aircraft	Unit	Base
Canberra B.Mk 2	5 Sqn	New Sarum
Hunter FGA.Mk 9	1 Sqn	Thornhill
Vampire FB.Mk 9	2 Sqn	Thornhill
Provost T.Mk 52	4 Sqn	Thornhill
C-47	3 Sqn	New Sarum
Alouette II	7 Sqn	New Sarum

▲ **English Electric Canberra B.Mk 2**

5 Sqn, Rhodesian AF / New Sarum, 1970

This Canberra was used for long-range bombing and reconnaissance missions against guerrilla groups, attacking targets within Rhodesia as well as in Angola, Botswana, Mozambique and Zambia. Two Rhodesian Canberras were lost during operations over Mozambique.

Specifications

Crew: 2

Powerplant: 2 x 28.9kN (6500lb) Rolls-Royce
Avon Mk 101 turbojets

Maximum speed: 917km/h (570mph)

Range: 4274km (2656 miles)

Service ceiling: 14,630m (48,000ft)

Dimensions: span 29.49m (63ft 11in); length
19.96m (65ft 6in); height 4.78m (15ft 8in)

Weight: 24,925kg (54,950lb) loaded

Armament: bomb bay with provision for up to
2727kg (6000lb) of bombs, plus 909kg
(2000lb) of underwing pylons

South Africa
1961–1988

Ostracized by the international community, apartheid South Africa faced cross-border attacks for over two decades, and air power was used widely in order to put down hostile guerrillas.

ULTIMATELY ABLE TO strike well beyond South Africa's borders from the air, and over land, the COIN forces of the South African military were the best equipped in Africa, their capabilities resting in a powerful indigenous arms industry and covert cooperation with foreign powers including Israel.

South Africa left the British Commonwealth in 1961 after which the UN imposed sanctions. These were counter-productive, hardening white South African resolve against Marxist-leaning neighbours and guerrillas. From the early 1960s, South Africa's armed forces were used to prevent infiltration from

across the northern borders with Angola, Botswana, Mozambique, Zambia and Zimbabwe. Prior to sanctions, South Africa had received warplanes from the UK, including Canberras and Buccaneers. These were later complemented by French Mirage IIIs and F1s, together with licence-built Impalas for COIN work, the latter based on the Italian M.B.326.

SWAPO standoff

From autumn 1965 the nationalist South West African People's Organization (SWAPO) group infiltrated Namibia, which was illegally administered by South Africa. SWAPO waged its war against South Africa from bases in Angola and Zambia, and these were targets for South African forces. A low-intensity COIN campaign was fought in Namibia throughout the 1960s and 1970s, before South Africa's cross-border campaign saw SWAPO forces pursued deep into neighbouring countries.

After 1975 Angola became the main base for anti-South African groups disputing control of Namibia. Within Angola the pro-western Frente Nacional da Libertação de Angola (FNLA) and UNITA (itself recipient of South African arms) fought the Marxist

MPLA in a civil war that commenced after Angolan independence. This ultimately pitched large numbers of Cuban troops against South African forces.

By spring 1976 most of Angola was controlled by the MPLA, and the South African AF responded by deploying aircraft to bases in northwestern South Africa. As the MPLA – supported by the Soviet-equipped Angolan AF – stepped up its campaign against the FNLA, fighting crossed over into South Africa. Between 1974 and 1987 South Africa mounted commando raids and air strikes against MPLA strongholds, and air combat pitched South

Specifications

Crew: 1	Dimensions: span 11.58m (38ft);
Powerplant: 1 x 32.35kW (7275lb) Avro Orenda	length 11.58m (38ft); height 4.57m (15ft)
Mark 14 engine	Weight: 6628kg (14.613lb) loaded
Maximum speed: 975km/h (606mph)	Armament: 6 x 12.7mm (0.50in) M2 Browning
Range: n/a	machine guns; 2 x AIM-9 missiles; 2400kg
Service ceiling: 15,450m (50,700ft)	(5300lb) of payload

▲ Canadair Sabre Mk 6

1 Sqn, South African AF / Pietersburg, 1970s

When the South African AF first became involved in the campaign against insurgents in neighbouring countries, the Sabre Mk 6 remained in use, primarily in the air defence role. 1 Sqn flew the fighter from Waterkloof between 1956 and 1967, before moving to Pietersburg, where the type was flown until 1975.

▲ Aérospatial Alouette III

South African AF / early 1980s

The Alouette III was used throughout South Africa's 'Bush War' beginning with the first attack against SWAPO camps in northern Namibia in August 1966, when the helicopters delivered South African security forces during a raid on a camp in Ovamboland. At least three squadrons operated the Alouette III.

Specifications

Crew: 2	Dimensions: rotor diameter 11.02m (36ft 2in);
Powerplant: 1 x 649kW (870hp) Turbomeca	length 10.03m (32ft 11in); height 3m
Artouste IIIB turboshaft	(9ft 10in)
Maximum speed: 220km/h (137mph)	Weight: 2200kg (4950lb) loaded
Range: 604km (375 miles)	Armament: 20mm cannons, carried in the rear
Service ceiling: 3200m (10,500ft)	cabin and fired over the side

SOUTH AFRICAN AF, FIGHTER/BOMBER UNITS, 1966–88		
Aircraft	**Unit**	**Base**
Buccaneer S.Mk 50	24 Sqn	Waterkloof
Canberra B(I).Mk 12	12 Sqn	Waterkloof
Sabre Mk 6, Impala I, Mirage F1AZ/CZ	1 Sqn	Waterkloof, Pietersburg, Hoedspruit
Mirage F1CZ	3 Sqn	Waterkloof
Mirage IIIAZ/BZ/CZ/DZ/RZ	2 Sqn	Waterkloof
Mirage IIIDZ/EZ, Impala II	85 AFS	Pietersburg

African AF jets against Angolan fighters and helicopters. Supply of Soviet SAMs and AAA to the SWAPO provided a particular hazard.

Major South African AF pre-emptive operations took place in the early 1980s, with deep penetrations into Angola involving Buccaneers, Canberras, Mirages and Impalas in combined arms offensives. After the departure of Cuban troops from Angola, South African forces left Namibia in 1988, and Namibia itself was in turn granted independence.

▲ Atlas AM.3C Bosbok

42 Sqn, South African AF / Potchefstroom, early 1980s

Locally built under Italian licence, the Atlas Bosbok (based on the Aermacchi AM.3C) and the closely related Kudu single-engined types were used for light transport and liaison tasks respectively. The South African AF also used the Bosbok for forward air control and casualty evacuation duties.

Specifications

Crew: 2

Powerplant: 1x 236kW (340hp) Lycoming GSO-480-B1B6 piston engine

Maximum speed: 278km/h (173mph)

Range: 990km (619 miles)

Service ceiling: 2440m (8000ft)

Dimensions: span 11.73m (38ft 6in); length 8.73m (28ft 8in); height 2.72m (8ft 11in)

Weight: 1500kg (3300lb) loaded

Armament: Up to 2 machine gun pods, up to 4 smoke-rocket pods and up to 170kg (375lb) bombs

▲ Atlas C4M Kudu

41 Sqn, South African AF / Swartkop/Lanseria, early 1980s

The robust Kudu short take-off and landing (STOL) transport was used widely from unprepared strips in support of ground forces through the provision of air-dropping, medical evacuation and the delivery of small teams of troops. The South African AF received 40 Kudus up to 1979, for use with two front-line squadrons.

Specifications

Crew: 1

Powerplant: 1 x 253kW (340hp) Avco Lycoming GSO-480-B1B3

Maximum speed: 260km/h (161mph)

Range: 1297km (806 miles)

Service ceiling: n/a

Dimensions: span 13.08m (42ft 9in); length 9.31m (30ft 5in); height 3.66m (12ft)

Weight: 2040kg (4498lb) loaded

Armament: None

Kenya
1952–1955

Kenya, a former British colony, saw a rebellion in the Kikuyu province, which was mercilessly suppressed by the UK, with 11,000 Mau Mau casualties recorded in a period between 1952-55.

THE REMOVAL OF the leader of the Kenya African Union in 1952 did not put an end to the Kikuyu uprising, and Britain declared an emergency. Suspected tribal leaders were arrested, together with Kikuyu radicals, and the rebels, known as the Mau Mau, began to be relentlessly pursued.

Starting in April 1953 air power was used in a large-scale COIN campaign, with an initial group of RAF Harvards being forward deployed from Rhodesia. Used for ground attack, the Harvards completed 2000 sorties in a year. In November 1953 heavy bombers arrived in the form of Lincolns, which operated from Eastleigh on three-month rotations. Normally based at Khormaksar, Aden, a small number of Vampire fighter-bombers were provided by the RAF's Middle East Air Force, together with photo-reconnaissance Meteors.

Rebellion suppressed

Aided by Austers, Pembrokes and Valettas – plus Sycamore helicopters – used in support of forces on the ground, the RAF helped to put an end to the rebellion by 1955. However, the true results of the military operations cannot be easily calculated, since there was very little means of effectively discriminating between Mau Mau rebel and innocent local, and certain British Army commanders were reported to offer bounty money for dead Mau Mau.

After becoming independent within the Commonwealth, Kenya became a republic in 1965.

RAF, KENYA, 1952–56		
Aircraft	**Unit**	**Base**
Lincoln B.Mk 2	21 Sqn	Eastleigh2
Lincoln B.Mk 2	49 Sqn	Eastleigh
Lincoln B.Mk 2	61 Sqn	Eastleigh
Lincoln B.Mk 2	100 Sqn	Eastleigh
Lincoln B.Mk 2	214 Sqn	Eastleigh
Vampire FB.Mk 9	8 Sqn (Det)	Eastleigh
Meteor PR.Mk 10	13 Sqn (Det)	Eastleigh
Lancaster PR.Mk 1, Dakota Mk 3	82 Sqn	Eastleigh
Harvard Mk 2B	1340 Flt	Eastleigh
Anson C.Mk 21, Proctor Mk 4, Valetta C.Mk 1, Dakota Mk 3, Auster AOP.Mk 6, Pembroke C.Mk 1, Sycamore HR.Mk 14	Comms Flt	Eastleigh

Specifications

Crew: 7

Powerplant: 4 x 1305kW (1750hp) Rolls Royce Merlin 68, 68A or 300 piston engines

Maximum speed: 491km/h (305mph)

Range: 4506km (2800 miles)

Service ceiling: n/a

Dimensions: span 36.58m (120ft 0in); length 23.85m (78ft 3in); height n/a

Weight: 37,195kg (82,000lb) loaded

Armament: 2 x 20mm cannon and 4 x 7mm (0.5in) MGs; provision for up to 6350kg (14,000lb) of bombs

▲ **Avro Lincoln B.Mk 2**

214 Sqn, RAF / Eastleigh, 1954

The first RAF Lincolns were from 49 Sqn and were detached to Eastleigh, Kenya, in November 1953. The following year aircraft drawn from 110 and 214 Sqns replaced these. The Lincolns were used to pattern-bomb suspected Mau Mau supply dumps and terrorist strongholds.

Chapter 7

Southern Asia

While the series of wars fought between India and Pakistan during the course of the Cold War did not involve direct participation by the superpowers, the two belligerents on the Indian subcontinent made considerable use of advanced aircraft supplied by the U.S. and China (in the case of Pakistan) and by the Soviets (in the case of India). Events to the north would subsequently shift the focus in the region towards Afghanistan, where the Soviet Union became entrenched in a costly war of attrition fought against U.S.-supported Islamic insurgents.

◀ **Shenyang F-6**

The series of wars fought between Indian and Pakistan during the years of the Cold War saw use made of some of the most advanced warplanes available from both Eastern and Western manufacturers. These Pakistan AF F-6s were licence-built versions of the MiG-19 supersonic interceptor.

Early India–Pakistan conflicts
1947–1948

Previously united under British rule, the Indian subcontinent was divided into three states, and political and religious differences saw three major wars fought between India and Pakistan.

THE BRITISH WITHDREW from India in August 1947, and the country was left divided into three independent states: mainly Muslim East and West Pakistan, and predominantly Hindu India. Chiefly Muslim, but ruled by a Hindu Maharajah, Kashmir was one of a number of border areas the boundaries of which were subject to dispute by the rival states.

After independence, the Indian AF and Pakistan AF set about equipping themselves, both receiving ex-RAF Tempest FB.Mk 2 fighters (89 for India in 1947, 24 for Pakistan in 1948). Initially, both air arms would receive considerable support from Britain in terms of equipment and training. Other early aircraft types included Liberators, Dakotas, Austers, Harvards and Tiger Moths for India, and Furies, Halifaxes, Dakotas, Austers, Devons and Harvards for Pakistan, most of the Pakistan AF units being located at airfields in West Pakistan.

In October 1947 Pakistan-backed Pathan tribesmen from the Northwest Frontier began to move on Srinagar, the Kashmiri capital, which was relieved by Indian airborne forces flown in by Dakotas and civilian aircraft. Further Kashmiri insurrection was carried out by Muslim 'Free Kashmiri' groups, which were countered by Indian AF Tempest FB.Mk 2 and Spitfire Mk XIV fighters.

By early 1948 Pakistan had entered the conflict more overtly, providing artillery support and later airlift using its Halifaxes. The campaign had ended in stalemate by 31 December 1948, before the UN intervened to establish a ceasefire line that was recognized as the border between the two countries.

Northwest Frontier

At the same time as Pakistan and India were fighting over Kashmir, Pakistani air power was involved in policing the borders of the Northwest Frontier with Afghanistan, where tribes were also in open revolt.

In order to counter the insurrection, the Pakistan AF deployed Tempests to Peshawar, and these fighters were in action in a policing role over the Khyber Pass starting in December 1947. Transport of Pakistan Army formations in the area was the responsibility of Pakistan AF Dakotas, and Halifaxes were also available for bombing. Pakistan was still engaged on the Northwest Frontier between 1948-49, sending Tempest units to the front in rotation, before Furies superseded these fighters beginning in 1950.

▲ **Consolidated B-24J Liberator**

5 Sqn, Indian AF / Cawnpore/Poona, 1948-49

In addition to its ex-RAF Tempest fighters, India set about developing a strategic air arm, through the fielding of Liberator bombers. These were mainly assembled using wartime airframes that were retrieved from storage yards at Kanpur. Used for bombing and reconnaissance, 5 Sqn Liberators served at Cawnpore and Poona.

Specifications

Crew: 8

Powerplant: 4 x 895kW (1200hp) Pratt & Whitney R-1830-65 14-cylinder two-row radial piston engines

Maximum speed: 483km/h (300mph)

Range: 3380km (2100 miles)

Service ceiling: 8535m (28,000ft)

Dimensions: span 33.53m (110ft); length 20.47m (67ft 2in); height 5.49m (18ft)

Weight: 29,484kg (65,000lb) maximum takeoff

Armament: 2 x .5in MGs in each of nose, dorsal, ventral and tail turrets, one .5in MG in each of waist positions; internal bomb load of 3992kg (8800lb)

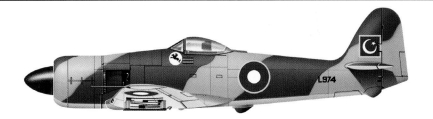

Specifications

Crew: 1

Powerplant: 1850kW (2480hp) Bristol
Centaurus XVIIC radial engine

Maximum speed: 740km/h (460mph)

Range: n/a

Service ceiling: 10,900m (35,800ft)

Dimensions: span 11.7m (38ft 5in);
length 10.6m (34ft 8in); height 4.9m
(16ft 1in)

Weight: 5670kg (12,500lb) loaded

Armament: 4 x 20mm (0.79in) Hispano Mk V
cannon; 12 x 76mm (3in) rockets or 908kg
(2000lb) of bombs

▲ **Hawker Fury FB.Mk 60**

9 Sqn, Pakistan AF / Peshawar, 1951

This Hawker Fury FB.Mk 60 was part of the second batch of deliveries that Pakistan received in 1951. Pakistan was the most important operator of the land-based Fury, taking 93 examples between 1949 and 1954. Subsequent British deliveries provided Halifax bombers, Attacker fighters and Bristol 170 transports.

India–Pakistan
1965

India and Pakistan went to war in 1965, once again over the issue of control of Kashmir. The 22-day war saw the outnumbered Pakistan AF perform well against Indian AF opposition.

THE CONFLICT BEGAN when Pakistan began arming and training irregulars to infiltrate Kashmir, hopeful of sparking a revolution that would see the territory fall into Pakistani hands. After supporting the insurgency with artillery, Pakistan launched an offensive against Indian military forces near Jammu.

During the conflict the Pakistan AF was able to field 12 combat squadrons (including reserve units)

▲ **Dassault Ouragan**

29 Sqn, Indian AF / Gahauti, 1965

India was the recipient of 104 French-built Ouragan jet fighters between 1953 and 1954, the type receiving the local designation Toofani. Together with Indian AF Vampires, Ouragans were relieved from front-line duties early in the 1965 campaign, after the former type proved vulnerable to Pakistan AF F-86s.

Specifications

Crew: 1

Powerplant: 1 x 22.2kN (4990lbf) Rolls-Royce
Nene 104B turbojet

Maximum speed: 940km/h (584mph)

Range: 920km (570 miles)

Service ceiling: 13,000m (42,650ft)

Dimensions: span 13.16m (43ft 2in); length
10.73m (35ft 2in); height 4.14m (13ft 7in)

Weight: 7404kg (16,323lb) loaded

Armament: 4 x 20mm (.787in) Hispano-Suiza
HS.404 cannon, rockets and up to 2270kg
(5000lb) of payload

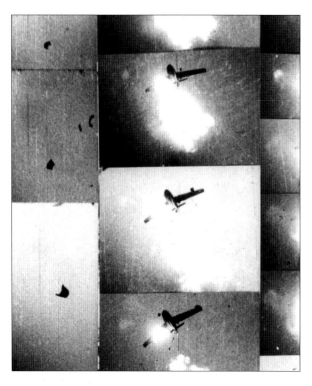

▲ F-86 Sabre

Gun camera footage reveals the final moments of a Pakistan AF F-86 as it falls to the guns of an Indian AF fighter. The backbone of the Pakistan AF in the 1965 war, additional ex-German Sabre Mk 6s were received in time for the 1971 conflict.

compared to the Indian AF's 14. However, Pakistan claimed a superior kill/loss rate in air combat, most victories being recorded by F-86s.

Most fighting took place along the northern Indo-Pakistan border, and the Indian AF held back much of its air power in the east, where fighting was limited. After 6 September both sides continued to launch raids into opposition territory, although these met little in the way of opposition. From now on, however, the Indian AF was able to generate a superior number of sorties, while the Pakistan AF regrouped and conserved its strength.

On the ground, an Indian Army counter-offensive pushed the Pakistani forces back across their own border in some areas, before the situation became one of stalemate, and a ceasefire was declared.

Inconclusive outcome

A subsequent treaty reinstated the pre-war borders of Kashmir. Outnumbered, the Pakistan AF had used skilful tactics to gain air superiority where it was needed. The Pakistan AF suffered losses of 25 aircraft during the war, compared to 60 for the Indian AF. However, Pakistan AF losses had removed around 17 per cent of its front-line strength. Equally damaging was the fact that as a result of the fighting Pakistan was denied military aid by the U.S., which would have a major impact on the course of the next conflict.

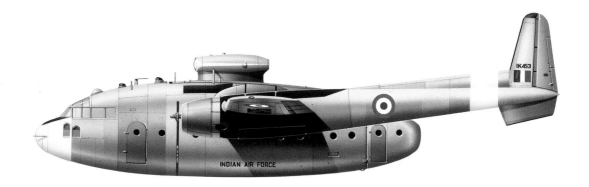

Specifications

Crew: 6–8

Powerplant: 2 x two 2610kW (3500hp) Wright R-3350-85 piston engines and one 22kN (4850lb) thrust Bristol Orpheus turbojet

Maximum speed: 470km/h (292mph)

Range: 3669km (2280 miles)

Service ceiling: 7300m (23,950ft)

Dimensions: span 33.3m (109ft 3in); length 26.37m (86ft 6in); height 8m (26ft 3in)

Weight: 33,747kg (74,700lb) loaded

Armament: none

▲ Fairchild C-119G Flying Boxcar

Indian AF

Three Indian AF squadrons were ultimately equipped with the C-119, these aircraft being fitted with an additional turbojet engine for improved performance under 'hot and high' conditions. At the time of the 1965 war, the Indian AF maintained two Flying Boxcar units, 12 and 19 Sqns.

▲ **Martin B-57B**

7 Sqn, Pakistan AF

A licence-built U.S. version of the British Canberra that was operated by the
Indian AF, the B-57 served the Pakistan AF in both reconnaissance and bomber
versions. The B-57B was widely used during the course of the 1965 campaign to
attack Indian airfields, flying from bases at Mauripur, Risalspur and Sargodha.

Specifications

Crew: 2	length 20m (65ft 6in); height 4.52m
Powerplant: 2 x 32.1kN (7220lbf) Wright J65-	(14ft 10in)
W-5 turbojets	Weight: 18,300kg (40,345lb) loaded
Maximum speed: 960km/h (598mph)	Armament: 4 x 20mm (0.787in) M39 cannon;
Range: 4380km (2720 miles)	2000kg (4500lb) in bomb bay; 1300kg
Service ceiling: 13,745m (45,100ft)	(2800lb) on four external hardpoints,
Dimensions: span 19.5m (64ft 0in);	including unguided rockets

India–Pakistan
1971

**In 1971 Pakistan and India went to war again, this time over mainly Bengali-populated East
Pakistan, separated from West Pakistan by more than 1600km (1000 miles) of Indian territory.**

IN EAST PAKISTAN Indian forces supported the
Mukti Bahani secessionist rebels and there was
widespread support for a Bengali breakaway from
West Pakistan.

Instigated by Pakistan, the 1971 war saw the
Pakistan AF severely hampered by the fact that fighting
took place a considerable distance from its primary
bases in the west. India had meanwhile prepared for

▲ **Canadair Sabre Mk 6**

17 Sqn, Pakistan AF / Rafiqui, 1971

Pakistan's fleet of Sabres played a major role during the fighting in 1971, as they
had in 1965. However, faced with numerical inferiority, the Pakistan AF suffered in
the air at the hands of Indian AF Hunters and Gnats, while aircraft were bombed
on their airfields by Indian Canberras, MiG-21s and Su-7s.

Specifications

Crew: 1	Dimensions: span 11.58m (38ft);
Powerplant: 1 x 32.35kN (7275lb) Avro Orenda	length 11.58m (38ft); height 4.57m (15ft)
Mark 14 engine	Weight: 6628kg (14.613lb) loaded
Maximum speed: 975km/h (606mph)	Armament: 6 x 12.7mm (0.50in) M2 Browning
Range: n/a	machine guns; 2 x AIM-9 missiles; 2400kg
Service ceiling: 15,450m (50,700ft)	(5300lb) of payload

the conflict, with a chain of heavily defended airfields along the borders with East and West Pakistan. The Indian AF planned two phases: an initial wave of airfield attacks followed by a campaign of interdiction against Pakistani forward areas and communications.

On 3 November, Indian interceptors scrambled in response to a Pakistan AF airspace infringement in the west. The first notable air combat came on 23 November, when four Pakistan AF Sabres on a strafing mission clashed with four Gnats northeast of Calcutta. Three Sabres were claimed shot down.

A full-scale assault was launched by Pakistan after it had accused India of launching attacks against East Bengal in support of the Mukti Bahani. Pre-emptive strikes were made against forward Indian AF airfields and radar sites in the west. The aim was to deny the Indian AF bases from which to launch attacks against

Pakistani ground formations in the north. The results of the first wave of airfield attacks were limited, however. Follow-on raids involved Pakistan AF B-57s launching nocturnal attacks against airfields and other Indian military targets in the west.

War on two fronts

War was officially declared on 4 December and the Indian AF launched its own wave of attacks against targets in the west and east, using Canberras and Su-7s. Sheer weight of numbers forced the Pakistan AF to operate on the defensive, and it was compelled to fight on both fronts. East Bengal hosted 10 Indian AF squadrons, while the carrier INS *Vikrant* also provided Sea Hawks and Alizés in the Bay of Bengal.

Hunters, MiG-21s and Su-7s targeted Pakistan AF bases at Tezgaon and Kurmitola beginning on

Specifications

Crew: 1	height 3.88m (12ft 8.75in)
Powerplant: 2 x 31.9kN (7165lb) Shenyang	Weight: 10,000kg (22,046lb) maximum
WP-6 turbojets	Armament: 3 x 30mm NR-30 cannon; four
Maximum speed: 1540km/h (957mph)	external hardpoints with provision for up to
Range: 1390km (864 miles)	500kg (1102lb) of stores, including air-to-air
Service ceiling: 17,900m (58,725ft)	missiles, 250kg (551lb) bombs, 55mm (2.1in)
Dimensions: span 9.2m (30ft 2.25in);	rocket-launcher pods, 212mm (8.34in)
length 14.9m (48ft 10.5in);	rockets or drop tanks

▲ Shenyang F-6

11 Sqn, Pakistan AF / Sargodha, 1971

In the absence of U.S. aircraft deliveries, Pakistan re-equipped with Chinese-supplied F-6 fighters (licence-built Chinese versions of the Soviet MiG-19), the first arriving in December 1965. This Pakistani F-6 was one of 135 delivered, and was reportedly one of the first to be received by the Pakistan AF, in 1966.

▲ Dassault Mirage IIIEP

5 Sqn, Pakistan AF / Sargodha, 1971

Additional new equipment in service with the Pakistan AF at the time of the 1971 war were French Mirage IIIs, a single squadron of which became operational in June 1969. As well as missile-armed Mirage IIIEP interceptor versions, the 1971 war saw Pakistan make use of the Mirage IIIRP version for reconnaissance.

Specifications

Crew: 1	Dimensions: span 8.22m (26ft 11.875in);
Powerplant: 1 x 60.8kN (13,668lb) SNECMA	length 16.5m (56ft); height 4.5m (14ft 9in);
Atar 9C turbojet	Weight: 13,500kg (29,760lb) loaded
Maximum speed: 1390km/h (883mph)	Armament: 2 x 30mm DEFA 552A cannon with
Range: 1200km (745 miles)	125rpg; three external pylons with provision
Service ceiling: 17,000m (55,755ft)	for up to 3000kg (6612lb) of stores

4 December. Outnumbered, Pakistani Sabres (some of which were missile-armed) put up stiff resistance.

On 6 December an Indian strike against Tezgaon and Kurmitola effectively put both bases out of action. Conversely, Pakistan only managed to launch five raids against India's major airfield in the west, Pathankot, which remained in operation.

Subsequent aerial activity focused on airfield denial, anti-radar and close support missions by both combatants, while Pakistan AF C-130s and B-57s and Indian AF Canberras and An-12s maintained nocturnal raids. The Indian AF Marut jet fighter-bomber made its debut, attacking Pakistani armour. Used for combat air patrols, Sidewinder-armed F-6s made claims against MiG-21s and Su-7s, and Mirages also proved their value in aerial combat, but

Pakistan was denied overall air superiority. On 7 December Indian infantry were lifted by Mi-4 and Mi-8 helicopters, in additionn to Alouette escorts, and helicopters also carried infantry to the western side of the Megha River on 10 December. A day later, Indian forces around Dacca launched an airborne assault, troops being delivered by An-12 and C-119G. The Indian AF kept up the pace of its raids in the following days, striking Pakistani forward bases, although the focus was now on interdicting lines of communication and close support.

After 14 days of fighting, the Indian AF had comprehensively bettered its Pakistani opposition, and contributed to Pakistan's military defeat. With the country's 'eastern wing' lost, East Pakistan now re-emerged as Bangladesh.

Specifications

Crew: 1

Powerplant: 1 x 60.8kN (13,668lb) thrust
 Tumanskii afterburning turbojet

Maximum speed: 2050km/h (1300mph)

Range: 1800km (1118 miles)

Service ceiling: 17,000m (57,750ft)

Dimensions: span 7.15m (23ft 5.5in);

length (including probe) 15.76m (51ft 8.5in);

height 4.1m (13ft 5.5in)

Weight: 9400kg (20,723lb) loaded

Armament: 1 x 23mm cannon, provision for
 about 1500kg (3307kg) of stores, including
 air-to-air missiles, rocket pods, napalm tanks
 or drop tanks

▲ MiG-21PF

1 Sqn, Indian AF / Adampur, 1971

As well as receiving MiG-21s from the USSR in the form of export deliveries, licence production of the fighter was undertaken by HAL in India. This MiG-21PF wears a hastily applied camouflage scheme for combat in the 1971 war, and is armed with a GSh-23 fuselage gun pack and R-13 air-to-air missiles.

▲ English Electric Canberra B.Mk 66

5 Sqn, Indian AF / Agra, 1971

While the B(I).Mk 58 bomber-interdictor served in the 1965 war, the 1971 conflict also saw the involvement of the B.Mk 66 version of the Canberra. The aircraft was active on both eastern and western fronts during 1971, and also saw service in a reconnaissance capacity, in the form of the Canberra PR.Mk 57 version.

Specifications

Crew: 3

Powerplant: 2 x 33.23kN (7490lb) thrust
 turbojet engine Avon R.A.7 Mk.109 turbojet
 engines

Maximum speed: 933km/h (580mph)

Range: 5440km (3380 miles)

Service ceiling: 15,000m (48,000ft)

Dimensions: span 19.51m (65ft 6in); length
 19.96m (65ft 6in); height 4.77m (15ft 8in)

Weight: 24,948kg (55,000lb) loaded

Armament: 4 x 20mm cannon; two rocket pods
 or up to 2772kg (6000lb) of bombs

Specifications

Crew: 1

Powerplant: 1 x 24kN (5400lb) Rolls-Royce
  Nene 103 turbojet

Maximum speed: 969km/h (602mph)

Range: 370km (230 miles)

Service ceiling: 13,565m (44,500ft)

Dimensions: span 11.89m (39ft);

length 12.09m (39ft 8in); height 2.64m
(8ft 8in)

Weight: 7348kg (16,200lb) loaded

Armament: 4 x 20mm Hispano cannon;
provision for 4 x 227kg (500lb) bombs, or
2 x 227kg (500lb) bombs and 20 x 76mm
(3in) or 16 x 127mm (5in) rockets

▲ **Hawker Sea Hawk FGA.Mk 6**

300 Sqn, Indian Navy / INS Vikrant, *1971*

This Indian Navy Sea Hawk fighter-bomber operated from the carrier INS *Vikrant* during the 1971 conflict fought against Pakistan. Beginning operations on 4 December, the Sea Hawks claimed the destruction of seven ships and a submarine, and also mounted strikes against coastal installations and airfields.

Afghanistan
1979–1989

Sometimes dubbed 'Russia's Vietnam', the conflict waged by the USSR in Afghanistan saw air power deployed in force in a battle for supremacy against a resourceful guerrilla enemy.

THE ORIGINAL OBJECTIVE of the Soviet invasion of Afghanistan in December 1979 was the removal of President Hafizullah Amin, and restoration of order following the installation of a new regime. In the first instance the Soviets succeeded, aided by around 1000 Soviet 'advisors' already based in Afghanistan. However, they were unable to subjugate the country, which was soon gripped by a powerful Islamic insurgency and a rapidly escalating war.

Until withdrawal of the final Soviet troops in February 1989, the Red Army was bogged down in a guerrilla war, in which air power was put to use in various forms in an effort to extinguish resistance.

Guerrilla tactics

Although Soviet air power proved effective in certain instances, the mountainous terrain gave the insurgents the upper hand on the ground, and the Mujahideen guerrillas regularly exposed Soviet Army units to ambushes and hit-and-run attacks. In order to regain the initiative, the Soviet AF was employed not only to provide troops with direct support where required, but to maintain a bombing offensive,

deploying the Tu-16, Tu-22 and Tu-22M as free-fall bombers in order to weaken opposition resolve and deny it the resources needed to wage its campaign.

In direct support of troops on the ground, the Soviet AF used MiG-27, Su-17M, Su-24 and Su-25 aircraft in a close support role to target insurgents' positions. Meanwhile extensive use was made of rotorcraft to transport troops and also to provide organic fire support via the employment of helicopter gunships, such as the Mi-24 and heavily armed versions of the Mi-8. As well as increasing use of aircraft, the Soviet presence on the ground grew from 6000 troops in December 1979 to more than 130,000 troops by the mid-1980s. An-12, An-22 and Il-76 airlifters of Transport Aviation provided intra-theatre logistic support throughout. These transports came under increasing threat from the guerrillas as they complemented AAA with man-portable SAMs obtained via CIA channels.

In addition to Soviet AF assets, a more minor role was played by the Afghan AF itself, which was allied with the Soviets and equipped with similar types, including MiG-17s, MiG-21s, Mi-8s and Mi-24s.

Facing challenging weather conditions, the Soviets typically made use of the onset of spring to launch renewed offensives against the guerrillas, the first being initiated in 1980. By the end of 1980, it was reported that Soviet Mi-24 numbers had quadrupled to 240, with six airfields under construction.

Soviet tactics were increasingly reliant on helicopter gunships and heliborne assault, while a new facet to the air war was represented by the arrival of the Su-25 dedicated ground attack aircraft in spring 1981. In a similar timeframe, Soviet tactical jets began to make increasing use of precision-guided

weapons. Other popular stores included thermobaric (fuel-air explosive) weapons, particularly for use against cave complexes and buildings.

After major operations that included the siege of Khost in 1983 and a combined-arms offensive against Najrab in the early months of 1984, a spring bombing offensive was launched against the Panjshir valley in 1984. The guerrillas waged a campaign of attrition for the next four years, prior to the beginning of the Soviet withdrawal in 1988. By the end of the Cold War the situation was stalemate, with the Mujahideen left to battle the Afghan military.

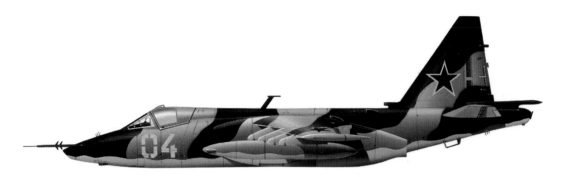

Specifications

Crew: 1
Powerplant: 2 x 44.1kN (9921lb) Tumanskii
R-195 turbojets
Maximum speed: 975km/h (606mph)
Range: 750km (466 miles)
Service ceiling: 7000m (22,965ft)
Dimensions: span 14.36m (47ft 1.5in); length

15.53m (50ft 11.5in); height 4.8m (15ft 9in)
Weight: 17,600kg (38,800lb) loaded
Armament: 1 x 30mm GSh-30-2 cannon with
250 rounds; 8 x external pylons with provision
for up to 4400kg (9700lb) of stores, including
AAMs, ASMs, ARMs, anti-tank missiles,
guided bombs and cluster bombs

▲ **Sukhoi Su-25**
Soviet Frontal Aviation

The Su-25 ground attack aircraft received its combat debut in Afghanistan, where it was first observed by Western analysts. A successor to the wartime Il-2 Shturmovik, the Su-25 was tailored for survivability in a battlefield environment, and proved useful against the Mujahideen, on occasion working alongside Mi-24s.

Specifications

Crew: 5–6
Powerplant: 4 x 11,030kW (15,000hp)
Kuznetsov NK-12MA turboprops
Maximum speed: 740km/h (460mph)
Range: 5000km (3100 miles)
Service ceiling: 8000m (26,240ft)

Dimensions: 64.4m (211ft 3in);
length 57.9m (190ft); height 12.53m
(41ft 1in)
Weight: 250,000kg (551,000lb) loaded
Payload: 80,000kg (180,000lb)

▲ **An-22**
Soviet Transport Aviation

Flying into Kabul and Shindand, the An-22 was the most capable strategic airlifter available to the Soviets at the time of the invasion of Afghanistan. The initial combat force of 6000 troops was sent to Afghanistan in around 300 sorties flown by transport aircraft between 24-26 December 1979.

Chapter 8

The Far East

During the years of the Cold War, Southeast Asia and the Far East saw the frequent application of air power in localized conflicts and post-colonial insurgencies. On the Korean peninsula, UN forces assembled to repulse a communist invasion of South Korea, while in Indo-China, the departure of the French colonizers left a power vacuum, and a guerrilla war in which the U.S. would rapidly become entrenched. Colonial history also led to British involvement in Malaya and Borneo, where air power was once again used to put down communist-inspired, nationalist insurrection.

◀ **Republic F-105 Thunderchief/Douglas B-66 Destroyer**
Four USAF F-105s formate on a B-66 pathfinder that guided the strike fighters to their targets using advanced navigation and attack electronics. The Vietnam air war was typified by America's deployment of increasingly advanced weapons and warplanes against a consistently elusive enemy.

Korean War
1950–1953

Divided in 1945 along the 38th Parallel, North and South Korea went to war in 1950 when the communist North invaded its neighbour, with support from both the USSR and China.

THE UN RESPONSE to the invasion of 25 June 1950 was to send a military coalition to attempt to drive the North Korean forces back across the 38th Parallel. The initial air power available to the UN forces comprised USAF Far East Air Force units based in Japan, the Philippines and Okinawa, its fighter units equipped with three squadrons of F-82Gs and five wings of F-80Cs. The Republic of Korea AF in the south was not in possession of any combat types. As North Korean forces moved towards the South Korean

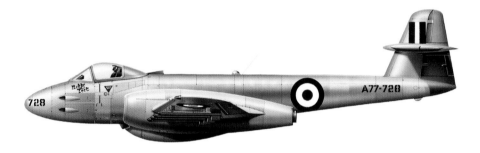

▲ **Gloster Meteor F.Mk 8**

77 Sqn, Royal Australian AF / K14 (Kimpo), 1951–53

Based at K14, the Royal Australian AF contingent supporting the UN forces in Korea flew the British-built Meteor F.Mk 8. Outclassed in air combat after the appearance of the MiG-15, the Meteor was switched from fighter sweeps and B-29 escort missions to ground attack, flying over 15,000 sorties in total.

Specifications

Crew: 1

Powerplant: 2 x 16kN (3600lb) Rolls-Royce
  Derwent 8 turbojets

Maximum speed: 962km/h (598mph)

Range: 1580km (980 miles)

Service ceiling: 13,106m (43,000ft)

Dimensions: span 11.32m (37ft 2in); length
  13.58m (44ft 7in); height 3.96m (13ft)

Weight: 8664kg (19,100lb) loaded

Armament: 4 x 20mm Hispano cannon, foreign
  F.8s often modified to carry two iron bombs or
  eight rockets

Specifications

Crew: 1

Powerplant: 1 x 26.3kN (5952lb) Klimov VK-1
  turbojet

Maximum speed: 1100km/h (684 mph)

Range: 1424km (885 miles)

Service ceiling: 15,545m (51,000ft)

Dimensions: span 10.08m (33ft .75in); length
  11.05m (36ft 3.75in); height 3.4m (11ft 1.75in)

Weight: 5700kg (12,566lb) loaded

Armament: 1 x 37mm N-37 cannon and
  2 x 23mm NS-23 cannon, plus up to 500kg
  (1102lb) of stores on underwing pylons

▲ **MiG-15**

People's Liberation Army AF

The first MiG-15s to be encountered by the UN forces in Korea were Chinese-flown examples, which began to cross the Yalu on 1 November 1950. The Soviet-built fighter quickly showed its superiority over the USAF's F-80 and as a result the first F-86As were hurried to Korea, the 4th FIW arriving on 11 November.

capital, Seoul, USAF fighters covered a civilian evacuation, F-82s and F-80s clashing with North Korean AF Yak-9s and Il-10s in the first aerial engagements of the war on 27 June.

With General Douglas MacArthur appointed head of the UN forces and Seoul fallen to the communists, the U.S. began to take a harder line. The F-80 formed the mainstay of UN fighter power, supported by F-51s flown by USAF, Australian and South African units. Such was UN air supremacy that the North Korean AF was restricted to only limited operations for several months starting in July.

The outbreak of the Korean War saw the USAF bomber force in the Far East equipped with a single B-29 wing on Guam, plus two squadrons of B-26s.

Early in the war the B-29s and Japan-based B-26s were directed against North Korean AF airfields in the north, where they succeeded in destroying many aircraft on the ground. North Korean AF opposition was limited, and the B-29s were able to raid North Korean industry almost unmolested.

Close support in Korea

On the ground, the UN air assets were struggling to blunt the advance by the North Koreans, with fighter-bombers targeting bridges and other transport infrastructure as well as columns of troops and armour. Although the UN air arms were dominant in the air, there was little they could do to prevent North Korean progress on the ground despite round-the-

Specifications
Crew: 1

Powerplant: 1 x 26.3kN (5952lb) Klimov VK-1 turbojet

Maximum speed: 1100km/h (684 mph)

Range: 1424km (885 miles)

Service ceiling: 15,545m (51,000ft)

Dimensions: span 10.08m (33ft .75in); length 11.05m (36ft 3.75in); height 3.4m (11ft 1.75in)

Weight: 5700kg (12,566lb) loaded

Armament: 1 x 37mm N-37 cannon and 2 x 23mm NS-23 cannon, plus up to 500kg (1102lb) of stores on underwing pylons

▲ MiG-15
North Korean AF

'2057' was a Korean-operated MiG-15, although UN forces would encounter examples of the fighter flown by Soviet, Chinese and North Korean pilots. Raids by the U.S. Fifth Air Force against North Korean airfields meant that the communists never dared to operate the MiGs from bases south of the Yalu River.

Specifications
Crew: 2

Powerplant: 1 x 26.7kN (6000lb) Allison J33-A-33 turbojet

Maximum speed: 933km/h (580mph)

Range: 1850km/h (1150 miles)

Service ceiling: 14,630m (48,000ft)

Dimensions: span not including tip tanks 11.85m (38ft 10.5in); length 12.2m (40ft 1in); height 3.89m (12ft 8in)

Weight: 7125kg (15,710lb) loaded

Armament: 4 x .5in machine guns

▲ Lockheed F-94B Starfire
319th Fighter Interceptor Squadron, USAF / K13 (Suwon), 1952–53

The first F-94 all-weather fighters arrived in Korea in March 1951 although the type's use was initially restricted, with the U.S. fearful that the E-1 fire control radar might fall into communist hands. Mounting B-29 losses then saw the two-seat F-94 fighters used as escorts for the USAF bombers.

Specifications

Crew: 1

Powerplant: 1 x 32.36kN (7275lb) thrust Avro
Orenda Mark 14 turbojet engine

Maximum speed: 965km/h (600mph)

Range: 530km (329 miles)

Service ceiling: 14,600m (48,000ft)

Dimensions: span 11.58m (39ft); length
11.4m (37ft 6in); height 4.4m (14ft 8in)

Weight: 6628kg (14,613lb) loaded

Armament: 6 x .5in (12.7mm) machine guns

▲ North American F-86F Sabre

2 Sqn, South African AF / K55 (Osan), 1952–53

In addition to the USAF, Sabres were operated over Korea by the South African AF, which replaced its F-51Ds with F-86Fs that were based at K55. The South African jets were primarily used in a fighter-bomber role, 2 Sqn being operated under the command of the USAF's 18th Fighter Bomber Group.

clock air attacks. By September, the UN forces were pinned back to a pocket around Pusan located in the far south of the Korean peninsula.

The UN regained the initiative on 15 September when, under the protection of air superiority, MacArthur launched an amphibious landing at Inchon further up the coast. With the North Korean forces overstretched on the ground, the UN started to make progress, the landings being followed by a counter-attack at Pusan, while air power continued to hit the North Korean forces on the ground. Carriers of the U.S. Navy and Royal Navy, operating F4U-4Bs, AD-4s, F9F-2s, Fireflies and Seafires provided air support at Inchon. These types were aided over the beachhead by OY-1 forward air control aircraft, F7F-3N night-fighters and HO3S-1 helicopters.

China intervenes

The audacious Inchon landings led to the recapture of the important airfield at Kimpo, and by the end of September most of the North Korean invasion force had been rolled back to positions just beyond the 38th Parallel. This was the signal for communist China to intervene on behalf of its ally, and Chinese troops were assembled north of the Yalu River. At the same time, MacArthur announced his objective of occupying the entire Korean peninsula, rather than a return to the 1945 border as originally envisaged by the UN. U.S.-led forces advanced deep into the

north, the North Korean capital, Pyongyang, being occupied by UN forces on 19 October.

On 1 November the UN forces encountered the MiG-15 fighter for the first time. Soviet-flown and operating out of Chinese bases north of the Yalu, which were immune to air attack, the swept-wing MiGs were superior to any UN fighter then in theatre. At the time of the MiG's combat debut, the USAF fighter arm in Korea comprised three wings of piston-engined F-51s, and two of F-80 jets. Further F-51s were operated by a single Royal Australian AF (RAAF) unit under the command of the USAF 35th Fighter Bomber Group.

Concurrent with the deployment of the MiG-15 was the arrival on the ground of Chinese troops, and

USAF FIGHTERS, KOREAN WAR		
Aircraft	Unit	Base
F-82G	4th F(AW)S	Naha
F-82G, F-94B	68th F(AW)S	Itazuke, K13 (det)
F-82G	339th F(AW)S	Yokota
F-51D, F-80C	8th FBW	Itazuke
F-51D	35th FIG	Johnson AB, K2
F-51D, F-80C	35th FIG	Johnson AB, K1, K3, K13
F-86A/E	4th FIG	K14, Japan, K2, K13
F-86E/F	51st FIG	K13, K14
F-94B	319th FIS	K13

UN aircraft stepped up their close support activity, land-based fighter-bombers being joined by carrier-based aircraft from Task Force 77 (including the British carrier HMS *Theseus*) at the mouth of the Yalu. Using B-29s to attack the Chinese assault over the Yalu was considered too high of a risk so it was left to the carrier-based fighter-bombers to attack bridges on the river. The raids were conducted by ADs and F4Us with top cover provided by F9Fs.

The first-ever confirmed jet-versus-jet combat pitched an F-80C against a MiG-15 over the Yalu on November 8, and in the following days, the

USAF FIGHTER-BOMBERS, KOREAN WAR, 1950		
Aircraft	Unit	Base
F-51D, F-80C	8th FBG	Itazuke, K2, K13
F-51D, F-80C	35th FIG	Johnson AB, K1, K2, K3
F-80C	44th FBS	Clark AB
F-51D, F-80C	18th FBG	K2, K24, K10
F-80C	49th FBG	K2, Misawa
F-80C	51st FIW	K14, K13
F-84E/G	27th FEG	Itazuke, K2

Specifications

Crew: 1

Powerplant: 1 x 24kN (5400lb) Allison
    J33-A-35 turbojet

Maximum speed: 966km/h (594mph)

Range: 1930km (1200 miles)

Service ceiling: 14,000m (46,000ft)

Dimensions: span 11.81m (38ft 9in); length
    10.49m (34ft 5in); height 3.43m (11ft 3in)

Weight: 5738kg (12,660lb) loaded

Armament: 6 x 0.50 in (12.7mm) M2 Browning
    MGs; 2 x 1000lb (454kg) bombs;
    8 x unguided rockets

▲ F-80C Shooting Star

36th Fighter Bomber Squadron, 8th Fighter Bomber Group, USAF / K13 (Suwon), 1951

At the outset of the Korean War the F-80 comprised the backbone of the USAF's fighter forces deployed in theatre. The appearance of the MiG-15 saw the F-80 outclassed in the air-to-air role, and it was thereafter used for fighter-bomber missions. This F-80C-5 flew with the 36th FBS, 8th FBG at K13.

Specifications

Crew: 1

Powerplant: 1 x 21.8kN (4900lb) thrust Allison
    J35-A-17 turbojet engine

Maximum speed: 986km/h (613mph)

Range: 2390km (1485 miles)

Service ceiling: 13,180m (43,240ft)

Dimensions: span 11.1m (36ft 5in); length
    11.41m (36ft 5in); height 3.91m (12ft)

Weight: 10,185kg (22,455lb) loaded

Armament: 6 x .5in (12.7mm) machine guns;
    2 x 454kg (1000lb) bombs or 8 x 2.75in
    rockets

▲ F-84E Thunderjet

9th Fighter Bomber Squadron, 49th Fighter Bomber Group, USAF / K2 (Taegu), 1951

Part of the 49th FBG, this F-84E fighter-bomber was based at K2 in late 1951. Visible beneath the cockpit canopy is a marking that commemorates the wing's first aerial victory against a MiG-15, achieved by Captain Kenneth L. Skeen on 19 September 1951. Note the bomb carried under the wing of this particular jet.

communist fighters exacted an increasing toll on B-29 bombers. By the end of the month the Chinese presence on the ground meant that the UN forces were matched in terms of numbers, while the introduction of the MiG-15 had threatened to conclusively turn the tables in terms of air superiority.

On 26 November the communists launched their new offensive, involving 250,000 Chinese troops as well as North Korean formations. The communist offensive caught the UN off guard, and its supply lines were now dangerously overstretched. The UN began to withdraw its troops from the north, using both transport aircraft and ships. By January 1951 the situation had returned to a standoff just north of the 38th Parallel, while UN air power had been increased through the addition of further aircraft carriers and the deployment of the F-86A. A match for the MiG-15, the F-86A had first arrived in Korea with the 4th Fighter Interceptor Group at Kimpo in December 1950. Within a similar timeframe the USAF began to deploy F-84E fighter-bombers, while the RAAF unit re-equipped with Meteors. The Meteor was soon outclassed in aerial combat, and switched to ground attack, a role in which the F-84 would excel. F-84s would prove versatile, and its other missions included interdiction, armed reconnaissance and close support.

▲ **Ilyushin Il-10**

North Korean AF

At the outbreak of the war in June 1950 it was assumed that the North Korean AF included 70 single-seat piston-engined fighters (Yak-9s, La-7s and La-11s) plus around 65 Il-2 and Il-10 attack aircraft. An Il-10 is illustrated, examples of this type being among the first to be claimed by U.S. fighters on 27 June 1950.

Specifications

Crew: 2

Powerplant: 1 x 1320kW (1770hp) Mikulin
AM-42 liquid-cooled V-12 engine

Maximum speed: 550km/h (342mph)

Range: 800km (550 miles)

Service ceiling: 4000m (13,123ft)

Dimensions: span 13.40m (44ft); length

11.12m (36ft 6in); height 4.10m (13ft 5in)

Weight: 6345kg (14,000lb) loaded

Armament: 2 x 23mm (0.9in) Nudelman-
Suranov NS-23 cannons; 1 x 12.7mm (0.5in)
UBST cannon in the BU-9 rear gunner station;
up to 600kg (1320lb) bomb load

▲ **Yakovlev Yak-18**

North Korean AF

Designed as a trainer, the Yak-18 was used by North Korea for nocturnal harassment raids over UN airfields, with similar missions also being carried out by Po-2 utility biplanes. These nuisance raiders were dubbed 'Bedcheck Charlies' by the UN forces and proved to be challenging targets for Allied fighters.

Specifications

Crew: 2

Powerplant: 1 x 224kW (300hp) Ivchenko AI-
14RF radial piston engine

Maximum speed: 300km/h (187mph)

Range: 700km (436 miles)

Service ceiling: 5060m (16,596ft)

Dimensions: span 10.6m (34ft 9in);
length 8.35m (27ft 5in);
height 3.35m (11ft)

Weight: 1320kg (2904lb) maximum
takeoff

Armament: none

MiG-15 and F-86A first clashed in the air on 17 December, and successive marks of these fighters would contest air superiority until the end of the conflict, the principal area of combat being over the Yalu, a sector known as 'MiG Alley'.

A further communist advance forced the evacuation of the F-86s from Kimpo to Johnson AFB in Japan and temporarily out of the action. In the meantime it was left to the UN carriers to bring the air war to the North Korean forces, with close support missions being undertaken by ADs and F4Us, among others. At the same time the communists set about improving their airfields in North Korea, to extend the reach of air power beyond that offered by aircraft based in Manchuria, and further units were equipped with MiG-15 fighters. Meanwhile, USAF RB-26Cs were used for reconnaissance missions, flying from Japan, and latterly from Taegu and Kimpo in Korea.

Thunderjet offensive

Starting in January 1951 F-84Es of the 27th Fighter Escort Group were in action in an offensive role, interdicting communist supply routes, but also enjoying some success when tangling with MiGs in the air-to-air arena. Flying from Taegu in the south, the 27th FEG flew around 12,000 combat missions by the end of May 1951. The 27th FEG then returned to SAC command, and its place in Korea was taken by the 136th Fighter Bomber Wing, also with F-84Es. An additional Thunderjet group also arrived at around the same time, with the deployment of the 49th FBG, which had previously

been equipped with F-80Cs, and had been in Korea since the outbreak of the war.

By the time the communist spring offensive began in March 1951 the USAF still only had a single F-86 wing committed to the conflict. The F-86As returned to Korea from Japan in March, at which time B-29s were suffering losses to the MiGs. Because the communist MiG-15s were primarily held back at bases in the north and west, most air-to-air action was confined to the skies over the Yalu. However, some MiG-15s were closer to the front at Antung, and aerial fighting escalated in April, the MiG revealing itself to be superior to the F-84E, as well as being a lethal bomber-destroyer. In the latter role, MiGs were involved in the largest aerial battle of the war so far when they met B-29s, plus F-84E escorts and F-86A top cover over the Yalu on 12 April. Despite losses, the three B-29 wings – and to a lesser extent the two wings of B-26s – kept up their harassment of the communist forces, most missions being flown during the day, with fighter escorts provided.

As a result of the increasing intensity of the air war, a second F-86A squadron was moved forward to Suwon, and tactics were modified, ensuring that greater numbers of Sabres were in the air at any one time. The F-86s were soon showing their worth in the aerial fighting, posting claims for 22 MiGs destroyed by the end of May, in the course of over 3500 sorties.

With the spring offensive of 1951 stalled on the ground, the communists were forced into

USAF BOMBERS, KOREAN WAR		
Aircraft	Unit	Base
B-29A	19th BG(M)	Kadena
B-29A	22nd BG(M)	Kadena
B-29A	92nd BG(M)	Yokota
B-29A	98th BG(M)	Yokota
B-29A	307th BG(M)	Kadena
B-26B/C	3rd BG(L)	Iwakuni, K8, K16
B-26B/C	452nd BG(L)	Miho, K1
B-26B/C	17th BG(L)	K1

◀ Douglas B-26 Invader

First introduced to combat during the final stages of World War II, the B-26 remained the most important USAF light bomber during the conflict in Korea and was also used for reconnaissance missions and interdiction.

negotiation. In the meantime, both sides attempted to gain air superiority, and June and July saw pitched air battles in 'Mig Alley'. In the quest for air supremacy, the UN forces would eventually be able to call on an improved version of the Sabre, the F-86E model with a power-boosted 'flying tail', although they would have to wait until September 1951 for the fighter to become available in Korea.

The UN air forces staged a major air operation in June 1951 under the codename Strangle, with the aim of cutting off the communist forces from their supply lines and communications. To achieve this, the operation targeted road and rail targets, bridges and tunnels, and aircraft involved included USAF bombers, land-based U.S. Marine Corps aircraft and

U.S. Navy carrier aircraft from Task Force 77. An ambitious operation, Strangle failed to sever supply lines (although it did succeed in drawing MiG-15s into battle), but it continued to be pursued until September. The major drawback of Operation Strangle was the fact that the communists relied on roads rather than rail for transport of supplies, and there were simply too many targets for the U.S. air forces to address.

'Bedcheck Charlies'
With the F-86s operating from Suwon, the communists attempted to destroy the fighters on the ground, operating Po-2s and Yak-18s under the cover of darkness. Such raids began on 17 June, and the

Specifications
Crew: 1	Dimensions: span 11.6m (38ft); length 11.3m
Powerplant: 1 x 26.5kN (5950lb) thrust Pratt &	(37ft 5in); height 3.8m (11ft 4in)
Whitney J42-P-6/P-8 turbojet engine	Weight: 7462kg (16,450lb) loaded
Maximum speed: 925km/h (575mph)	Armament: 4 x 20mm M2 cannon; up to 910kg
Range: 2100km (1300 miles)	(2000lb) bombs, 6 x 5in (127mm) rockets
Service ceiling: 13,600m (44,600ft)	

▲ Grumman F9F-2 Panther
VF-781, US Navy / USS Bonne Homme Richard, 1951
This F9F-2 served with VF-781 aboard the carrier USS *Bonne Homme Richard*, part of Carrier Air Group 102, on station in Korea between May and November 1951. Together with the F2H Banshee, the Panther was the major U.S. Navy carrier-based fighter deployed in Korea, and scored several aerial victories.

▲ Supermarine Seafire FR.Mk 47
800 NAS, Royal Navy / HMS Triumph, 1950
The ultimate development of the Spitfire/Seafire line, the FR.Mk 47 was mainly used for ground attack work in Korea. This example flew from HMS *Triumph*, the first Royal Navy carrier to be deployed to Korea, arriving on station in July 1950 with an air wing comprising Seafires and the Firefly F.Mk 1s of 827 NAS.

Specifications
Crew: 1	Dimensions: span 11.25m (36ft 11in);
Powerplant: 1 x 1752kW (2350hp) Rolls-Royce	length 10.46m (34ft 4in); height 3.88m
Griffon 88 piston engine	(12ft 9in)
Maximum speed: 727km/h (452mph)	Weight: 4853kg (10,700lb) loaded
Range: 2374km (1375 miles)	Armament: 4 x 20mm Hispano V cannon; up to 8
Service ceiling: 13,135m (43,100ft)	x RP-3 rockets; up to 3 x 230kg (500lb) bombs

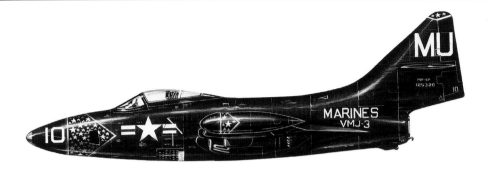

Grumman F9F-5P Panther

VMJ-3, U.S. Marine Corps / Itami, 1953

The F9F-5P was a camera-equipped version of the Panther, and this example was
operated by VMJ-3 of the U.S. Marine Corps over Korea, based at Itami, Japan. The
'VMJ' of the unit designation signified a Marine Photo-Reconnaissance Squadron.
Carried-based U.S. Navy F9F-2Ps were also active over Korea in the same role.

Specifications

Crew: 1

Powerplant: 1 x 27.7kN (6250lb) thrust Pratt &
Whitney J48-P-6A turbojet engine

Maximum speed: 972km/h (604mph)

Range: 2093km (1300 miles)

Service ceiling: 13,045m (42,800ft)

Dimensions: span 11.6m (38ft); length 12.1m
(40ft); height 3.7m (12ft 2in)

Weight: 8057kg (17,776lb) loaded

Armament: none

UN air forces were unable to develop an effective
counter to the slow-flying nuisance raiders. In the
same month, the Yalu was scene to frenetic aerial
combats, as F-86s again clashed with MiG-15s, and
on 20 June communist Il-10s escorted by Yak-9s
attacked a UN-held island off the Korean coast.

Chinese involvement meant that the UN could no
longer hope to unify north and south as a single
Korean entity. Stalemate on the ground led to both

sides beginning peace talks in July 1951, MacArthur
by now having been replaced by General Matthew B.
Ridgway as the leader of the UN military contingent.

Summer 1951 saw continued B-29 raids against
North Korean targets, the bombers now facing MiGs
as well as increasingly accurate, radar-directed AAA.
In June and July alone, 13 B-29s were damaged
while, in August, a series of raids was staged by B-29s
against the port and rail marshalling yard at Wojin,

Grumman F7F-3N Tigercat

HEDRON 1, U.S. Marine Corps / K3 (Pohang), 1950–53

A specialist night-fighter, the F7F-3N was deployed to Korea in small numbers by
the U.S. Marine Corps, serving exclusively from land bases. The aircraft carried air
interception radar in the nose, and was armed with 30mm cannon in the wings.
This Tigercat served with the headquarters squadron, HEDRON 1, at K3.

Specifications

Crew: 2

Powerplant: 2 x 1566kW (21000hp) Pratt &
Whitney R-2800-34W radial piston engines

Maximum speed: 700km/h (435mph)

Range: 1545km (960 miles)

Service ceiling: 12,405m (40,700ft)

Dimensions: span 15.7m (51ft 6in); length
13.8 (45ft 4in); height 4.6m (15ft 2in)

Weight: 11,880kg (26,190lb) loaded

Armament: 4 x 30mm cannon; up to 1814kg
(4000lb) of bombs

ultimately with escort provided by U.S. Navy F2H-2 and F9F fighters. A further F-84 group was also available to the UN beginning in July, with the 116th Fighter Bomber Group arriving in the Far East.

August 1951 also saw the deployment of a new MiG-15 regiment at Antung, and in response F-86s

were moved forward to Kimpo. The following month witnessed the arrival of the F-86E, with the 4th Fighter Interceptor Group, initially as attrition replacements for the F-86A. A first complete F-86E wing, the 51st FIG, was fully equipped before the end of the year. In the latter group the new F-86Es replaced the F-80C.

Improved MiGs arrive

Operation Strangle was superseded by a new UN air campaign that sought to destroy rail communications in the north, cutting off supplies before they began to be transported by road to the North Korean front line. In response to the new campaign, the communists deployed a further regiment of MiGs, by now equipped with the improved MiG-15bis variant. The new fighter was directed against the B-29s, and in October losses of the bomber again began to mount.

The largest air battle of the campaign took place on 22 October, and saw an estimated 100 MiGs clash with B-29s and F-84 and F-86 escorts. For the claimed destruction of six MiGs, the USAF lost three B-29s, with four more damaged, plus an F-84 destroyed. Eventually, the sheer numbers of MiGs now being put up by the communist air arms forced the USAF to abandon daylight raids by the B-29s. As an alternative, the UN began to rely increasingly on night-time attacks flown by carrier-based aircraft.

US MARINE CORPS, KOREAN WAR (MAG UNITS ONLY)		
Aircraft	**Unit**	**Base**
F9F-2B, F9F-4	VMF-115	K3, K6
F9F-2B	VMF-311	K3
F4U-4, AU-1	VMF-212	USS *Badoeng Strait*, K14, Wonsan, K3
F4U-4	VMF-312	K14, Wonsan, K27, K1, various carriers inc. USS *Badoeng Strait*
F4U-4	VMF-214	K9, Ashiya, USS *Sicily*, K1, K6
F4U-4, AU-1	VMF-323	K9, Ashiya, USS *Sicily*, USS *Badoeng Strait*, K1, K6
F4U-4N, F4U-5N, F7F-3N	VMF-542	K14, Wonsan, K27, K8
F7F-3N, F4U-5N, F3D-2N	VMF-513	Itazuke, Wonsan, K1, K6
AD-3	VMA-121	K3
F4U-4	VMA-332	USS *Bairoko*
AD-3	VMA-121	K3
HO3S-1, OY-2, OE-1	VMO-6	K9, USS *Sicily*, K14

Specifications

Crew: 6–8

Powerplant: 2 x 2610kW (3500hp) Pratt & Whitney R-4360-20 piston engines

Maximum speed: 476km/h (296mph)

Range: 3669km (2280 miles)

Service ceiling: 7300m (23,950ft)

Dimensions: span 33.3m (109ft 3in); length 26.37m (86ft 6in); height 8m (26ft 3in)

Weight: 29,029kg (64,000lb) loaded

Payload: 4500kg (10,000lb) of cargo

▲ **Fairchild R4Q-1 Flying Boxcar**

VMR-253, U.S. Marine Corps / Itami, 1950–53

The U.S. Marine Corps version of the C-119 was the R4Q-1, and 41 examples of the type served in two squadrons, VMR-252 and VMR-253. Outfitted as an assault transport, the R4Q-1 was operated from Itami between 1950 and 1953. Other USMC transports in theatre were the R4D (C-47), R5D (C-54) and R5C (C-46).

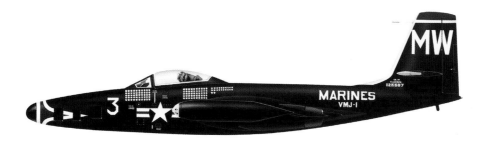

▲ McDonnell F2H-2P Banshee

VMJ-1, U.S. Marine Corps / K3 (Pohang) and K14 (Kimpo), 1952–53

Displaying 122 mission markings on the fuselage, this photo-reconnaissance Banshee was operated by VMJ-1 over Korea from bases at K3 and K14. Operating under the command of the U.S. Fifth Air Force, VMJ-1 provided the USMC with an organic reconnaissance capability when it arrived in theatre in March 1952.

Specifications

Crew: 1	Dimensions: span 13.6m (44ft 11in);
Powerplant: 2 x 1474kg (3250lb) Westinghouse	length 12.9m (42ft 5in); height 4.4m
J34-WE-34 turbojets	(14ft 5in)
Maximum speed: 851km/h (529mph)	Weight: 9342kg (20,600lb) loaded
Range: 1930km (1200 miles)	Armament: none
Service ceiling: 14,785m (48,500ft)	

These involved night-capable U.S. Navy F4U-5N and AD-4N aircraft, while the U.S. Marine Corps provided land-based AD-3s for the first time, with an initial unit operating from K3 (Pohang).

Further offensive air power was made available by the basing of two B-26 groups at Kunsan and Pusan from May 1951. These units had previously been based in Japan and now began to undertake mainly nocturnal raids against communist convoys on their way to the front. At the same time, the B-29 force switched from primarily daylight missions to nocturnal raids, in an effort to reduce the losses at the hands of MiGs and AAA.

Night-fighter war

In the nocturnal realm, March 1951 saw the arrival in the Far East Air Force of the F-94A/B night-fighter as a successor to the ageing, propeller-driven F-82, which had been active within three Fighter (All Weather) Squadrons since the onset of hostilities, mainly flying out of Itazuke, Japan. Operational deficiencies kept the F-94 out of the fray until December 1951, however, when a pair of F-94Bs took up alert duties at Suwon with the 68th Fighter Interceptor Squadron.

In March 1952 the 319th Fighter Interceptor squadron arrived at Suwon, with F-94Bs, although these were prohibited from flying over enemy territory for fear that their sensitive radar equipment may end up in communist hands. B-29 losses to

MiGs continued at night, however, despite the presence of U.S. Marine Corps F7F-3N night-fighters of VMF(N)-513, and in December 1952 it was agreed that the F-94s could operate without restriction, the night-fighters forming patrols between the Chongchon and Yalu rivers in support of the night-bombing offensive.

Based at Misawa and Chitose, the primary mission of the 116th Fighter Bomber Group's F-84s was the air defence of Japan. However, it later undertook operations over Korea, aided by in-flight refuelling from KB-29P tankers. Project High Tide, as these missions were known, commenced in May 1952,

USAF RECONNAISSANCE, KOREAN WAR		
Aircraft	**Unit**	**Base**
RB-29A, RB-50A, RB-36A, WB-26, RB-45C, KB-29A	91st SRS	Yokota, Misawa
RB-29A	31st SRS	Yokota
RB-17G	6204th PMF	Yokota
RB-26C	162nd TRS	Itazuke, K2
RB-26C	12th TRS	K2
RF-80A	8th TRS	Yokota, Itazuke
RF-80A	15th TRS	K2
F-6D (RF-51D), RF-80C	45th TRS	Itazuke, K2
AT-6G, LT-6G	6148th TCS	K16, K47
AT-6G, LT-6G	6149th TCS	K47

Specifications

Crew: 1

Powerplant: 1 x 24kN (5400lb) Allison J33-A-35 turbojet

Maximum speed: 966km/h (594mph)

Range: 1328km (825 miles)

Service ceiling: 14,265m (46,800ft)

Dimensions: span 11.81m (38ft 9in); length 10.49m (34ft 5in); height 3.43m (11ft 3in)

Weight: 7646kg (16,856lb) loaded

Armament: none

▲ **Lockheed RF-80A Shooting Star**

67th Tactical Reconnaissance Wing, USAF / K13 (Suwon)

Wearing an experimental water-based drab olive paint scheme that was applied in theatre, this USAF RF-80A was on strength with the 67th Tactical Reconnaissance Wing at Suwon, Korea. The RF-80 proved itself capable of absorbing considerable battle damage and was also used on long-range missions with tanker support.

with a raid against Sariwon in North Korea. The same month also saw the first use of the USAF's F-86E in the fighter-bomber role, when bomb-equipped Sabres attacked Sinuiju airfield.

A significant large-scale UN raid on 23 June 1952, involved over 200 ground attack aircraft from USAF U.S. Navy, U.S. Marine Corps and Republic of Korea AF units, escorted by over 100 F-86Es. Their objective was the hydroelectric plant at Suiho. Surprisingly, the North Korean AF put up no resistance, the MiGs instead focusing on defending Manchuria's industries. In general, MiG activity was decreasing, but the arrival of the F-86E ensured that the USAF had a qualitative edge over the communist air forces.

New Sabres

Peace talks continued into 1953, the final year of the war, while the communists attempted to gain the upper hand in the air war, while brokering an agreement concerning the repatriation of prisoners of war. In the air war, however, they were denied superiority by the UN air forces, which were boosted in particular by the arrival of an improved Sabre variant, the F-86F, in June and July 1952. This model introduced a more powerful engine for improved performance, and could better the MiG in terms of agility at all altitudes.

August 1952 saw an increase in MiG activity, met by additional F-86 sorties, while the F-86F was

further improved through the introduction of a modified wing, supplied in kit form from October. As well as the new wing, which boosted manoeuvrability, the Sabre began to be outfitted for offensive missions, with the 8th and 18th Fighter Bomber Groups receiving F-86Fs as replacement for their F-80s and F-51s. After a lengthy period of crew conversion, the 'fighter bomber' F-86F flew its first combat missions in February 1953.

By the time the F-86F was in action as a fighter-bomber, MiG activity had begun to increase once again. However, the Chinese approach to the war situation changed with the death of Stalin in March, after which the People's Republic lost valuable political support from the USSR. Fighting on the ground continued, with air support for the UN contingent now being supplied by the improved F-84G model, based at Taegu and Kunsan starting in the summer of 1952, as well as B-26s at Kunsan and Pusan. Off the Korean coast, Task Force 77 kept at

US ARMY HELICOPTERS, KOREAN WAR		
Aircraft	**Unit**	**Base**
H-13, H-23A	MASH	various
H-19C	THC-6	various
H-5A/G, H-19	3rd ARS	Japan, K14, K96, Cho-do
H-19A	3rd ARS	Japan, Cho-do

▲ **Sikorsky HO3S-1**

MAMS-33, U.S. Marine Corps / Korea

Aircraft Maintenance Squadron (MAMS) 33 was equipped with a number of
different U.S. Marine Corps types, including the HO3S-1 and the fixed-wing F9F
and AD-2. Named *Southern Comfort*, this example of the former was used for ship
guard and rescue duties. The HO3S-1 was similar to the USAF's H-5F Dragonfly.

Specifications

Crew: 1

Powerplant: 1 x 335kW (450shp) Pratt &
 Whitney R-985-AN-5 turboshaft

Maximum speed: 172km/h (107mph)

Range: 442km (275 miles)

Service ceiling: 4510m (14,800ft)

Dimensions: rotor diameter 14.9m (49ft);
 length 17.6m (57ft 8in); height 3.9m
 (12ft 11in)

Weight: 2495kg (5500lb) loaded

Armament: none

▲ **Sikorsky HRS-1**

HMR-161, U.S. Marine Corps / K18 (Kangnung), 1951–53

An assault transport with capacity for up to eight troops, 60 examples of the
HRS-1 served with nine U.S. Marine Corps transport helicopter squadrons before
the end of the war in Korea. The HRS-1 was also used for rescue missions, and
operations were based out of K18 from September 1951.

Specifications

Crew: 2

Powerplant: 1 x 450kW (600hp) Pratt &
 Whitney R-1340-57 radial engine,

Maximum speed: 163km/h (101mph)

Range: 652km (405 miles)

Service ceiling: 3200m (10,500ft)

Dimensions: Rotor diameter 16.16m (53ft);
 length 62ft 7in (19.1m); height 4.07m
 (13ft 4in)

Weight: 3266kg (7200lb) loaded

Armament: none

least three carriers on station, with the more advanced
F9F-5 fighter deployed beginning in October 1952.

June 1953, the final full month of fighting, saw the
F-86s maintain their superiority, with almost 8000
sorties flown. In July, the communists gave up on the
issue of repatriation at the peace talks, and fighting
came to an end on 27 June. The final claims made for
victories in aerial combat have long been disputed,
but it is clear that the UN air forces more than held

their own, and gained air superiority, despite being
heavily outnumbered by the end of the conflict.

The war also served as a compelling warning to
the U.S. military machine, which set about
modernizing its equipment and strengthening its
presence in key trouble spots, as well as granting
additional equipment and expertise to U.S. allies,
and to states seen to be at risk of communist invasion
or insurrection.

China and Taiwan
1946–1958

The end of World War II left power in China divided between the Soviet-backed communists, and the Nationalists of Chiang Kai-Shek, armed and supported by the U.S.

AFTER A PAUSE during the years of World War II, the Chinese Civil War resumed in 1946, following the departure of U.S. forces from China. Armed by the U.S., the Nationalists gained some early victories, but by 1949 Peking and Tienstsin had both fallen into communist hands. The People's Republic of China was established on 1 October 1949, and the nationalist force evacuated the

Specifications

Crew: 1

Powerplant: 1 x 1264kW (1695hp) Packard
 Merlin V-1650-7 V-12 piston engine

Maximum speed: 703km/h (437mph)

Range: 3347km (2080 miles)

Service ceiling: 12,770m (41,900ft)

Dimensions: span 11.28m (37ft); length 9.83m
 (32ft 3in); height 4.17m (13ft 8in)

Weight: 5488kg (12,100lb) loaded

Armament: 6 x 12.7mm (.5in) MGs in wings,
 plus up to 2 x 454kg (1000lb) bombs

▲ **North American P-51D Mustang**

People's Liberation Army AF

The P-51D was supplied in quantity to the Chinese AF during 1944-45. After the end of World War II, these aircraft were flown by the Chinese Nationalists as well as by the post-revolution People's Republic, as illustrated by this example. Prior to the arrival of MiG-15s, PLAAF fighters also included La-11s and Yak-9s.

Specifications

Crew: 4

Powerplant: 2 x 1500kW (2000hp) Pratt &
 Whitney R-2800-51 radial piston engines

Maximum speed: 433km/h (269mph)

Range: 4750km (2950 miles)

Service ceiling: 8410m (27,600ft)

Dimensions: span 32.9m (108ft 1in);
 length 23.27m (76ft 4in);
 height 6.63m (21ft 9in)

Weight: 22,000kg (48,000lb) maximum

Armament: none

▲ **Curtiss C-46 Commando**

Transport Wing, Chinese Nationalist AF, Taipei

At the time of the Chinese Civil War in 1948, the Chinese Nationalist AF included two transport groups equipped with C-46s and C-47s. This ex-USAAF example was one of those that participated in the evacuation from mainland China to Taiwan in 1949. The Commando remained in CNAF service long into the 1950s.

mainland for the island of Formosa, to form the Republic of China (Taiwan). The People's Liberation Army AF played a significant role in the Korean War starting in 1950 and retained U.S.-built equipment at the outbreak of this conflict, before receiving new equipment from the USSR, beginning with MiG-15 jet fighters.

While the communists were recipients of military aid from the USSR, the U.S. supplied Taiwan with advanced weaponry as of 1951 in order to establish itself as a bulwark against the communist threat, while the U.S. 7th Fleet sailed in the Taiwan Straits.

Covert operations

Through the Taiwan-based Civil Air Transport (CAT), a CIA-operated front airline, the U.S. was able to maintain a covert military presence in Southeast Asia, supporting the French in Indo-China and inserting U.S. agents on the Chinese mainland.

Fighting between China and Taiwan broke out in 1958 over the issue of the islands of Quemoy and Matsu, which were claimed by the Nationalists. The PLA began an artillery bombardment against the island in September 1954, the nationalists responding with counter-bombardment and air raids. In August 1958 fighting erupted again, and China announced plans for a invasion of the islands, to be followed by an occupation of Taiwan.

The Chinese Nationalist AF mounted patrols over the disputed islands, and Sidewinder-armed F-86s

CHINESE NATIONAL AF, 1958		
Aircraft	Unit	Base
F-86F	1st FW	Taipeh
F-86F	2nd FW	Taipeh
F-86F	3rd FW	Tainan
F-84G	5th FBW	n/a
RF-84F	TRS	Taipeh
C-46D, C-47, SA-16A	TW	Taipeh

fought aerial engagements against Chinese MiG-15s and MiG-17s. On 24 September the CNAF claimed a number of MiGs destroyed, these victories marking the first successful combat usage of air-to-air missiles. In October the CNAF was recipient of more advanced U.S.-supplied equipment, including B-57s, F-100Ds, F-104As, F-101Cs and RF-101Cs.

The crisis surrounding Quemoy and Matsu passed, yet relations between the two Chinas remained tense. Further air-to-air confrontations were recorded in July 1959, when Sabres fought with MiG-17s. In 1967 CNAF F-104As battles against PLAAF MiG-19s, claiming two destroyed. As of 1959, the CNAF operated U-2 spyplanes over mainland China on behalf of the CIA, and at least eight were downed by Chinese air defences. Hostility would last until the end of the Cold War. The U.S. eventually withdrew overt support for Taiwan, but continued to supply the Nationalists with combat aircraft.

Specifications

Crew: 3

Powerplant: 2 x 26.3kN (5952lb) Klimov
VK-1 turbojets

Maximum speed: 902km/h (560mph)

Range: 2180km (1355 miles)

Service ceiling: 12,300m (40,355ft)

Dimensions: span 21.45m (70ft 4in); length

17.65m (57ft 10.75in); height 6.7m (21ft
11.8in)

Weight: 21,200kg (46,738lb) loaded

Armament: 4 x 23mm cannon; internal bomb
capacity 1000kg (2205lb), max bomb
capacity 3000kg (6614lb)

▲ **Ilyushin Il-28**

People's Liberation Army AF

Received from the Soviets and locally built under licence as the H-5, the Il-28 was the first jet bomber to serve with the PLA. By far the largest export operator of the Il-28, China began to receive several hundred examples of the light bomber from the USSR in the late 1950s, with local manufacture beginning in 1967.

Specifications

Crew: 1

Powerplant: 2 x 31.9kN (7165lb) Shenyang
WP-6 turbojets

Maximum speed: 1540km/h (957mph)

Range: 1390km (864 miles)

Service ceiling: 17,900m (58,725ft)

Dimensions: span 9.2m (30ft 2.25in); length
14.9m (48ft 10.5in); height 3.88m (12ft 8.75in)

Weight: 10,000kg (22,046lb) maximum

Armament: 3 x 30mm NR-30 cannon; four
external hardpoints with provision for up to
500kg (1102lb) of stores, including air-to-air
missiles, 250kg (551lb) bombs, 55mm (2.1in)
rocket-launcher pods, 212mm (8.34in) rockets
or drop tanks

▲ **Shenyang J-6**

People's Liberation Army AF

Entering service in the early 1960s, PLA J-6 fighters (licence-built versions of the
MiG-19) were involved in a number of Cold War skirmishes against Nationalist
Chinese and other air arms. In addition to clashes against the CNAF and USAF, the
J-6 was used in combat during China's border conflict with Vietnam as of 1979.

France in Indochina
1946–1954

**In the wake of World War II, tensions emerged between the French colony of Indo-China and its
European occupier and the Viet Minh forces that had fought previously against the Japanese.**

SERIOUS FIGHTING BROKE out between the French
and the communist Viet Minh in late 1946 when
the guerrillas tried to take control of Hanoi and other
cities. Among the first aircraft deployed to Indo-

China were French AF Spitfire Mk IXs, which arrived
at Saigon in 1946, joining a number of Ki-43s seized
from the Japanese. The Spitfires, serving with four
escadrilles, performed well in the anti-guerrilla role, in

▲ **Grumman F6F-5 Hellcat**

Escadrille 1F, French Navy / Arromanches, 1951-52

Serving from the aircraft carrier *Arromanches*, this French Navy F6F saw action
over Indo-China in 1954. The carrier arrived on station off Indo-China in 1953 and
provided an air wing that included Flotilles 11F (F6Fs) and 3F (SB2Cs). These
were joined by the AU-1 Corsairs of 14F for the fighting at Dien Bien Phu.

Specifications

Crew: 1

Powerplant: 1 x 1491kW (2000hp) Pratt &
Whitney R-2800-10W Double Wasp
18-cylinder two-row radial engine

Maximum speed: 603km/h (375mph)

Range: 2559km (1590 miles)

Service ceiling: 11,705m (38,400ft)

Dimensions: span 13.06m (42ft 10in); length
10.24m (33ft 7in); height 3.99m (13ft 1in)

Weight: 7025kg (15,487lb) maximum

Armament: 4 x 0.50in (12.7mm) Browning
machine guns

contrast to the Mosquitoes. The latter arrived in 1947 but soon proved unsuitable for tropical operations. In addition to French AF types in theatre, the French Navy provided SBD-5 dive-bombers, PBY flying boats, Sea Otter amphibians and ex-Japanese E13A1 floatplanes.

The first wave of fighting ended in spring 1947 with French troops still in control of the cities. Later in 1947 the French began an offensive in order to defeat the guerrillas, who in turn began to establish strongholds in rural areas, led by Vo Nguyen Giap.

Throughout the campaign, French air power was used exclusively in support of the troops on the ground, and in 1949 the U.S. began to deliver war materiel, including P-63 fighters. As of June 1950, aircraft were organized into three autonomous tactical organizations (GATAC), one in the north, one in the south, and one in the central region. All answered directly to local commanders on the ground. The French Navy was also modernizing its force in the same period, now fielding carrier-based F6Fs and SB2Cs as well as land-based PB4Y-2 patrol aircraft.

Rural resistance

By 1950 the Viet Minh were influential across much of the rural north and central regions, while the French were in control in the south; the same year saw the arrival of the F6F as a replacement for the Spitfire and P-63. Also in 1950 the French began to deploy bombers to the war zone, in the form of the B-26B/C, which arrived in November, and eventually equipped four *groupes*. Other aircraft types on strength at this time included RB-26 and NC.701 reconnaissance types, assorted observation and communications types, and a number of helicopters, including the UH-12A, H-23A/B, S-51 and S-55.

Towards the end of 1950 the Viet Ming took Cao Bang and Lang Son, while French troops followed up with victories at Vinh Yen and Mao Khe in 1951.

In 1952-53 the fighting was focused on Tonkin and Laos, and the French began to establish garrisons in Viet Minh territory to encourage attacks in which the French would overcome the guerrillas with superior firepower. Initially successful, this concept would be defeated in humiliating circumstances at Dien Bien Phu, between Tonkin and Laos, in May 1954. In 1953 the French AF had re-equipped with the F8F as a replacement for the F6F that was phased out in January that year.

By the time of the siege of Dien Bien Phu the French had some 400 aircraft in Indo-China. Of particular importance from now on would be the French AF transport fleet, based around C-47s, plus smaller numbers of Ju 52/3ms. No fewer than 100 C-47s were involved in the final evacuation from Dien Bien Phu. The garrison fell on the evening of 7 May, after a bayonet charge by the last 600 French troops, facing encirclement by 40,000 Viet Minh. The loss of Dien Bien Phu sealed Viet Minh victory in Indo-China, and a ceasefire was agreed in July.

▲ **Grumman F8F-1 Bearcat**

GC II/21, French AF / Tan Son Nhut, 1953–54

Based at Tan Son Nhut, this French AF F8F was in action over Indo-China during 1953-54. First appearing with the French AF in Southeast Asia in 1951, the F8F was undoubtedly the most effective close support aircraft deployed by the French AF in Indo-China. Armament included rockets, bombs and napalm.

Specifications

Crew: 1	Dimensions: span 10.92m (35ft 10in); length
Powerplant: 1 x 156kW (2100hp) Pratt &	8.61m (28ft 3in); height 4.21m (13ft 9in)
Whitney R-2800-34W Double Wasp radial	Weight: 5873kg (12,947lb) loaded
piston engine	Armament: 4 x .5in (12.7mm) M2 machine
Maximum speed: 678km/h (421mph)	guns; up to 454kg (1000lb) of bombs or 4 x
Range: 1778km (1105 miles)	127mm (5in) rockets
Service ceiling: 11,796m (38,700ft)	

U.S. in Vietnam
1959–1975

After the French collapse, Indo-China was divided into four: North and South Vietnam, Cambodia and Laos. With North Vietnam 'lost' to communism, the U.S. expected the others to follow.

SOUTH VIETNAM WAS supported by the U.S., fearful it might go the way of the Viet Min-ruled North. U.S. military advisors remained in the South after the French withdrawal, providing support to the local regime, which maintained its own air power in the form of F8Fs, C-47s, H-19s, L-19s and others.

In 1959 the North Vietnamese leader, Ho Chi Minh, announced his intention to reunify the two Vietnams, and the North Vietnamese Army (NVA) began to support the communist Viet Cong (VC) guerrillas operating in South Vietnam. As the South descended into civil war, the U.S. sent more advisors, together with AD-6 (A-1) attack aircraft in September 1960, followed by H-34 helicopters. Before the end of the war rotorcraft would transform the concept of U.S. Army air-mobility, as well as

serving in other diverse roles including close support, re-supply, casualty evacuation and command.

The trigger for increased U.S. military involvement in Vietnam was the inauguration of President Kennedy in 1961. The first unit deployed was a USAF mobile command unit sent to Tan Son Nhut in October, followed by Project Farm Gate, under which jungle warfare specialists and COIN aircraft were sent to Bien Hoa. The first jet equipment were RF-101C photo-reconnaissance aircraft. The U.S. Army presence began with H-21 helicopters, together with heliborne troops. Further equipment for the VNAF included T-28s, with C-123s to boost local airlift capacity. As of 1962 the latter type was used to deliver defoliant under Project Ranch Hand, denying the VC jungle cover.

USAF IN VIETNAM, 1961–64			
Project	**Aircraft**	**Unit**	**Base**
Pipe Stem	RF-101C	15th TRS	Tan Son Nhut
Abel Mabel	RF-101C	45th TRS	Don Muang, Tan Son Nhut
Farm Gate	T-28D, SC-47, B-26B, RB-26C, U-10A, RB-26L	4400th CCTS	Bien Hoa
Farm Gate	T-28B, SC-47, B-26B, RB-26C/L, U-10A, A-1E	4410th CCTS	Bien Hoa, Pleiku
Farm Gate	O-1E	19th TASS	Bien Hoa, Can Tho
Mule Train	C-123B	346th TCS	Tan Son Nhut, Dan Nang
Mule Train	C-123B	776th TCS	Tan Son Nhut
Mule Train	C-123B	310th TCS	Tan Son Nhut
Mule Train	C-123B	309th TCS	Tan Son Nhut
Mule Train	C-123B	777th TCS	Dan Nang, Don Muang
Mule Train	C-123B	311th TCS	Dan Nang, Don Muang
Ranch Hand	UC-123B/K	SASF	Tan Son Nhut
Water Glass	TF/F-102A	509th FIS	Tan Son Nhut
Water Glass	AD-5Q	VAW-35	Tan Son Nhut
Patricia Lynn	RB-57E	33rd TG	Tan Son Nhut
Dragon Lady	U-2A/C	4080th SRW	Bien Hoa

Attacks on U.S. Navy destroyers by NVA torpedo boats in the Gulf of Tonkin in August 1964 were the catalyst for full-scale U.S. military intervention. In the first instance, F-8Es from USS *Ticonderoga* sank one torpedo boat, with attacks made by A-1s from the same carrier days later. Finally, U.S. Navy A-1s and A-4 attack aircraft from USS *Ticonderoga* and *Constellation* raided North Vietnamese naval bases and oil depots. Carrier air power would be an ever-present for the remaining eight years of the conflict.

Increasing presence

After the Gulf of Tonkin incident the Pentagon sent USAF B-57s to Bien Hoa in August, followed by F-100s and F-102s to Da Nang, while other aircraft were stationed in Thailand, using the Royal Thai AF bases at U-Tapao and Udorn. As airbases came under attack from VC, the U.S. planned Operation Flaming Dart, a series of retaliatory air strikes in February 1965. In response, U.S. Navy carrier aircraft hit NVA targets in the first of countless air attacks that would be launched by U.S. air power against communist positions in the coming years.

The F-100D bore the brunt of much of the early bombing sorties, as well as providing defensive low-level combat air patrols (CAPs). Less successful in the early days of the war was the F-104C, which was soon switched from its defensive mission to the role of low-level tactical bomber as of the autumn of 1965.

In Laos, meanwhile, the U.S. supplied T-28s for use against the North Vietnam-backed Pathet Lao guerrillas starting in 1965, supported from late 1964 by a U.S. air campaign codenamed Barrel Roll.

March 1965 saw the start of a new campaign of bombing against the NVA, known as Rolling Thunder. This aimed to break communist resolve, but was less than successful, merely hardening anti-U.S. feeling in the North, and failing to find enough targets of genuine military value. Furthermore, Hanoi and other cities were considered 'off bounds', together with North Vietnamese airfields and SAM sites – the U.S. unwilling to risk the loss of life of Chinese or Soviet advisors.

A final level of inefficiency in the Rolling Thunder campaign was ensured by the fact that targets had to be selected and approved in Washington, with little regard for local conditions. In terms of air combat, the hands of the U.S. pilots were further tied by a ruling that demanded that

▲ **Republic F-105 Thunderchief**
A line-up of bare-metal F-105 Thunderchiefs deployed to Southeast Asia

U.S. NAVY IN VIETNAM, 1964–65		
Aircraft	**Unit**	**Carrier**
F-8E	VF-191	USS *Bonne Homme Richard*
F-8C	VF-194	USS *Bonne Homme Richard*
A-4C	VA-192	USS *Bonne Homme Richard*
A-4C	VA-195	USS *Bonne Homme Richard*
A-1H/J	VA-196	USS *Bonne Homme Richard*
E-1B	VAW-11	USS *Bonne Homme Richard*
RF-8A	VFP-63	USS *Bonne Homme Richard*
A-3B	VAH-4	USS *Bonne Homme Richard*
UH-2A	HU-1	USS *Bonne Homme Richard*
F-4B	VF-142	USS *Constellation*
F-4B	VF-143	USS *Constellation*
A-4C	VA-144	USS *Constellation*
A-1H/J	VA-145	USS *Constellation*
A-4C	VA-146	USS *Constellation*
E-1B	VAW-11	USS *Constellation*
RF-8A	VFP-63	USS *Constellation*
A-3B	VAH-10	USS *Constellation*
UH-2A	HU-1	USS *Constellation*
F-8E	VF-51	USS *Ticonderoga*
F-8E	VF-53	USS *Ticonderoga*
A-1H/J	VA-52, VA-56	USS *Ticonderoga*
A-4B	VA-55	USS *Ticonderoga*
A-4E	VA-56	USS *Ticonderoga*
E-1B	VAW-11	USS *Ticonderoga*
RF-8A	VFP-63	USS *Ticonderoga*
A-3B	VAH-4	USS *Ticonderoga*

positive visual identification be acquired before an engagement could take place.

Another key event of March 1965 was the deployment of large numbers of ground troops, with 3500 U.S. Marines arriving at Da Nang to join the advisors already committed. Vital to the build-up and the subsequent support of the war effort was the USAF's fleet of airlifters, including the C-141 that entered service in 1965 and replaced the piston-engined C-124 and C-133. As well bringing troops and materiel from the U.S. to the war zone, the C-141 was responsible for flying casualties home. Once cargo and troops were brought to Southeast Asia it was the job of the C-130 and C-123 to bring these cargoes forward to airstrips near the front lines.

Throughout 1965 the air war escalated, and began to encompass aerial combat between the U.S. air arms and the North Vietnamese AF, and the use of SAMs and electronic countermeasures against them. The NVAF expanded starting in early 1965, and its MiG-15s and MiG-17s were increasingly sent into battle against U.S. aircraft, the first recorded instance being on 17 June when two F-4Bs from the USS *Midway* met four MiG-17s, claiming two shot down.

The first USAF fighter-bomber to be deployed to Vietnam in large numbers was the F-105, the basic F-105D being joined later by the Thunderstick II modification with enhanced mission avionics, and the two-seat F-105G for the defence suppression, or Wild Weasel role, analyzing and attacking North Vietnamese air defence radars by active or passive means. Early bombing tactics saw the use of formations of aircraft flying at medium level, and typical scenarios involved a B-66 formation leader guiding a force of F-105s to the target. The EB-66C model was used to jam enemy air defence radars, in order to protect the attack formations. As an alternative to the formation leader, targets could be identified by forward air controllers (FACs), which would circle the combat area in slow-flying aircraft and call in strikes by tactical fighters.

Reconnaissance missions

Finding the targets in the first instance – and studying the results of the bombing raids – was the responsibility of reconnaissance aircraft, including the A-26A (a redesignated, COIN development of the B-26), the RF-101C and the U.S. Navy's carrier-based RA-5C and RF-8. More exotic reconnaissance assets were the Teledyne Ryan 147 series of remotely piloted vehicles (RPVs), equipped with a variety of sensors and used to fly hazardous, low-level missions over both Vietnam and China after launch from a specially equipped DC-130 drone carrier. After the mission, recovery was effected through the use of an HH-3E helicopter that snatched the drone after it had shut down its engine and deployed a parachute.

An almost insurmountable challenge for the U.S. was the Ho Chi Minh trail, a vast network of supply routes, which was crucial to the communist war

▲ **Douglas A-1H Skyraider**

83rd Special Operations Group, VNAF / Tan Son Nhut, 1966

Wearing an unusual low-visibility camouflage scheme, this A-1H was used for close support, attack and forward air control missions by the 83rd Special Operations Group, VNAF. Originally built for the U.S. Navy, this particular aircraft was based at Tan Son Nhut in 1966.

Specifications

Crew: 1

Powerplant: 1 x 2013kW (2700hp) Pratt & Whitney R-3350-26WA radial piston engine

Maximum speed: 520km/h (320mph)

Range: 2115km (1315 miles)

Service ceiling: 8660m (28,500ft)

Dimensions: span 15.25m (50ft); length 11.84m (38ft 10in); height 4.78m (15ft 8in)

Weight: 11,340kg (25,000lb) maximum

Armament: 4 x 20mm cannon; up to 3600kg (8000lb) of bombs, rockets, or other stores

Aircraft	Wing	Squadrons	Base
USAF FIGHTERS AND ATTACK, VIETNAM			
B-57B/C/E	405th TBW, 6252nd TFW	8th TBS, 13th TBS	Tan Son Nhut, Bien Hoa Da Nang, Phan Rang
F-102A	–	16th FIS	Tan Son Nhut
TF/F-102A	–	509th FIS	Tan Son Nhut, Bien Hoa
TF/F-102A	–	64th FIS	Bien Hoa
F-102A	–	82nd FIS	Da Nang
F-105D	4th TFW	36th TFS, 80th TFS	Takhli, Korat
F-104C	–	435th TFS, 476th TFS	Da Nang
F-105D	18th TFW	12th TFS, 44th TFS, 67th TFS	Korat
F-100D	405th TFW	511th TFS	Takhli
F-100D/F, B-57B/C/E	35th TFW	612th TFS, 614th TFS, 615th TFS, 352nd TFS, 8th TBS, 13th TBS, 120th TFS	Phan Rang, Da Nang, Tuy Hoa
F-105D	23rd TFW	562nd TFS, 563rd TFS	Da Nang
F-4C	12th TFW	45th TFS, 43rd TFS, 557th TFS, 558th TFS, 559th TFS, 389th TFS, 480th TFS	Ubon, Cam Ranh Bay, Phu Cat
F-100D	474th TFW	429th TFS, 481st TFS	Bien Hoa, Tan Son Nhut
F-100D/F, F-5A, A-37B	3rd TFW	307th TFS, 308th TFS, 510th TFS, 531st TFS, 90th TFS, 4503rd TFS, 8th AS, 90th AS	Bien Hoa
F-105D/F, F-111A	355th TFW	333rd TFS, 334th TFS, 335th TFS, 354th TFS, 357th TFS, 428th TFS, 44th TFS	Takhli
F-105D/F/G, F-4C/D/E, A-7D	388th TFW	421st TFS, 13th TFS, 469th TFS, 561st TFS, 561st TFS, 44th TFS, 12th TFS, 34th TFS, 6010th TFS, 17th TFS, 44th TFS, 354th TFS, 67th TFS, 25th TFS, 561st TFS, 3rd TFS	Korat
F-4C/D/E, B-57G	8th TFW	433rd TFS, 497th TFS, 25th TFS, 555th TFS, 435th TFS, 13th TBS, 35th TFS, 336th TFS, 334th TFS	Ubon, Korat
F-4C/D/E	366th TFW	389th TFS, 390th TFS, 480th TFS, 4th TFS, 421st TFS, 35th TFS, 7th TFS, 9th TFS, 417th TFS	Phan Rang, Da Nang, Takhli
F-104C	479th TFW	435th TFS, 476th TFS	Da Nang
F-100D/F	31st TFW	306th TFS, 308th TFS, 309th TFS, 355th TFS, 416th TFS, 136th, TFS, 188th TFS	Tuy Hoa
F-100D/F	37rd FTW	612 TFS, 355 TFS, 416 TFS, 174 TFS	Phu Cat
F-4C/D/E	432nd TRW	13th TFS, 555th TFS, 524th TFS, 8th TFS, 308th TFS, 307th TFS, 58th TFS, 523rd TFS, 4th TFS	Udorn
F-111A	347th TFW	429th TFS, 430th TFS	Takhli, Korat
A-7D	354th TFW	353rd TFS, 355th TFS, 356th TFS	Korat
F-5A, A-27A/B	3rd TFW	10th FCS, 604th ACS, 8th AS, 90th AS	Bien Hoa

Specifications

Crew: 1

Powerplant: 1 x 104.5kN (23,500lb) Pratt & Whitney J75 turbojet

Maximum speed: 2018km/h (1254mph)

Range: 370km (230 miles)

Service ceiling: 15,850m (52,000ft)

Dimensions: 10.65m (34ft 11.25in); length 19.58m (64ft 3in); height 5.99m (19ft 8in)

Weight: 18,144kg (40,000lb) maximum

Armament: 1 x 20mm M61 cannon; internal bay with provision for up to 3629kg (8000lb) of bombs; external load of 2722kg (6000lb)

▲ **North American F-100A Super Sabre**

208th TFS, 31st TFW / Tuy Hoa, 1970

This F-100A-61-NA, named *Jeanne Kay*, was typical of the type serving in Southeast Asia. The 'Hun' was in action over Vietnam almost from the outset and proved a robust ground attack platform, which bore the brunt of offensive operations in the early years of the conflict.

effort in South Vietnam. Arms and supplies were carried along the Trail to the front line, typically via Laos. Directing air power against the Trail was a difficult task, and the supply lines were never successfully broken. From 1965-67 U.S. air power focused on attacking particularly important targets along the Trail, raids being directed by FACs flying in aircraft such as the O-1 and its eventual replacement, the O-2. As well as running the gauntlet of AAA and SAMs, the FACs would have to approach close enough to the target to mark it with rockets.

One innovative method of interdicting supplies on the Trail was the Igloo White sensor that detected noise or vibration after having been dropped into the jungle by an OP-2E, or by a tactical jet. An EC-121R relay aircraft then picked up transmissions from these sensors, before they were transmitted to a ground station for analysis. Starting in 1971 a number of EC-121s were replaced by the smaller QU-22 under a programme known as Pave Eagle. Some QU-22s were also adapted to fly as pilotless RPVs. In addition to the data gathered by the Igloo White sensors, further inputs were delivered by AQM-34L (Ryan 147) RPVs, with their signals sent via the DC-130 drone controllers.

Even with the target identified, prosecuting an attack with a tactical jet was not easy, and most lacked the capacity for precision ordnance delivery. An exception was the A-6A, flown from U.S. Navy carriers and also operated from land bases by USMC units, which was equipped with sophisticated radar

U.S. MARINE CORPS FIGHTERS AND ATTACK, VIETNAM		
Aircraft	**Unit**	**Base**
MAG-11		
TF-9J, TA-4F	H&MS-11	Da Nang
F-8E	VMF-235	Da Nang
F-4B/J	VMFA-542	Da Nang
F-4B	VMFA-531	Da Nang
A-6A	VMA-242	Da Nang
OV-10A	VMO-2	Marble Mountain
A-6A	VMA-225	Da Nang
A-4E	VMA-311	Da Nang
MAG-12		
A-4C	VMA-224, VMA-225, VMA-214	Chu Lai
A-4E	VMA-311, VMA-223, VMA-211, VMA-121	Chu Lai, Bien Hoa
A-6A	VMA-533	Chu Lai
MAG-13		
F-4B	VMFA-323, VMFA-115, VMFA-122	Chu Lai
F-8E	VMF-232	Da Nang, Chu Lai
F-4J	VMFA-232	Chu Lai
MAG-15		
F-4B	VMFA-115	Da Nang, Nam Phong
F-4J	VMFA-232	Da Nang, Nam Phong
A-6A	VMA-533	Nam Phong

and attack navigation equipment. The A-6A's combat debut came in March 1965.

Precision bombing

In terms of USAF assets, the best-equipped aircraft in terms of navigation/attack avionics were a small number of considerably modified B-57Gs, and the sophisticated F-111A, which was first detached to Takhli with the 482nd Tactical Fighter Squadron in March 1968. After a dismal combat debut in which a number of losses were suffered, the all-weather-capable F-111 only completed a relatively small number of operational missions before two additional squadrons arrived at Takhli towards the end of 1972.

A less sophisticated method of interdicting the Trail was expressed by gunship conversions of

transport aircraft. The first of these to see combat was the AC-47, dubbed 'Puff the Magic Dragon', deployed to Tan Son Nhut in November 1965. The AC-47 was followed by the Shadow and Stinger, gun-toting modifications of the C-119. The ultimate gunship deployed in Vietnam was the AC-130, which carried an increasingly heavy armament of 7.62-mm rotary Miniguns, 40-mm cannon and 105-mm howitzers. As well as carrying their own sensors, the AC-130s worked on the basis of target coordinates established using the Igloo White sensors.

In addition to gunship versions, the venerable C-47 also served in Southeast Asia as the EC-47 electronic warfare platform, used for eavesdropping on communications along the Ho Chi Minh and Sihanouk supply lines. Others served in the

Specifications

Crew: 5	Dimensions: span 56.4m (185ft); length 48m
Powerplant: 8 x 44.5kN (10,000lb) Pratt &	(157ft 7in); height 14.75m (48ft 3in)
Whitney J57 turbojets	Weight: 204,120kg (450,000lb) loaded
Maximum speed: 1014km/h (630mph)	Armament: remotely controlled tail mounting
Range: 9978km (6200 miles)	with 4 x .5in MGs; internal bomb capacity
Service ceiling: 16,765m (55,000ft)	12,247kg (27,000lb) to 31,750kg (70,000lb)

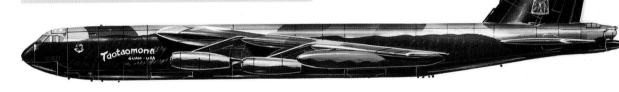

▲ **Boeing B-52D Stratofortress**

60th Bomb Squadron, 43rd Strategic Wing, USAF / Andersen AFB

B-52D 55-0069 is illustrated as it appeared at the height of the war in Vietnam. Operating out of Guam, the bomber received a coat of black paint to reduce its conspicuity for nocturnal missions over Southeast Asia. The aircraft's unit, the 60th Bomb Squadron, was part of the 43rd Strategic Wing, the final operator of the B-52D variant.

▲ **Boeing B-52G Stratofortress**

72nd Strategic Wing (Provisional), USAF / Andersen AFB, 1972–73

Operating out of Guam during the Linebacker offensive, this B-52G lacks the 'Big Belly' modification that was found on converted B-52Ds. As a result, its warload was decreased. The B-52G also lacked certain ECM equipment, so was assigned less heavily defended targets. However, the variant offered increased range.

Specifications

Crew: 5	Dimensions: span 56.4m (185ft); length 48m
Powerplant: 8 x 61.1kN (13,750lb) Pratt &	(157ft 7in); height 12.4m (40ft 8in)
Whitney J57-P-43W turbojets	Weight: 221,500kg (448,000lb) loaded
Maximum speed: 1014km/h (630mph)	Armament: 4 x .5in MGs; normal internal bomb
Range: 13,680km (8500 miles)	capacity 12,247kg (27,000lb); external pylons
Service ceiling: 16,765m (55,000ft)	for 2 x Hound Dog missiles

psychological warfare role, fitted with loudspeakers or carrying propaganda leaflets. Additional 'psy-war' assets included the smaller O-2B, the AU-23A and the U-10. Based on the O-2A observation/FAC aircraft, the O-2B arrived in theatre in 1967, fitted with loudspeakers and a leaflet dispenser. The AU-23A, meanwhile, was able to carry stores including guns and rockets, as well as psy-war equipment, and was also operated by Thailand. Finally, the U-10 was a dedicated STOL type used for psy-war and other specialist missions including the insertion of agents and paradropping. A more powerful development of the U-10 was the AU-24A, a dedicated COIN aircraft with various weapons options available.

The 'heavies' at war

U.S. air power was deployed over Vietnam in an almost exclusively tactical role, and the B-52 was no exception. The strategic bombers were soon adapted for the carriage of vast loads of conventional bombs, and were attacking targets across Southeast Asia under operations codenamed Arc Light, Linebacker and Linebacker II. As early as February 1965 two B-52F wings were forward-deployed to Andersen Air Base on Guam in the Marianas. Arc Light primarily involved the B-52F and began on 18 June 1965, the bombers using aerial refuelling to strike suspected VC bases in Binh Duong. Initial results of the bombing were less than satisfactory, but tactics were improved such that by November the B-52s were effectively

USAF HEAVY BOMBERS, VIETNAM		
Aircraft	Unit	Base
B-52D	3960th SW	Andersen AFB
B-52D/F	4133rd BW(P)	Andersen AFB
B-52D	43rd SW	Andersen AFB
B-52G	72nd SW(P)	Andersen AFB
B-52D	4252nd SW	Kadena AB
B-52D	376th SW	Kadena AB
B-52D	4258th SW	U-Tapao
B-52D	307th SW	U-Tapao
B-52D	310th SW(P)	U-Tapao

undertaking close support missions to relieve U.S. troops under fire from the NVA at Ia Drang.

In April 1966 the B-52D arrived at Guam, aircraft receiving the 'Big Belly' modification to carry even more bombs. The B-52 presence continued to grow, until there were 200 examples of the bomber on the island airbase by 1972. As of September 1967, however, the B-52s were under increasing threat from SAMs, and began to carry additional electronic warfare equipment. At the same time the focus of the bombers shifted from 'carpet bombing' to close support, necessitating the use of Combat Skyspot, a radar-directed bombing aid. In April 1967 B-52 missions were expanded through the addition of U-Tapao as an operating facility for the B-52D, which reduced the duration of the sorties.

▲ **Douglas A-1H Skyraider**

VA-145, US Navy, USS Constellation, *1964–65*

Built for the U.S. Navy as an AD-6, this aircraft was redesignated as an A-1H in 1962. During the early years of the Vietnam War this aircraft served with VA-145 'Swordsmen' aboard USS *Constellation*. Despite its antiquated appearance, the A-1 offered a very useful endurance and carried a heavy warload.

Specifications

Crew: 1

Powerplant: 1 x 2013kW (2700hp) Pratt & Whitney R-3350-26WA radial piston engine

Maximum speed: 520km/h (320mph)

Range: 2115km (1315 miles)

Service ceiling: 8660m (28,500ft)

Dimensions: span 15.25m (50ft); length 11.84m (38ft 10in); height 4.78m (15ft 8in)

Weight: 11,340kg (25,000lb) maximum

Armament: 4 x 20mm cannon; up to 3600kg (8000lb) of bombs, rockets or other stores

In order to prevent the entry of war equipment to the North Vietnamese port of Haiphong, the U.S. launched a campaign to mine its entrances. Mining the port itself was prohibited, however, so instead the mines were deposited around the mouths of waterways. The first mines were delivered by A-6As from the USS *Enterprise* in February 1967.

In 1968 the OV-10A joined the ranks of the USMC in Vietnam, this purpose-designed COIN aircraft proving its value in both offensive and reconnaissance missions, for which it was able to operate from semi-prepared airstrips. In addition to USMC service, the OV-10 saw action with the USAF, with the most advanced versions being equipped with improved night vision and targeting equipment under the Pave Nail programme.

Vietnam is popularly remembered as a 'helicopter war', and the UH-1 'Huey' became an icon of the conflict, employed by the U.S. Army, U.S. Navy and USMC in all arenas of the war. The original UH-1B was joined in 1963 by the UH-1D with provision for 14 rather than seven troops. In 1967 the further improved UH-1H became available. Air Cavalry missions involved UH-1s (including at least one outfitted for command duties), aided by USAF close support assets, such as the A-37B. UH-1s were also backed by observation helicopters, such as the OH-6A, which would provide support around the landing

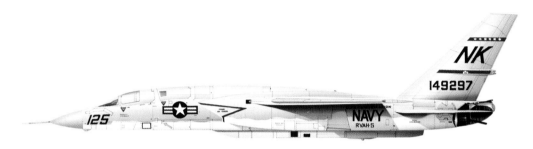

Specifications

Crew: 2	Dimensions: span 16.15m (53ft); length
Powerplant: 2 x 79.4kN (17,860lb) General	23.11m (75ft 10in); height 5.92m (19ft 5in)
Electric J79-GE-10 turbojets	Weight: 36,285kg (80,000lb) loaded
Maximum speed: 2230km/h (1385mph)	Armament: none
Range (with drop tanks): 5150km (3200 miles)	
Service ceiling: 20,400m (67,000ft)	

▲ North American RA-5C Vigilante

RVAH-5, US Navy, USS Constellation, *1968–69*

Providing the carrier air wing with a useful reconnaissance-gathering capability was the RA-5C, this example serving aboard USS *Constellation* in the Gulf of Tonkin in 1968–69. The RA-5C's mission equipment included a large sideways-looking airborne radar (SLAR) and an infrared line-scanner.

▲ Grumman EA-6A Intruder

VMCJ-2, US Marine Corps / Da Nang, 1972–73

Part of a composite reconnaissance squadron, this EA-6A was deployed to Vietnam in 1966 to operate from Da Nang. An electronic warfare adaptation of the A-6A Intruder, the EA-6A was used for jamming enemy radio transmissions and for intelligence-gathering, replacing the EF-10 Skyknight in USMC service.

Specifications

Crew: 4	Dimensions: span 16.15m (53ft); length
Powerplant: 2 x 37.8kN (8500lb) Pratt &	16.90m (55ft 6in); height 4.7m (15ft 6in)
Whitney J52-P-6 turbojets	Weight: 18,918kg (41,715lb) loaded
Maximum speed: 1016km/h (631mph)	Armament: none
Range: 3254km (2021 miles)	
Service ceiling: 11,580m (38,000ft)	

zone, carrying both its own weaponry and delivering small numbers of troops to extinguish resistance on the ground and to serve as observers.

From September 1969 the OH-6A was complemented by a new light observation type, the OH-58A, widely used thereafter for reconnaissance and liaison duties. Protecting the UH-1 and OH-6 was the AH-1 HueyCobra gunship, which was first employed in Vietnam in autumn 1967. Carrying a wide array of offensive weaponry, the AH-1 provided airmobile companies with organic firepower. In addition to the lighter helicopters, the U.S. Army made good use of the CH-47 for movement of up to 44 fully equipped troops or equipment including light vehicles or artillery. One noteworthy development of the CH-47 was the ACH-47, a powerfully armed gunship with both fixed and

trainable armament. Only a handful was completed, and the concept did not prove successful. In addition, both the CH-47, and the CH-54 flying crane were put to use in the recovery of downed aircraft. If a landing zone was not available, the helicopters could put down in a clearing made in the jungle by a 'Daisy

USAF RECONNAISSANCE, VIETNAM

Aircraft	Unit	Base
U-2A/C/F	4028th SRS	Bien Hoa
U-2C/F/R	349th SRS	Bien Hoa, U-Tapao
SR-71A	1st SRS	Kadena
RB-47H, KC-135R, RC-135C	55th SRW	Kadena
RC-135M/U	82nd SRS	Kadena
RC-135D	6th SW	Kadena
EC-121R	553rd RW	Nakhon Phanom
RB-57D, C-130A-II	6091st RS	Don Muang
EB-57E, C-130B-II	556th RS	Yokota, Don Muang
RB-57E	33rd TG	Tan Son Nhut
RF-101C	45th TRS	Tan Son Nhut
RF-4C	16th TRS	Tan Son Nhut
RF-101C	20th TRS	Tan Son Nhut, Udorn
RF-101C, RF-4C	12th TRS	Tan Son Nhut
RF-101C, RF-4C	15th TRS	Udorn
RF-4C	6461st TRS	Udorn
RF-4C	11th TRS	Udorn
RF-4C	14th TRS	Udorn
F-4D	25th TFS	Ubon
QU-22B	554th RS	Nakhon Phanom
DC-130A, CH-3E, AQM-34	4025th SRS	Bien Hoa
DC-130A/E, CH-53A, AQM-34	350th SRS	Bien Hoa, U-Tapao

U.S. ELECTRONIC WARFARE, VIETNAM

Aircraft	Unit	Base
Early warning		
EC-121D/M	522 AEWCW, USAF	Tainan, Tan Son Nhut, Ubon, Udorn, Korat
C-130E-II	7 ACCS, USAF	Udorn
EC-121K	VW-1, U.S. Navy	Da Nang
USAF electronic warfare		
KC-135A, EC-135L	n/a	Kadena, Taiwan
EC-135L	70 ARS	U-Tapao
EC-121J	n/a	Cam Ranh Bay
RB-66B/C	41 TRS	Tan Son Nhut
EB-66C/E	41 TEWS	Takhli
RB-66B	6460 TRS	Takhli
EB-66B/E	42 TEWS	Takhli, Korat
EB-66E	39 TEWS	Korat
F-105F	44 TFS	Korat
EC-47N/P	360 TEWS	Pleiku, Tan Son Nhut
EC-47N/P	361 TEWS	Nha Trang, TSN, Phu Cat
EC-47N/P	362 TEWS	Pleiku, Da Nang
USAF defence suppression		
F-100F, F-105F/G	561 TFS	Korat
F-105F	357 TFS	Takhli
F-105F/G	6010 TFS	Korat
F-105G	17 TFS	Korat
F-4C	67 TFS	Korat
USMC		
EF-10B, EA-6A, RF-8A, RF-4B	VMCJ-1	Da Nang
EA-6A	VMCJ-2	Da Nang
EA-6B	VAQ-132	Cam Ranh Bay
TF-9J, TA-4F	H&MS-11	Da Nang
TF-9J	H&MS-13	Chu Lai
TF-9J	H&MS-17	Da Nang
U.S. Navy		
AP-2H	VAH-21	Cam Ranh Bay

Cutter' bomb – the most powerful weapon deployed during the conflict. Rolled from the rear ramp of a C-130, the bomb weighed 6800kg (15,000lb), and was triggered before impacting the ground.

'Jolly Green Giants'

One helicopter mission pioneered during the Vietnam War was combat search and rescue (CSAR), in which the USAF picked up downed airmen. The first helicopter dedicated to the role was the HH-3E 'Jolly Green Giant', outfitted with armour, external fuel tanks, a refuelling probe and a hoist. The type entered service in 1968 and the helicopter was armed in recognition of the hazardous nature of the missions it was called upon to undertake. Flying deep into enemy territory the HH-3Es were often escorted by slow-flying A-1H/J close support aircraft, known by

their call sign 'Sandy'. Refuelling was conducted using HC-130P or KC-130 tankers. The successor to the HH-3E was the HH-53B/C 'Super Jolly', offering increased range and a greater payload. Also used for rescue was the HU-16 amphibian, operated in coastal areas, and also used for general transport duties. Another flying boat operated in Vietnam was the U.S. Navy's SP-5, which undertook offshore patrols during Operation Market Time, a blockade of South Vietnam designed to prevent infiltration from the sea. The SP-5 was eventually replaced by the land-based P-2 and P-3.

In addition to an assortment of light types, such as the C-12, U-8 and U-12 that were used for liaison, and the OV-10 used for battlefield surveillance, fixed-wing U.S. Army types in Vietnam included the CV-2 (DHC-4 Caribou), a transport that offered good

▲ **Bell AH-1G HueyCobra**

1st Air Cavalry Division, U.S. Army / Vietnam

The AH-1G was the first HueyCobra model to see action in Vietnam. Powered by a single engine, the AH-1G was outfitted to carry the M28 armament subsystem, comprising a chin turret that could carry either a pair of 40-mm grenade launchers, a pair of 7.62-mm Miniguns, or a combination of both weapons.

Specifications
Crew: 2
Powerplant: 1 x 820kW (1100shp) Lycoming T53-L-13 turboshaft
Maximum speed: 352km/h (219mph)
Range: 574km (357 miles)
Service ceiling: 3475m (11,400ft)
Dimensions: rotor diameter: 13.4m (44ft); length 13.4m (44ft 5in); height 4.1m (13ft 6in)
Weight: 4500kg (10,000lb) loaded
Armament: 2 x 7.62mm MGs; 70mm (2.75in) rockets; M18 7.62mm Minigun pod

Specifications
Crew: 2
Powerplant: 1 x 820kW (1100shp) Lycoming T53-L-11 turboshaft engine
Maximum speed: 236km/h (147mph)
Range: 418km (260 miles)
Dimensions: main rotor diameter 13.4m (44ft); length 12m (39ft 7in); height 4.4m (14ft 7in)
Weight: 3854kg (8500lb) loaded
Armament: none

▲ **Bell UH-1B Iroquois**

'A' Company, 1st Aviation Battalion, 1st Infantry Division, US Army / Vietnam, 1960s

An iconic participant in the US war in Southeast Asia, the 'Huey' is illustrated here in the form of a 'slick' (unarmed) UH-1B model. Configured for transport duties, the helicopter wears the 'Big One' insignia of the 1st Infantry Division on its tail. 'Slicks' were typically escorted to more hazardous landing zones by gun- and rocket-armed UH-1 'hogs'.

STOL performance, permitting use from rough or semi-prepared airstrips. Later transferred to USAF service as the C-7, the Caribou was particularly useful for supporting outlying villages or isolated pockets of troops. The Caribou was also operated in Vietnam by the Royal Australian AF, alongside Canberra B.Mk 20 bombers used for ground attack and bombing.

With much of neighbouring Cambodia used as safe areas by the VC, the U.S. turned its offensive against this neutral country, President Richard Nixon ordering a B-52 bombing campaign after his election victory in November 1969. The raids against Cambodia were undertaken clandestinely and were followed by tactical air strikes and an invasion by ground troops. The Sihanouk regime collapsed as a result of the offensive, precipitating the regime of terror by Pol Pot's Khmer Rouge.

The huge C-5A airlifter was available for participation as of 1969, and in the first half of 1972 almost the entire fleet was engaged in supporting the war effort. The transport was also to play a key role in the final evacuation of the U.S. forces.

In March 1972 the NVA launched a major new offensive, and the U.S. responded by sending B-52Gs to Guam. These offered longer range and could reach most targets without refuelling. The Linebacker missions of 1972 saw the B-52 used to hit targets north of the Demilitarized Zone, although these missions were curtailed in October while peace talks took place in Paris. When the North Vietnamese left the talks Linebacker II began. This operation was the largest mounted by B-52s during the war, with groups of around 100 aircraft flying 729 sorties between 18-29 December, in the course of which over 15,000 tons of bombs were dropped on key targets, including the port of Haiphong. The attentions of MiG-21s and SAMs combined to claim 15 B-52s destroyed.

Laser-guided bombs

Towards the end of their involvement, the U.S. armed forces began to call upon increasingly sophisticated weaponry to aid their cause. Among the weapons making its debut was the laser-guided bomb (LGB), the first operational examples of which were used by USAF F-4Es on 27 April 1972. The raid in question targeted the Thanh Hoa railway bridge that had survived numerous previous bombing raids. The Paveway LGBs succeeded in destroying it.

In May 1972 the U.S. changed its policy towards mining Haiphong, and mines were now sown in the harbour itself. This had the effect of bringing the North Vietnamese to the negotiating table, but it also meant that the U.S. had to remove the mines in turn once they had done their job, for which it deployed RH-53D mine countermeasures helicopters, equipped with mine sleds to drag the harbour.

With the tide of public opinion at home turning against the U.S. involvement in Southeast Asia, the forces in theatre were gradually drawn down. The war against the NVA and VC was left to the South

▲ Douglas A-1H Skyraider
56th Special Operations Wing, USAF / Nakhon Phanom, 1968

This A-1H was flown by the 56th Special Operations Wing from Nakhon Phanom in 1968. The most prominent missions undertaken by the wing's Skyraiders involved 'Sandy' air support for aircrew rescue missions. The aircraft depicted was originally built for the U.S. Navy as an AD-6.

Specifications

Crew: 1	Dimensions: span 15.25m (50ft); length
Powerplant: 1 x 2013kW (2700hp) Pratt &	11.84m (38ft 10in); height 4.78m (15ft 8in)
Whitney R-3350-26WA radial piston engine	Weight: 11,340kg (25,000lb) maximum
Maximum speed: 520km/h (320mph)	Armament: 4 x 20mm cannon; up to 3600kg
Range: 2115km (1315 miles)	(8000lb) of bombs, rockets or other stores
Service ceiling: 8660m (28,500ft)	

Vietnamese. Nixon's process of 'Vietnamization' planned to withdraw U.S. troops and leave the South Vietnamese to tackle the communist forces. In order to fulfil this remit, the South Vietnamese military, trained by U.S. advisors, would be equipped with primarily U.S.-supplied equipment.

By 1970 the South Vietnamese AF had been expanded to include around 700 aircraft, including T-28 and A-37B COIN/light attack types, A-1s, AC-47s, C-47, C-119s and O-1s. Another type flown by the South Vietnamese was the F-5 light attack jet, which was also operated in small numbers by the USAF under a project codenamed Skoshi Tiger.

The fielding of an effective South Vietnamese AF foundered, however, and the U.S. was forced to continue providing air power, together with 40,000 troops. However, there was no turning back from the drawdown, and after a final wave of B-52 raids, a ceasefire was finally signed on 27 January 1973.

The U.S. continued to provide South Vietnam with financial support, although aid packages were much reduced from 1974. North Vietnam was now free to fulfil its objective of reunifying the two countries. Beginning in March 1975, the North launched a series of attacks into the South, overwhelming the defenders. The South Vietnamese military and the administration rapidly crumbled,

U.S. FORWARD AIR CONTROL, VIETNAM		
Aircraft	Unit	Base
USAF		
O-1E/G, O-2A, OV-10A	19th TASS	Bien Hoa
O-1E/F, O-2A	20th TASS	Da Nang
O-1E/F, O-2A	21st TASS	Phu Cat, Tan Son Nhut
O-1E/F, O-2A	22nd TASS	n/a
O-2A, OV-10A	23rd TASS	Nakhon Phnom
U.S. Marine Corps		
OV-10A	VMO-6	Quang Tri, Chu Lai
OV-10A/D	VMO-2	Marble Mountain

and by the end of April the last of the U.S. presence in Saigon was being evacuated. A huge airlift evacuated refugees and U.S. civilians, and after the last airports had fallen to the communists, Operation Frequent Wind provided UH-1, H-53 and CH-46 helicopters to carry the evacuees out of Tan Son Nhut and to ships offshore.

At dawn on 30 April the last helicopter out of South Vietnam left the roof of the U.S. embassy in Saigon. One day later Saigon was renamed Ho Chi Minh City. Despite the overwhelming military superiority of the U.S. and its air arms, the communist insurgents and NVA had succeeded in their aims.

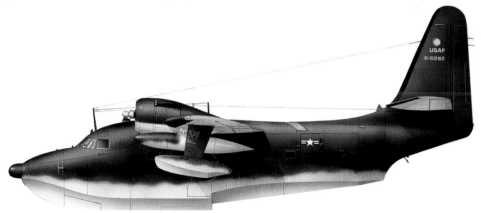

▲ **Grumman HU-16B Albatross**

3rd Air Rescue and Recovery Group, USAF / Vietnam

One of the more unusual USAF types to see service in Vietnam was the HU-16B amphibian. This particular aircraft was used for command post duties, and wears a low visibility paint scheme. The insignia on the tail of this aircraft is that of Pan Am, reflecting the fact that it was operated by Air Force Reserve crews.

Specifications

Crew: 2

Powerplant: 2 x 1063kW (1425hp)

Wright R-1820-76 Cyclone 9 radial engines;

2 or 4 x 4.4kN (1000lb) 15KS1000 rocket

motors

Maximum speed: 380km/h (236mph)

Range: 4587km (2850 miles)

Service ceiling: 6553m (21,500ft)

Dimensions: span 24.4m (80ft); length 19.16m

(62ft 10in); height 7.8m (25ft 10in)

Weight: 14,968kg (33,000lb) maximum

Armament: none

▲ Sikorsky HH-53C

3rd Air Rescue and Recovery Group, USAF / Vietnam

Known as the 'Super Jolly Green Giant', the HH-53C was equipped for flying long-range aircrew rescue missions in Southeast Asia, carrying additional armour, defensive armament and fitted with an in-flight refuelling probe. The HH-53C could also recover downed aircraft, using its external cargo hook.

Specifications

Crew: 6

Powerplant: 2 x 2927kW (3925shp) General
Electric T64-GE-7 turboshafts

Maximum speed: 315km/h (196mph)

Range: 869km (540 miles)

Service ceiling: 6220m (20,400ft)

Dimensions: main rotor diameter 22.02m
(72ft 3in); fuselage length 20.47m (67ft 2in);
height overall 7.6m (24ft 11in)

Weight: 19,050kg (42,000lb) loaded

Armament: 3 x 7.62mm Miniguns or .50 BMG
(12.7mm) machine guns

USAF RESCUE, VIETNAM

Aircraft	Unit	Base
HH-43B/F, HU-16B, CH-3C	33rd ARRS	Bien Hoa, Nakhon Phanom, Korat, Takhli, Udorn, Da Nang, Pleiku
HH-43B/F, HU-16B, HH-3E, HH-53B/C	37th ARRS	Udorn, Da Nang
HH-43B/F, HC-54, HC-130H, HH-3E	38th ARRS	Tan Son Nhut, Bien Hoa, Korat, Da Nang
HC-130P	39th ARRS	Tuy Hoa
HH-43B, HH-3E, HH-53C	40th ARRS	Nakhon Phanom, Udorn
HC-130P	56th ARRS	Korat
HC-54, HC-130H	31st ARRS	Clark AB
HH-43B, HC-54, HC-130H	36th ARRS	Tachikawa AB
HC-54, HC-130H	79th ARRS	Andersen AFB

USAF SPECIAL OPERATIONS, VIETNAM

Aircraft	Unit	Base
T-28D, A-1E/G	1st SOS	Bien Hoa, Pleiku
A-1E/H	6th SOS	Pleiku
A-37B	8th SOS	Bien Hoa
A-37A/B	604th SOS	Bien Hoa
AC-47D	4th SOS	Bien Hoa, Nha Trang, Tan Son Nhut, Da Nang
AC-47D	14th ACS	Nha Trang
AC-47D	3rd SOS	Pleiku
AC-130A, NC-123K	16th SOS	Ubon, Nha Trang
AC-119G	71st SOS	Nha Trang
AC-119G	17th SOS	Phu Cat
AC-119G/K	18th SOS	Phan Rang
AC-47D, U-10A	5th SOS	Nha Trang
AC-47D, O-2B	9th SOS	Tan Son Nhut
UH-1B/F/P, CH-3C	20th SOS	Tuy Ha, Nha Trang, Cam Ranh Bay, Nakhon Phanom
C-130E-I	15th SOS	Nha Trang
A-1E/G/H/J	602nd SOS	Bien Hoa, Nakhon Phanom
A-1E/G/H/J	1st SOS	Nakhon Phanom
A-1E/G/H/J	22nd SOS	Nakhon Phanom
T-28D, C-123K, A-26A	606th SOS	Nakhon Phanom
T-28D, A-26A	609th SOS	Nakhon Phanom
CH-3C/E	21st SOS	Nakhon Phanom
AC-119K	18th SOS	Nakhon Phanom
AC-130A/E/H	16th SOS	Ubon, Korat
MC-130E	318th SOS	Nha Trang, Korat
AC-47D	4th SOS	Udorn
UC-123B/K	12th SOS	Bien Hoa
UC-123K	310th TAS	Tan Son Nhut

Malaya
1948–1960

The Malayan Emergency pitted the British in a campaign of jungle warfare against primarily Chinese communist rebels who sought to gain independence from the colonial administration.

THE BRITISH BEGAN their campaign against the rebels in 1948, suppressing trade unions before the guerrillas adopted jungle warfare tactics. When the Emergency began the RAF maintained eight squadrons in Singapore and at Kuala Lumpur, spearheaded by Spitfire Mk 18s and Beaufighter Mk 10s. The terrorists' locations were uncovered using Mosquito PR.Mk 34s and in 1949 the RAF launched Operation Firedog to defeat the terrorists.

Dakotas delivered troops into the jungle, the same aircraft then dropping supplies. Brigands replaced the Beaufighters in 1949 and the Brigand was employed widely as an anti-terrorist weapon; in the same year the Tempest fighter-bomber began to arrive. By 1950 the RAF had 160 aircraft in theatre, while the terrorists strengthened their presence in the rural areas, operating out of village strongholds. Guerrilla movements off the coast were tracked by RAF Sunderland flying boats.

Hornet fighter-bombers were in action as of early 1951 as successors to the Tempest, while the first jets in theatre were Vampires, replacing the Spitfires

starting in December 1950. Beginning in 1952 the British and Commonwealth forces assumed the upper hand, aided by a refinement of tactics. Valettas meanwhile replaced Dakotas while helicopters appeared in the form of the Dragonfly from early 1953, rotorcraft being used to insert small units rapidly into the jungle. Reconnaissance work was passed from the Mosquito to the Meteor PR.Mk 10 in late 1953, and Pioneer STOL transports began to work the jungle airstrips from early 1954, by which time the RAF had committed 242 front-line aircraft. Further air support was provided by Australia, with Lincolns and Dakotas, and New Zealand, with Vampires, Venoms and Bristol 170s.

While British and Malay forces held on to the towns, the rebels were limited to a terror campaign against British interests. Eventually, a British programme of resettling Chinese populations left the guerrillas isolated. By the conclusion of the campaign in 1960, deployed assets included RAF and RAAF Canberras, Hastings and Twin Pioneer transports, Meteor night-fighters and Whirlwind helicopters.

▲ **De Havilland Hornet F.Mk 3**

33 Sqn, RAF / Tengah/Butterworth, 1951–55

Normally stationed at Tengah, this de Havilland Hornet single-seat fighter was deployed to Butterworth during the Malayan Emergency. The aircraft is armed with underwing rockets, typical weapons used in the campaign waged against the terrorists, who exploited the dense jungle of Malaya to their advantage.

Specifications

Crew: 1	Dimensions: span 13.72m (45ft 0in);
Powerplant: 2 x 1551kW (2080hp) Rolls-Royce	length 11.18m (36ft 8in); height 4.3m
Merlin 130/131 12-cylinder engines	(14ft 2in)
Maximum speed: 760km/h (472mph)	Weight: 9480kg (20,900lb) loaded
Range: 4828km (3000 miles)	Armament: 4 x 20mm Hispano Mk. V cannons;
Service ceiling: 10,668m (35,000ft)	2 x 454kg (1000lb) bombs; 8 x rockets

Borneo
1962–1966

Coming in the wake of the Malayan Emergency, the Indonesian Confrontation was sparked by a border dispute between Britain and Indonesia, which began in December 1962.

AFTER OUTBREAKS OF violence in British-protected Brunei in northern Borneo, and in the British colony of Sarawak, the British faced hostility from Indonesia, with which it shared long borders on the island of Borneo.

Britain hoped to create a Greater Malaysia that would include its colonies of Sarawak and Sabah in the north of Borneo. Indonesia opposed the plan and hoped to gain control of these two territories, plus independent Brunei. Each territory supported anti-Malaysian, pro-communist factions, and Indonesia decided to foment rebellion by infiltrating these groups and providing support and training in Kalimantan, Indonesian territory in southern Borneo.

As well as dealing with the anti-colonialist groups in the northern territories, the UK had to guard the borders with Indonesia to prevent infiltration. At the time of the Emergency, the RAF's Far East Air Force was based around Hunter and Javelin fighters, Canberra bombers and reconnaissance aircraft,

RAF IN BORNEO, 1962–66		
Aircraft	Unit	Base
Canberra B.Mk 15	45 Sqn	Tengah, Labuan, Kuching
Canberra B.Mk 15	32 Sqn	Tengah, Kuantan
Hunter FGA.Mk 9	20 Sqn	Labuan, Kuching, Tengah
Javelin FAW.Mk 9	60 Sqn, 64 Sqn	Labuan, Kuching, Tengah
Meteor F.Mk 8	1574 Flt	Changi
Shackleton MR.Mk 2	205 Sqn	Labuan, Changi
Canberra PR.Mk 7	81 Sqn	Labuan, Tengah
Pioneer C.Mk 1, Twin Pioneer CC.Mk 1	209 Sqn	Labuan, Kuching, Brunei
Belvedere HC.Mk 1	66 Sqn	Labuan, Kuching, Seletar
Belvedere HC.Mk 1	26 Sqn	Seletar

▲ **Scottish Aviation Pioneer CC.Mk 1**

209 Sqn, RAF / Seletar/Bayan Lepas, late 1950s

Normally based at Seletar in Singapore, this Pioneer was flown operationally in Borneo during the confrontation with Indonesia. The aircraft's excellent STOL capability allowed it to operate from rough airstrips in support of ground troops fighting in the dense jungle of Borneo. The type also saw action in Malaya.

Specifications

Crew: 1

Powerplant: 1 x 388kW (520hp) Alvis Leonides 502/4 radial engine

Maximum speed: 261km/h (162mph)

Range: 676km (420 miles)

Service ceiling: 7010m (23,000ft)

Dimensions: span 15.17m (49ft 9in); length 10.47m (34ft 4in); height 3.13m (10ft 3in)

Weight: 2636kg (5800lb) loaded

Capacity: 4 passengers

Specifications

Crew: 2

Powerplant: 2 x 1092kW (1465hp) Napier
Gazelle N.Ga.2 turboshaft engines

Maximum speed: 231km/h (145mph)

Range: 740km (460 miles)

Service ceiling: 5275m (17,302ft)

Dimensions: rotor diameter, each 14.91m
(49ft); length rotors turning 27.36m
(90ft); height 5.26m (17ft)

Weight: 9072kg (19,958lb) maximum

Armament: none

▲ **Bristol Belvedere HC.Mk 1**

66 Sqn, RAF / Labuan/Kuching/Seletar, 1962-67

The RAF refined its helicopter tactics during the campaign in Malaya and rotorcraft played a major role in the Borneo campaign. 66 Sqn flew the Belvedere in Borneo from 1962 until 1969, transporting both troops and equipment and operating from forward bases in the jungle.

Specifications

Crew: 2

Powerplant: 2 x 48.94kN (11,007lb-thrust)
Armstrong Siddeley Sapphire 203 turbojets

Maximum speed: 1130km/h (702mph)

Range: 1600km (994 miles)

Service ceiling: 16,000m (52,493ft)

Dimensions: span 15.85m (52ft);
length 17.15m (56ft 3in); 4.88m (16ft)

Weight: 19,578kg (43,162lb) loaded

Armament: 2 x 30mm (1.18in) ADEN cannon
in each wing; 4 x de Havilland Firestreak
heat-seeking air-to-air missiles

▲ **Gloster Javelin FAW.Mk 9**

64 Sqn, RAF / Tengah/Kuching/Labuan, 1963-66

In order to counter the threat posed by Indonesian AF Il-28 and Tu-16 bombers, and MiG-17 and MiG-19 fighters, the RAF sent Javelin all-weather fighters to operate from Kuching and Labuan. The units involved were 60 and 64 Sqns, this 64 Sqn aircraft being armed with Firestreak air-to-air missiles.

Shackletons for maritime patrol, as well as a transport fleet. The main operating base was Tengah in Singapore. Support was provided by the RAAF, with Sabres and Canberras at Butterworth, and the RNZAF with Canberras and Bristol Freighters.

COIN campaign

From December 1962 UK forces entered Borneo to put down the insurgencies in the north. Order was soon restored in Sarawak, before attentions turned to Brunei. Using transport aircraft to deliver troops

where they were most needed, Brunei was steadily returned to government control, with Hunters flying mock attacks over the rebels. Canberras, meanwhile, kept a check on infiltration across the land border from Kalimantan, and bases were set up along the border and supplied by air, with extensive use of helicopters. In the air, Hunters and Javelins policed the borders. Indonesian forces staged a series of naval landings and paradrops through 1964-65, but by 1966 the Confrontation had run its course, and a peace treaty was signed in August.

Chapter 9

Latin America

To some extent on the periphery of the Cold War, Central and South America nonetheless played host to some critical air battles during the postwar years, with Cuba more than once a major flashpoint in the superpower standoff of the 1960s, and the Falklands campaign in 1982 seeing modern air power deployed in action in a wide variety of roles. Meanwhile, the U.S. took a particular interest in the region as it sought to extinguish a number of regimes and guerrilla organizations it regarded as being dangerously pro-Soviet.

◄ **British Aerospace Sea Harrier FRS.Mk 1**
Although the Falklands conflict was little more than a sideshow in terms of the overall Cold War confrontation, it was notable for the deployment of a number of advanced warplanes and weapons, with undoubtedly the most successful being the Royal Navy Sea Harrier, seen here on the carrier HMS *Hermes*.

Cuba
1959–1962

Fidel Castro's revolution in Cuba brought the threat of communism to 'America's backyard', and tensions surrounding the Caribbean island brought the world to the brink of nuclear war.

WITH THE CORRUPT, pro-American regime of President Batista overthrown in 1958, Castro's Marxist Cuba increasingly became a Soviet outpost in the Caribbean. Located less than 160 kilometres (100 miles) from the coast of Florida, events in Cuba prompted a predictable reaction in Washington.

CIA air assets were used to wage a clandestine war in Cuba. In November 1959 U.S. aircraft dropped propaganda leaflets over Havana and C-46 transports began to drop weapons in support of counter-revolutionary forces on the island. Starting in 1960 the Agency meanwhile built up an armed force of around 1400 Cuban exiles who received training in Guatemala, for a planned invasion of Cuba.

Bay of Pigs invasion

The CIA-backed invasion was carefully staged in order to be 'plausibly deniable'. Various CIA front organizations operated C-46s and C-54s from Florida in support of the exile army, while B-26s that were to be used during the invasion proper received Cuban markings to give the impression that they had defected from Cuba. A Panamanian-registered PBY-5A flying boat was to serve as an aerial command post for the invasion, which would take place at the Bay of Pigs, on Cuba's southern coast.

President Kennedy approved invasion plans in March 1961, and on 15 April eight ex-USAF B-26Bs left Nicaragua, armed with guns, bombs and rockets. Forming three flights, the aircraft struck Cuban airfields at San Antonio de los Banos, Campo Libertad and Antonio Maceo. At the first base a T-33 and a number of B-26s were destroyed on the ground, with a Sea Fury and a civilian DC-3 hit at Antonio Maceo. One B-26 raider crashed into the sea, and two more were forced down by engine trouble and fuel shortage respectively.

At the same time an amphibious landing force of Cuban exiles was sailing from Puerto Cabezas, Nicaragua, with air support provided by 24 more B-26s, six C-46s and six C-54s. On April 16 B-26s struck ground targets in preparation for the invasion, two from a force of 11 bombers being lost in combat, one crash-landing, and two being lost on the return flight to Nicaragua. The amphibious landing took place on 17 April, while B-26s kept up their attacks on Cuban airfields and troops. The Cuban AF sunk two invasion vessels, although the invaders took the

▲ **Hawker Sea Fury FB.Mk 11**

Escuadron Persecucion y Combate, Fuerza Aérea Revolucionaria (Cuban AF)

The small force of British-supplied Sea Furies inherited from the Batista regime saw some action in the hands of the Fuerza Aérea Revolucionaria (FAR) during the abortive Bay of Pigs invasion. Cuba operated up to 12 Sea Furies, and these claimed at least two B-26Bs destroyed during the Bay of Pigs invasion.

Specifications

Crew: 1	Dimensions: span 11.7m (38ft 4in);
Powerplant: 1 x 1850kW (2480hp) Bristol	length 10.6m (34ft 8in); height 4.9m
Centaurus XVIIC 18-cylinder twin-row radial	(16ft 1in)
engine	Weight: 5670kg (12,500lb) loaded
Maximum speed: 740km/h (460mph)	Armament: 4 x 20mm (.79 in) Hispano Mk V
Range: 1127km (700 miles)	cannon; 12 x 76.2mm (3in) rockets or
Service ceiling: 10,900m (35,800ft)	907kg (2000lb) of bombs

beachhead and established a landing strip to receive C-46s carrying supplies. B-26 raids continued during 18–19 April, but there was no sign of a popular uprising that might threaten the leadership in Havana. The last B-26 attack was covered by unmarked U.S. Navy A4D-2s from USS *Essex*, but two Invaders were still destroyed, one falling to a Cuban AF T-33 and the other to AAA. Out of the invaders' force of 24 aircraft, half had been lost, and the amphibious assault ended in disaster, with 120 exiles killed and another 1200 captured.

Cuban Missile Crisis

Soviet premier Khrushchev upped the stakes in the Cold War standoff with the decision to place medium-range nuclear missiles on Cuba in 1962. With Cuba concerned by the threat posed by the U.S., Castro's regime received major arms shipments from the USSR, ultimately including nuclear-armed Il-28 jet bombers, SS-4 and SS-5 medium-range ballistic missiles, and surface-launched cruise missiles.

Aware of the military build-up on Cuba, the U.S. increased CIA-operated U-2 spyplane overflights, which detected the missiles in August 1962. At the same time, U.S. Navy and USAF patrol and reconnaissance aircraft carefully monitored shipping headed towards Cuba. On 29 August U-2s detected SA-2 SAM sites similar to those used to defend

strategic missile bases in the USSR, and on 4 September Kennedy informed Moscow that the U.S. would not tolerate the presence of Soviet strategic weapons on Cuba. Khrushchev told Washington that there were no such weapons on the island, but photo imagery gathered by U.S. Navy P-2s and CIA U-2s painted an altogether different picture.

With further missiles having arrived in mid-September, 10 October saw U-2 flights become the responsibility of the USAF rather than the CIA. These identified additional construction work associated with missile sites, and confirmation of the presence of SS-4s was provided to Kennedy on 16 October, after a U-2E flight from Patrick Air Force Base (AFB), Florida. In response, USAF RF-101Cs began low-level reconnaissance flights over Cuba from Shaw AFB, Arkansas.

The Soviets continued to insist that only defensive arms were deployed on Cuba, while the U.S. weighed up its options: invasion of Cuba, air attack, political ultimatum or blockade. A naval blockade duly began on 22 October, while SAC B-52 bombers were placed on alert. Task Force 138 was responsible for the blockade, enforced with the aid of the carrier USS *Essex*, with two squadrons of S2F-1s (S-2As) onboard. The 'quarantine' zone was established as a zone 800 kilometres (500 miles) off the Cuban coast, while additional photo-reconnaissance support

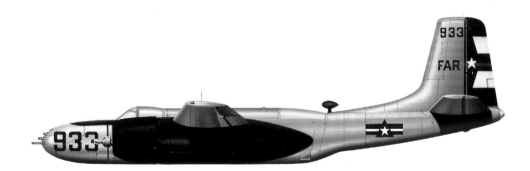

▲ **Douglas B-26B Invader**

'Cuban AF/CIA / Miami, April 1961

This 'Cuban' B-26 landed at Miami International after the attack on Cuban airfields on 15 April. The pilot claimed to be a defector, and that the raid had been planned by other defectors in collaboration with U.S.-based exiles. In fact, the ex-USAF Invader was part of a CIA operation, and the B-26B version was absent from the Cuban AF, which operated the B-26C model.

Specifications

Crew: 3	Dimensions: span 21.71m (71ft 3in); length
Powerplant: 2 x 1431kW (1920hp)	16.60m (51ft 3in); height 5.6m (18ft 6in)
Pratt & Whitney R-2800-43 radial engines	Weight: 16,782kg (37,000lb) loaded
Maximum speed: 453km/h (282mph)	Armament: 11 x 12.7mm (0.50in) M2 Browning
Range: 1850km (1150 miles)	MGs and up to 3628kg (8000lb) bomb load
Service ceiling: 6614m (21,700ft)	

arrived in the form of further USAF RF-101Cs, and U.S. Navy and Marine Corps RF-8As.

Khrushchev offered to remove the Soviet-manned strategic weapons on 26 October, in exchange for the removal of U.S. missiles from Turkey, but a day later tensions were increased after a SAM shot down a U-2 over Cuba, and the situation worsened when another U-2 overflew Siberia in error.

Finally, on the morning of 28 October the Soviets stepped down, and agreed to remove their offensive missiles from Cuba, together with Il-28 bombers, which were in the process of being assembled. The missiles were dismantled and were returned to the USSR in the course of November, and the naval blockade was lifted before the end of the month. The U.S. in turn agreed to remove its obsolescent Jupiter missiles from Europe, and pledged not to interfere in Cuban issues. A year later a 'hotline' telephone link was established between Moscow and Washington, with the aim of improving superpower relations.

▲ **Lockheed U-2A**

4080th Strategic Reconnaissance Wing, USAF / Laughlin AFB, 1961

The U-2 played a critical role during the Cuban Missile Crisis, with 102 USAF sorties being flown by the type in the period between 14 October and 6 December. Painted light grey overall, this USAF U-2A was operated by the 4080th SRW from Laughlin AFB, Texas, at the time of the crisis.

Specifications

Crew: 1

Powerplant: 1 x 48.93kN (11,000lb) thrust Pratt & Whitney J75-P-37A turbojet engine

Maximum speed: 795km/h (494mph)

Range: 3542km (2200 miles)

Service ceiling: 16,763m (55,000ft)

Dimensions: span 24.3m (80ft); length 15.1m (49ft 7in); height 3.9m (13ft)

Weight: 9523kg (21,000lb) loaded

Armament: none

Falklands
1982

When Argentina invaded the British overseas territory of the Falkland Islands almost unopposed on 2 April 1982, the Argentine administration did not expect a military response.

THE INITIAL ARGENTINE landings on the Falklands were achieved without air support, but on the same day there arrived at Port Stanley Argentine AF Pucára COIN aircraft, followed by an Army Puma, Air Force Bell 212 and CH-47C helicopters, Navy Skyvans and a Coast Guard Puma. The bases on the Falklands – Stanley, Goose Green and Pebble Island – were too small for Argentine AF fighter-bombers that instead had to operate at extreme range from the mainland. Three Pumas, two A.109s and a UH-1 that arrived by ship from 7–9 April later boosted army strength on the islands.

The Argentine carrier ARA *25 de Mayo* had set sail on 28 March, with A-4Qs embarked, but the loss of the cruiser ARA *General Belgrano* to a British submarine saw the carrier return to port before Navy

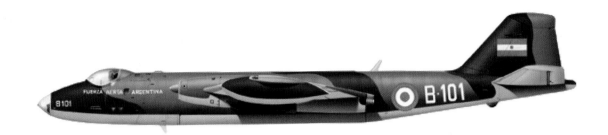

Specifications

Crew: 2

Powerplant: 2 x 28.9kN (6500lb) Rolls-Royce

Avon Mk 101 turbojets

Maximum speed: 917km/h (570mph)

Range: 4274km (2656 miles)

Service ceiling: 14,630m (48,000ft)

Dimensions: span 29.49m (63ft 11in); length

19.96m (65ft 6in); height 4.78m (15ft 8in)

Weight: 24,925kg (54,950lb) loaded

Armament: bomb bay with provision for up to

2727kg (6000lb) of bombs, plus 909kg

(2000lb) of underwing pylons

▲ **English Electric Canberra B.Mk 62**

Grupo 2 de Bombardeo (GB2), Argentine AF / Comodoro Rivadavia AB

The Argentine AF received 12 Canberras from BAC in 1970-71. On 1 May the type was involved in a combined attack against the Task Force, also involving A-4s, with Mirages and Daggers as top cover. In the ensuing air combats, a Canberra was shot down by an 801 NAS Sea Harrier, 240km (150 miles) northwest of Stanley.

A-4s could make an impact. On 11 April, GC4 A-4Cs were detached to San Julian, with GC5 moving to Rio Gallegos from 14 April, both airfields being around 1125 kilometres (700 miles) from Stanley.

With the British Maritime Exclusion Zone (MEZ) in force by 12 April, the Argentine garrison had to be supported by air, using C-130s, Air Force and Navy F.27s, Navy Electras and civil types, and further UH-1s were delivered. As the British Task Force approached, Argentine air power in the Falklands included two CH-47s, five Pumas, nine UH-1s and three A.109s, with 12 Pucáras at Goose Green joining the 12 at Stanley. By 24 April the Navy had deployed six M.B.339s and four T-34Cs, tasked with harassing shipping and defending against the landings.

Black Buck raids

Fourteen Victor tankers were based at Ascension Island by the end of April. Most took part in the Black Buck 1 raid, in which Vulcan bombers targeted Port Stanley airfield after 18 aerial refuellings. Leaving Ascension on 30 April, the two Black Buck 1 Vulcans were armed with 21 450-kilogram (1000-lb) bombs, with one primary attack aircraft and one back-up. After the successful first raid hit Stanley on 1 May, five more Black Bucks were flown, plus another mission abandoned after a refuelling unit broke. At the time, the 12,390-kilometre (7700-mile) Vulcan missions were the longest-ever point-to-point bombing sorties.

The first of May saw the Sea Harrier enter the fray. During a dawn raid on Stanley airfield an

inconclusive air action followed, involving two 801 NAS Sea Harriers and three T-34Cs that were carrying out a strafing attack on British warships. On the ground, 800 NAS Sea Harriers destroyed a Pucára at Goose Green, and put two more out of action. The afternoon of 1 May saw around 20 Argentine aircraft sent against the Task Force. A pair of Mirages tangled

ARGENTINE AF, 1982		
Aircraft	**Unit**	**Base**
Canberra B.Mk 62	GB2	Trelew, Rio Gallegos
Mirage IIIEA	GC8	Comodoro Rivadavia, Rio Gallegos
Dagger	Esc.2 GC6	San Julian
Dagger	Esc.3 GC6	Rio Grande
A-4C	GC4	San Julian
A-4B	GC5	Rio Gallegos
Pucará	GA3	Santa Cruz, Port Stanley, Goose Green, Pebble Island
B707	Esc.2 GTA1	Comodoro Rivadavia, El Palomar, Ezeiza
Learjet	GAF 1	Comodoro Rivadavia, Trelew, Rio Gallegos, Rio Grande
C-130E/H, KC-130H	Esc.1 GTA1	Comodoro Rivadavia
F.27, F.28, Twin Otter, BAC 1-11, B737	GTA9	Comodoro Rivadavia
CH-47C, Bell 212	GC17	Port Stanley

with Sea Harriers, one falling to a Sidewinder. The surviving Mirage was severely damaged before being finished off by friendly AAA. Minutes later, an 800 NAS Sea Harrier pair was bounced by Daggers, avoiding an Argentine missile, before destroying a Dagger. From now on the Dagger would be demoted to the air-to-ground role. A pair of 801 NAS Sea Harriers intercepted three Canberras on their way to attack British warships, one being destroyed.

1 May also saw a Pucará lost in a heavy landing and another destroyed by Sea Harrier on the ground. Two more Pucarás were damaged, and the survivors moved to Pebble Island. The same day also marked the first A-4 mission, four GC5 aircraft being escorted by Mirage IIIEA escorts. Another mission by GC4 and 5, plus escorts, similarly failed to find its targets before bombs from a GC5 aircraft missed a (friendly) ship off Stanley. The loss of two escorting Mirages to Sea Harriers combined with the Black Buck raid of 1 May saw Mirages held back from further action over the Falklands.

Naval gunfire forced the dispersal of the Argentine helicopters, whose subsequent use was limited, and between 3–4 May naval artillery put a Skyvan and a Puma out of action, while a Sea Harrier fell to AAA during a raid on Goose Green. The most significant action of 4 May was the sinking of HMS *Sheffield* by a combination of Super Etendard and Exocet anti-

Specifications

Crew: 1	Dimensions: span 8.47m (27ft 6in);
Powerplant: 1 x 49.8kN (11,200lb) Pratt &	length 12.58m (41ft 4in); height 4.57m (15ft)
Whitney J52-P-408 turbojet engine	Weight: 11,113kg (24,500lb) loaded
Maximum speed: 1110km/h (690mph)	Armament: 2 x 20mm cannon; 2721kg
Range: 4345km (2700 miles)	(6000lb) external bomb load
Service ceiling: 10,515m (34,500ft)	

▲ **Douglas A-4B Skyhawk**

Grupo 5 de Caza (GC5), Argentine AF / Rio Grande AB

Two Air Force and one Navy A-4 unit led the effort against the Task Force, destroying four ships and a landing craft and damaging four more. In return, they suffered 22 losses (three of which were Navy aircraft) in 289 sorties: 106 by Grupo 4, 149 by Grupo 5 and 34 by the Navy. Nineteen Skyhawks fell to British action.

▲ **Dassault Super Etendard**

2 Escuadrilla de Caza y Ataque (2ECA), Argentine Navy / Rio Grande AB, 1982

Argentina had received just five from a total order of 14 Super Etendards at the time of the conflict, the possibility of further deliveries being ended by a French arms embargo. The aircraft (and their five Etendard anti-ship missiles) were operated by 2 Escuadrilla, 3 Escuadra Aéronaval, which moved to Rio Grande.

Specifications

Crew: 1	length 14.31m (46ft 11.2in); height 3.86m
Powerplant: 1 x 49kW (11,023lb) SNECMA Atar	(12ft 8in)
8K-50 turbojet	Weight: 12,000kg (26,455lb) loaded
Maximum speed: 1180km/h (733mph)	Armament: 2 x 30mm cannon, provision for up
Range: 850km (528 miles)	to 2100kg (4630lb) of stores, including
Service ceiling: 13,700m (44,950ft)	nuclear weapons and Exocet air-to-surface
Dimensions: span 9.6m (31ft 6in);	missiles

ship missile. Two more Sea Harriers were destroyed in a mid-air collision after running into bad weather on 6 May. After the loss of an M.B.339 on an anti-ship patrol, a Sea Dart missile from HMS *Coventry* claimed another Puma on 9 May.

Poor weather limited further A-4 attacks until 12 May, following two operational losses (one aircraft flying into a cliff, another lost over the sea). On 12 May GC5 sent eight aircraft against British warships at Port Stanley. Despite flying at low level, Seawolf missiles from HMS *Brilliant* claimed two Skyhawks, and another crashed into the sea as it took evasive action. One bomb hit HMS *Glasgow*, forcing it to leave the battle, but friendly AAA then shot down the same A-4. This action was enough to dissuade the Royal Navy from continuing daylight bombardment.

SAS raid

The Pebble Island raid of 14–15 May saw two Sea King HC.Mk 4s deliver 45 British Special Air Service (SAS) troops and naval forward observers who would later direct shore bombardment. The SAS party also attacked Argentine aircraft at the airfield, destroying 11. Further SAS raiders were inserted by Sea King on 20–21 May, after which these helicopters remained on station to airlift equipment and stores during the invasion, including airlift of Rapier SAMs.

Originally configured for air defence, RAF Harriers had deployed to make up for possible Sea Harrier attrition. Joining the Task Force on 18 May, they transferred to HMS *Hermes* before assuming

ARGENTINE NAVY, FALKLANDS, 1982		
Aircraft	**Unit**	**Base**
Super Etendard	2 ECA	Bahia Blanca, Rio Grande
A-4Q	3 ECA	*25 de Mayo*, Bahia Blanca
MB.326GB, MB.339A	1 EA	Trelew, Bahia Blanca, Rio Grande, Port Stanley
T-34C-1	4 EA	PuntaIndio, Rio Grande, Port Stanley, Pebble Island
SP-2H	EE	Bahia Blanca, Rio Grande
Electra	1 ESLM	Rio Grande
F.28	2 ESLM	Rio Grande
S-2A	EAS	*25 de Mayo*, Bahia Blanca, Port Stanley, Rio Gallegos
S-61D-4	2 EH	Bahia Blanca, Almirante Irizar, *25 de Mayo*, Rio Grande
Lynx HAS.Mk 23, Alouette III	1 EH	various warships
Skyvan, Puma	PN	Port Stanley, Pebble Island

ground-attack duties on 20 May with a three-ship attack on an Argentine fuel dump on West Falkland.

21 May was the day of the Task Force's invasion, and landings began before dawn in Falkland Sound and San Carlos Water. Nimrods conducted surveillance, while Sea Kings monitored possible submarine activity. Other Sea Kings were used to deliver SAS teams from HMS *Hermes*, and the SAS also carried out a diversionary attack on Goose Green.

Specifications

Crew: 2

Powerplant: 1 x 17.8kN (4000lb thrust) Rolls-Royce Viper Mk. 632 turbojet

Maximum speed: 898km/h (558mph)

Range: 1760km (1093 miles)

Service ceiling: 14,630m (48,000ft)

Dimensions: span 10.86m (35ft 7in); length 10.97m (36ft); height 3.60m (11ft 9in)

Weight: 4400kg (9700lb) loaded

Armament: up to 1800kg (3968lb) of weapons

▲ **Aermacchi M.B.339A**

1 Escuadrilla de Ataque (1EA), Argentine Navy / Port Stanley, 1982

Argentine Navy M.B.339s were among the more capable combat aircraft stationed on the Falklands, with six examples from 1 Escuadrilla de Ataque (1 EA) based at Stanley by late April. An advanced trainer, the M.B.339 was also capable of undertaking ground attack and reconnaissance missions.

Specifications

Crew: 2

Powerplant: 2 x 729kW (978hp) Turbomeca
Astazou XVIG turboprop engines

Maximum speed: 500km/h (310mph)

Range: 3710km (2305 miles)

Service ceiling: 10,000m (31,800ft)

Dimensions: span 14.5m (47ft 6in); length
14.25m (46ft 9in); height 5.36m (17ft 7in);

Weight: 6800kg (14,991lb) loaded

Armament: 2 x 20mm Hispano-Suiza HS.804
cannon and four 7.62mm FM M2-20 MGs; up
to 1500kg (3300lb) of bombs or rockets

▲ FMA Pucará

Grupo 3 de Ataque (GA3), Argentine AF / Port Stanley, 1982

The first Pucára COIN aircraft arrived in the Falklands on 2 April, the day of the
Argentine invasion. By late April 24 Pucáras were operating from Stanley and
Goose Green, which were known by the Argentines as Base Aérea Militar (BAM)
Malvinas and BAM Condor respectively.

▲ Lockheed SP-2H Neptune

Escuadrilla Exploracion (EE), Argentine Navy / Bahia Blanca AB/Rio Grande AB

Argentina operated both SP-2H models on support missions during the Falklands
campaign, and an example was responsible for locating the destroyer HMS
Sheffield, which was sunk by an Exocet missile. After this successful outing,
however, maintenance problems effectively kept the Neptunes grounded.

Specifications

Crew: 9–11

Powerplant: 2 x 2759kW (3700hp) Wright R-
3350-32W Cyclone radial and 2 x 13.7kN
(3085kg) thrust Westinghouse J-34-WE-36
turbojet engines

Maximum speed: 586km/h (364mph)

Range: 3540km (2200 miles)

Service ceiling: 6827m (22,400ft)

Dimensions: span 31.65m (103ft 10in); length
27.9m (91ft 8in); height 8.9m (29ft 4in)

Weight: 79,895lb (35,240kg) loaded

Armament: up to 4540kg (10,000lb) of bombs,
mines or torpedoes

While RAF Harriers were to pin down Falklands-
based air assets, Sea Harriers would claim air
superiority. Although a Pucará fell to an SAS Stinger
SAM, it was an aircraft of this type that confirmed
that the Task Force had arrived.

Following an attack by eight Daggers, six A-4s
disabled HMS *Argonaut* and damaged HMS *Antrim*,
putting the warship temporarily out of action, for the
loss of one Dagger to a Seawolf missile. Two Goose
Green-based Pucarás then attacked *Ardent*, without
success, and one was shot down by Sea Harrier. The
next wave of Argentine attackers was a package of

eight A-4s. Two aircraft dropped out and another two
were shot down by Sea Harriers, with just one
abortive attack prosecuted against an Argentine ship.
Five Daggers were next on scene, one being lost to a
Sea Harrier, although *Ardent* was further damaged. A
second wave of three Daggers strafed *Brilliant*, but all
three fell to a combination of Sea Harriers and
Sidewinder AAMs soon after.

Three Navy A-4s left HMS *Ardent* sunk (the
warship had earlier been slightly damaged by a single
M.B.339), but at a cost of two of their own to Sea
Harriers, and one abandoned after sustaining

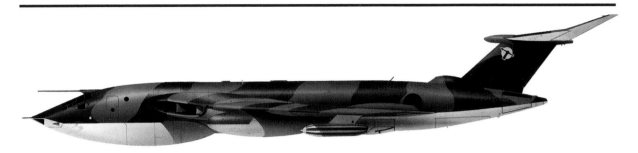

▲ **Handley Page Victor K.Mk 2**

55 Sqn, RAF / Marham

The RAF Victor K.Mk 2 tanker fleet comprised 23 aircraft at Marham, 22 of which were available for the Falklands campaign. As well as vital refuelling missions, four specially adapted Victors undertook maritime radar reconnaissance, and aided in the recapture of South Georgia, Operation Paraquat.

Specifications

Crew: 4

Powerplant: 4 x 91.6kN (20,600lb) Rolls-Royce Conway Mk 201 turbofans

Maximum speed: 1030km/h (640mph)

Range: 7400km (4600 miles)

Service ceiling: 18,290m (60,000ft)

Dimensions: span 36.58m (120ft); length 35.05m (114ft 11in); height 9.2m (30ft 1.5in)

Weight: 105,687kg (233,000lb) loaded

Armament: none

damage. RAF Harriers supported British troops landing at Port San Carlos, and also attacked Argentine helicopters near Mount Kent, destroying a Chinook and damaging a Puma and a UH-1, although one fell to a Blowpipe SAM. Despite the Argentine air attack, the transport vessels were generally unscathed, and a beachhead was established. Meanwhile, D-Day had seen Sea Harriers claim nine Argentine aircraft destroyed.

Also playing a key role during the landings were the helicopters of the Army Air Corps (AAC) and No. 3 Commando Brigade Air Squadron (CBAS) of the Royal Marines. Indeed, Gazelles from the landing ship *Sir Tristram* flew the first missions of the invasion, launching the SAS diversionary attack. Two more Gazelles from *Sir Galahad* helped secure sites for Rapier SAMs, and provided gunship escort for Sea Kings unloading stores from ships. One escort Gazelle was hit by small arms fire, becoming the first casualty of the day; a second Gazelle was also a victim of small arms fire near San Carlos.

Task Force under fire

In the wake of the British invasion, three Pumas and an A.109 were jumped by two Sea Harriers on 21 May, all but one Puma being destroyed. An RAF Harrier was also lost to AAA fire near Port Howard. Two days later a combined A-4 force hit HMS *Antelope* in San Carlos Water, and the vessel was later destroyed when an unexploded bomb detonated. However, two Skyhawks were lost, and a third limped home, while a Dagger was shot down by a Sea Harrier.

After three Daggers and an A-4 were destroyed on 24 May, A-4s attacked shipping off Pebble Island the next day, damaging HMS *Broadsword* and destroying HMS *Coventry*, which had been acting as a radar picket, but losing two aircraft in return. On the same day the container ship *Atlantic Conveyor* was destroyed by an Exocet anti-ship missile launched by Super Etendard, taking with it six Wessex, three Chinooks and a Puma helicopter, as well as other important stores, and Sea Harrier spares.

The A-4s switched to attacking British forces on the islands as of 27 May. On 28 May the Argentines attempted to reinforce Goose Green garrison (the first British objective after the breakout) with seven UH-1s, two A.109s, a Puma and a CH-47. On the same day Pucarás flew from Stanley to attack British troops, one claiming an Army Scout helicopter before being lost in bad weather. Scouts were the first British helicopters ashore, and were followed the next day by Gazelles, providing troop support from dispersed sites. An MB.339 was then lost to a Blowpipe SAM, with a Pucará downed by small arms fire.

After an attack on Argentine artillery near Goose Green on 28 May, the Argentine commander of the battery surrendered but losses to ground fire on 27 May and 30 May reduced the RAF Harrier fleet to three aircraft. Refuelled by Victor tankers, two reinforcements arrived on Hermes from Ascension on 1 June, and two more followed a week later.

By 30 May, the last airworthy M.B.339 had been withdrawn, with surviving Pucarás dispersed around Stanley town for protection. The final Exocet sortie

RAF, FALKLANDS, 1982		
Aircraft	Unit	Base
Vulcan B.Mk 2	44 Sqn 50 Sqn 101 Sqn	Ascension
Harrier GR.Mk 3	1 Sqn	Ascension, HMS *Hermes*, Stanley
Phantom FGR.Mk 2	29 Sqn	Ascension
Nimrod R.Mk 1	51 Sqn	Ascension, Chile
Canberra PR.Mk 9	39 Sqn	Punta Arenas
Hercules C.Mk 1/3	24 Sqn 30 Sqn 47 Sqn 70 Sqn	Ascension, Stanley
VC10 C.Mk 1	10 Sqn	Ascension, Stanley
Chinook HC.Mk 1	18 Sqn	Ascension, Port San Carlos
Nimrod MR.Mk 1	42 Sqn	Ascension
Nimrod MR.Mk 2	120 Sqn 201 Sqn 206 Sqn	Ascension
Victor K.Mk 2	55 Sqn 57 Sqn	Ascension
Sea King HAR.Mk 3	202 Sqn	Ascension

of the campaign, on 30 May, involved four A-4s accompanying two Super Etendards on an abortive attack against HMS *Invincible*. Two Skyhawks were shot down by SAMs, and the bombs missed the target (which was actually HMS *Avenger*).

With a beachhead established at Port San Carlos, an operating strip could be built, allowing Harriers and Sea Harriers to operate from dry land as of 5 June. RAF Harriers supported the British troops' advance on Stanley, their sorties including the first operational RAF use of laser-guided bombs.

On 8 June A-4s targeted the landing ships *Sir Tristram* (severely damaged) and *Sir Galahad* (destroyed) at Port Pleasant. Five A-4s caused much destruction; four more then attempted a follow-up raid, but three fell to Sea Harriers after sinking a landing craft – these were the Sea Harrier's final victories of the campaign. Meanwhile A-4s attacked troops at Port Pleasant. In the rescue that followed the attacks on the two troopships, Sea Kings were heavily involved in airlifting survivors.

Last Skyhawk raid

On 13 June eight Skyhawks attacked British positions at Mount Kent and Mount Longdon, in the final A-4 air raid of the war, and succeeded in damaging a number of helicopters.

Between 28–31 May the Argentines had evacuated Pebble Island, using a Twin Otter and two Sea Kings. In the same period the final Puma was shot down by 'friendly fire'. UH-1s continued casualty evacuation work from Stanley town, while CH-47s withdrew on 9 June. Night-time C-130 flights were conducted until 13 June, supported by Navy Electras and F.27s.

Helicopters again proved their value during the British advance on Port Stanley, with troop patrols supported by Scouts. The assault on Port Stanley also

▲ **Avro Vulcan B.Mk 2**

44 Sqn, RAF / Ascension Island, 1982

XM607 was the aircraft responsible for prosecuting the first Black Buck raid. Following two Black Buck sorties flown against the airfield at Port Stanley, to deny its access to the Argentines, two further Black Buck missions on 31 May and 3 June used Shrike anti-radar missiles to target long-range radars near the airfield.

Specifications

Crew: 5

Powerplant: 4 x 88.9kN (20,000lb) Olympus Mk.301 turbojets

Maximum speed: 1038km/h (645mph)

Range: about 7403km/h (4600 miles)

Service ceiling: 19,810m (65,000ft)

Dimensions: span 33.83m (111ft); length 30.45m (99ft 11in); height 8.28m (27ft 2in)

Weight: 113,398kg (250,000lb) loaded

Armament: internal weapons bay for up to 21,454kg (47,198lb) of bombs involved Sea Kings and Wessex, ferrying ammunition to Mount Kent. Only one Chinook was available throughout the campaign after the loss of the *Atlantic Conveyor*, and this was put to good use transferring supplies from ship to shore, ferrying ammunition and, on occasions, as many as 81 troops, which was twice its normal load. After a Gazelle spotted Argentine forces, Gurkhas were called in and transported by Sea Kings, while Scouts attacked

Argentine positions with AS.11 missiles and captured prisoners during vicious fighting that took place between 12–13 June. Scouts were heavily involved in the final hours of fighting, knocking out Argentine artillery, as well as conducting casualty evacuation from Tumbledown Mountain. A number of Pucára raids were staged between 10–13 June before the final collapse of the Argentine garrison and the Argentine surrender on 14 June.

FLEET AIR ARM, FALKLANDS, 1982		
Aircraft	**Unit**	**Base**
Sea Harrier FRS.Mk 1	800 NAS	HMS *Hermes*, Port San Carlos, Stanley
Sea Harrier FRS.Mk 1	801 NAS	HMS *Invincible*, Port San Carlos, Stanley
Sea Harrier FRS.Mk 1	809 NAS	HMS *Hermes*, HMS *Invincible*, HMS *Illustrious*
Sea King HAS.Mk 5	820 NAS	HMS *Invincible*, Ascension, Stanley
Sea King HAS.Mk 2	824 NAS	*Olmeda*, Port San Carlos, *Fort Grange*
Sea King HAS.Mk 2	825 NAS	*Queen Elizabeth 2*, *Atlantic Causeway*, Port San Carlos
Sea King HAS.Mk 5	826 NAS	HMS *Hermes*, Port San Carlos
Sea King HC.Mk 4	846 NAS	HMS *Hermes*, HMS *Fearless*, HMS *Intrepid*, *Canberra*, *Elk*, *Norland*, various island bases
Wessex HAS.Mk 3	737 NAS	HMS *Antrim*, HMS *Glamorgan*
Wessex HU.Mk 5	845 NAS	*Resource*, Stanley, *Fort Austin*, Port San Carlos, *Tidespring*, Ascension, *Tidepool*, various island bases
Wessex HU.Mk 5	847 NAS	*Engadine*, *Atlantic Causeway*, Port San Carlos, various island bases
Wessex HU.Mk 5	848 NAS	*Endurance*, *Regent*, *Olna*, *Fort Austin*, *Olwen*, *Atlantic Conveyor*, *Astronomer*, Port San Carlos
Lynx HAS.Mk 2	815 NAS	various warships
Wasp HAS.Mk 1	829 NAS	various warships

Specifications

Crew: 1

Powerplant: 1 x 95.6kN (21,500lb) Rolls-Royce Pegasus vectored thrust turbofan

Maximum speed: 1110km/h (690mph)

Range: 740km (460 miles)

Service ceiling: 15,545m (51,000ft)

Dimensions: span 7.7m (25ft 3in); length 14.5m (47ft 7in); height 3.71m (12ft 2in)

Weight: 11,884kg (26,200lb) loaded

Armament: 2 x 30mm cannon, provision for AIM-9 Sidewinder or Matra Magic air-to-air missiles, and two Harpoon or Sea Eagle anti-shipping missiles, up to a total of 3629kg (8000lb) bombs

▲ **Hawker Siddeley (BAe) Sea Harrier FRS.Mk 1**

809 NAS, Royal Navy / Falklands, 1982

Taking aircraft from storage and training units, 809 NAS was formed in April 1982 to reinforce 800 and 801 NAS. In total, 28 Sea Harriers flew over 2370 sorties in which they claimed 21 aircraft in aerial combat, as well as three helicopters and three Pucárs destroyed on the ground. This aircraft, ZA177, claimed two Mirages.

American Policing Actions
1954–1989

Whether working overtly or by clandestine means, during the Cold War the U.S. took a hard line against regimes in Latin America that it considered at risk from communism.

PUTTING INTO PRACTICE the 'domino theory', which proposed that the loss of one state to communism would lead to the spread of Marxism throughout a particular region, the U.S. participated in military action in Guatemala, overthrowing a left-wing government in 1954. Although U.S. air power was not deployed overtly in Guatemala, the CIA provided a B-26 bomber, which was operated from Nicaragua against government forces. A CIA-trained rebel army then invaded Guatemala from Honduras, supported by U.S.-supplied (and in some cases U.S.-flown) B-26, F-47, F-51 and C-47 aircraft operating out of Nicaragua. The operation was a success from a U.S. perspective, with Guatemala's left-wing government removed from power. The U.S. continued to take a military interest in Guatemala, supporting anti-guerrilla operations into the 1980s, and providing equipment including UH-1s and, later, gunship-equipped Bell 212 and 214 helicopters.

In 1961, U.S. forces put down a counter-revolution in Nicaragua. Next up was the Dominican Republic, where the U.S. intervened in 1965 in order to prevent a communist takeover. The U.S. deployed an invasion force to the Caribbean. This included the USS *Boxer*, carrying U.S. Marine Corps H-34, and UH-1 helicopters, which were used to effect a USMC landing on the island and to evacuate U.S. civilians.

Intervention in Grenada

As relations between the superpowers worsened in the early 1980s, the U.S. found itself once again embarking on military operations in Latin America, with an invasion of Grenada in 1983 to restore order after a coup. In particular, the presence of Cuban advisors on the island was a source of concern to the U.S., and SR-71A spyflights were followed by Operation Urgent Fury in October 1983, with the aim of evacuating U.S. citizens, neutralizing local military forces, and restoring order. The invasion force included C-130E/H transports for paradropping and C-141Bs and C-5As to bring follow-on supplies, while Marines were landed by CH-46E and CH-53D helicopters from USS *Guam*, escorted by AH-1Ts. Air support was provided by

▲ **Bell AH-1T SeaCobra**

U.S. Marine Corps

Four AH-1Ts were used in Grenada in support of the U.S. Marine Corps transport helicopters that delivered U.S. troops from the assault ship USS *Guam*. Two SeaCobras were shot down during the battle for Fort Frederick. The USMC helicopter component also included UH-1Ns for command and control duties.

Specifications

Crew: 2

Powerplant: 1 x 820kW (1100shp) Lycoming T53-L-13 turboshaft

Maximum speed: 352km/h (219mph)

Range: 574km (357 miles)

Service ceiling: 3475m (11,400ft)

Dimensions: rotor diameter: 13.4m (44ft); length 13.4m (44ft 5in); height 4.1m (13ft 6in)

Weight: 4500kg (10,000lb) loaded

Armament: 2 x 7.62mm MGs; 70mm (2.75in) rockets; M18 7.62mm Minigun pod

▲ Sikorsky CH-53D Sea Stallion
A US Marine Corps CH-53D is seen during the Grenada invasion, framed by a
Soviet-built, Cuban-operated ZSU-23 anti-aircraft gun. CH-53s operated from the
amphibious assault vessel USS *Guam* during the campaign.

▲ Lockheed C-130E Hercules
A C-130E of the USAF's 934th Airlift Wing over Panama in the wake of the 1989
military intervention, codenamed Operation Just Cause, during which USAF
C-130s, C-5s and C-141s had been used to deliver the first waves of US troops.

AC-130H gunships and air power from the USS *Independence*, and U.S. Army UH-60A helicopters made their combat debut. After eight days of fighting, the U.S. forces realized their objectives.

The U.S. operated more covertly during the civil wars fought in Nicaragua and El Salvador during the early 1980s. With military assistance provided through CIA channels, the U.S. backed the exiled right-wing Contra rebels operating against the left-wing Sandinista regime in Nicaragua, while propping up the government during El Salvador's civil war.

El Salvador was victorious in a brief war fought against Honduras in 1969, the air warfare having witnessed the last dogfights between piston-engined aircraft, but by 1980 El Salvador was suffering civil war, with military 'death squads' used to maintain internal security. U.S. military assistance resumed from 1981, including UH-1Hs, American military advisors and training for COIN teams. While the Salvadorean AF flew ground support missions against guerrillas, C-47s and helicopters were used to transport troops. A guerrilla raid destroyed many Salvadorean AF aircraft on the ground at Liopango in January 1982, and the U.S. supplied more helicopters, C-123s, O-2As and A-37Bs in response. UH-1s played perhaps the most significant role, not only transporting troops in pursuit of the guerrillas, but also serving as gunships. C-47 gunship conversions were also active as operations gathered pace by the mid-1980s. The election of a new president in El Salvador 1984 saw action reduced to skirmishes that would endure until the end of the Cold War.

In Nicaragua, the U.S. strove to topple the Sandinista regime as of 1981, with CIA-based Contra exile and mercenaries facing off against Nicaraguan military power, which included Soviet-supplied Mi-8 and Mi-24 helicopters. Salvadorean AF A-37Bs were used to stop infiltration by Nicaraguan guerrillas, with El Salvador also serving as a base for O-2As, and other types flown on clandestine missions by Nicaraguan exile crews. The Honduran AF was also active in support of the Contras. The civil war continued until 1990, when the Sandinistas were defeated in elections.

As the Cold War drew to a close, the U.S. was involved in yet another military action in Latin America, launching an operation against Panama in 1989. Again, USAF AC-130H, C-141B, C-5 and C-130 aircraft were involved in a successful campaign to oust General Manuel Noriega, and the December 1989 operation was notable for the first combat use of the USAF's F-117A stealth attack aircraft.

World Alliances
1950–1989

The ideological confrontation between the US and Soviet Union – and in turn, between their respective NATO and Warsaw Pact military alliances – formed the backdrop of the Cold War.

NORTH AMERICA

ATLANTIC OCEAN

PACIFIC OCEAN

■ Cuba

■ Dominican Republic

Guatemala ■ ■ Nicaragua
El Salvador ■

■ Grenada

■ Panama

SOUTH AMERICA

**World Alliances
1950–1989**

NATO   ■ Conflict
Warsaw Pact
Other U.S. ally
Socialist country allied with U.S.S.R.
Other ally of the U.S.S.R.
China
Non-aligned

However, the conflicts of the period were invariably fought by proxy, amid a complex political landscape of shifting allegiances, and with the superpowers typically becoming involved in actions that were initiated by local or civil strife, or by nationalist or anti-colonialist sentiment.

In Europe, the division created by the 'Iron Curtain' established the battle lines. The political situation in South America, seen as 'America's backyard', was closely controlled by the U.S. In Africa, as in the Middle East, the U.S. and U.S.S.R. time and again became involved in local conflicts in bids to undermine one another and to bolster their own divergent ideologies. A pattern of involvement in colonial struggles served as background to many of the conflicts fought in Southeast Asia.

Index

Page numbers in *italics* refer to illustrations.